UNSTUCK IN TIME

UNSTUCK IN TIME

On the Post-Soviet Uncanny

Eliot Borenstein

CORNELL UNIVERSITY PRESS   ITHACA AND LONDON

Copyright © 2024 by Cornell University

All rights reserved. Except for brief quotations in a review, this book, or parts thereof, must not be reproduced in any form without permission in writing from the publisher. For information, address Cornell University Press, Sage House, 512 East State Street, Ithaca, New York 14850. Visit our website at cornellpress. cornell.edu.

First published 2024 by Cornell University Press

Library of Congress Cataloging-in-Publication Data

Names: Borenstein, Eliot, 1966– author.
Title: Unstuck in time: on the post-Soviet uncanny / Eliot Borenstein.
Description: Ithaca : Cornell University Press, 2024. | Includes bibliographical references and index.
Identifiers: LCCN 2024018072 (print) | LCCN 2024018073 (ebook) | ISBN 9781501777882 (hardcover) | ISBN 9781501777899 (paperback) | ISBN 9781501777912 (epub) | ISBN 9781501777905 (pdf)
Subjects: LCSH: Popular culture—Russia (Federation) | Political culture—Russia (Federation) | Post-communism—Social aspects—Russia (Federation) | Time travel in mass media. | Soviet Union—In popular culture. | Russia (Federation)—Social conditions—1991–
Classification: LCC DK510.762 .B68 2024 (print) | LCC DK510.762 (ebook) | DDC 306.20947—dc23/eng/20240513
LC record available at https://lccn.loc.gov/2024018072
LC ebook record available at https://lccn.loc.gov/2024018073

To Louis Kandall and Fred Borenstein, for avoiding the grandfather paradox,

and

To Sonya Kandall and Sophie Borenstein, for not stepping on any butterflies

Why is today yesterday and not tomorrow?

—Rabfak, "Our Nuthouse Is Voting for Putin"

Contents

Acknowledgments	ix
Note on Translations and Transliteration	xi
Introduction: Time's Up	1
1. World War Me	16
2. History's Accidental Tourists	37
3. The Empire Never Ended	59
4. Not Dead Yet	86
5. The Return of the Radiant Future	123
Conclusion: Trading Russian Futures	166
Works Cited	179
Index	195

Acknowledgments

I owe a debt of gratitude to so many people who helped me while I wrote this book, and I am afraid there is no way I can remember them all (despite the running tally I try to keep during the writing process).

So let me start with the people I always thank, because these are the people who have always been supportive: my colleagues in New York University's Russian and Slavic Studies Department and the Jordan Center for the Advanced Study of Russia (Yevgenia Albats, Irina Belodedova, Rossen Djagalov, Bruce Grant, Boris Groys, Mikhail Iampolski, Ilya Kliger, Katya Korsounskaya, Yanni Kotsonis, Anne Lounsbery, Evelina Mendelevich, Anne O'Donnell, Jillian Porter, Leydi Rothman, Sasha Shpitalnik, Josh Tucker, Maya Vinokour, and Junlin Zhu), in the Office of Global Programs (Janet Alperstein, Zvi Ben-Dor Benite, Alejandra Gonzalez-Ariza, Nancy Morrison, Niyati Parekh, Libby Perkowski, Marianne Petit, and William Pruitt), and in the Offices of the President and the Provost (Gigi Dopico, Kate Hardy, Peter Holm, Linda Mills, Sabrina Sanchez, Josh Taylor, and Lisa Taylor).

Facebook, despite being evil, proved incredibly useful to me for my research on the various topics covered in *Unstuck in Time*. The hive mind answered my queries and commented on my posts, reminding me that I was not alone. Thanks to Yelena Abdullayeva, Alex Averbuch, Anna Dvigubski, Luke Ellenberg, Yevgeniy Fiks, Shawn Gilmore. Sergey Glebov, Kate Holland, Yuliya Ilchuk, Yelena Kalinsk, Pavel Khazanov, Paul Klanderud, Anna Krakus, Daniil Leiderman, Mark Lipovetsky, Mikhail Lipyanskiy, Angelina Lucento, Melissa Miller, Susan Mooney, Daria Kirjanov Mueller, Lucy Parts, Kevin M. F. Platt, Tamara Polyakova, Shannon Donally Quinn, Roberto Rabbia, Aaron Retish, Rebecca Stanton, Julia Trubikhina, Olga Vander, Jose Vergara, Meghan Vicks, and Emily Wang.

I am especially grateful to Amanda Lerner, whose dissertation on time travel in Russian fiction and film helped push me to write this book, and to Sofya Khagi, for her astute comments on the book before it went to press. Particular thanks go to the students and faculty who attended my talk at Wesleyan University and led me to rethink my conception of dysphoria. The first draft of the entire manuscript was serialized on eliotborenstein.net. A version of part of chapter 5 was published as "Dystopias and Catastrophe Tales after Chernobyl," in *Russian*

Literature since 1991, ed. Evgeny Dobrenko and Mark Lipovetsky (Cambridge: Cambridge University Press, 2015), 86–103 (https://www.eliotborenstein.net/s/Borenstein-Dystopias-and-Catastrophe-Tales-after-Chernobyl.pdf).

Working with Cornell University Press continues to be a delight, five books in. I keep expecting them to tell me they've had enough, but they remain inexplicably enthusiastic. Editor Mahinder Kingra has been a constant source of insight and suggestions. Susan Specter patiently shepherded the manuscript through all the requisite phases of production. And once again, Carolyn Pouncy's copy edits saved me from my own sloppiness.

As always, my family put up with my immersion in my various manuscripts. Fran somehow manages not to be annoyed by my juggling multiple projects, Lev provides useful pop cultural commentary, and Louie remains blissfully unaware of what I do for a living.

Note on Translations and Transliteration

The Library of Congress transliteration system is used in this book whenever unfamiliar Russian words are introduced, and whenever quotes are included in the original Russian. For the sake of easier reading, however, when Russian authors are named in the body of the text, I have chosen the most familiar English spelling ("Dostoevsky" rather than "Dostoevskii"); last names containing a Russian ё are rendered with the letters *yo* rather than *e* ("Fyodorov" rather than "Federov"). The "Works Cited" section and internal citations use the Library of Congress system for ease of bibliographic reference; thus, either of the brothers who wrote the most famous science fiction in the Soviet period are referred to in the text as "Strugatsky," but their Russian-language publications would be listed in the citations under "Strugatskii." Fictional characters' names are rendered in a more "reader-friendly" fashion so that non-Russian speakers can better pronounce the names ("Lyuda" rather than "Liuda").

All translations are my own unless otherwise noted.

Introduction

TIME'S UP

Scheduling Conflicts

On or about December 1991, the normal course of time in Russia stopped. To put it more precisely, the normal course of time in the Soviet Union ended along with the country itself, leaving Russia and the other fourteen successor states to reset their clocks for a new era. Not literally, of course, although the Russian state would occasionally tinker with the metaphorical timepieces established by the USSR.

Among the many aspects of the Soviet Union inherited by the Russian Federation was a voluntarist approach to time. In 1930, all clocks in the Soviet Union were moved ahead one hour, a phenomenon known as "decree time" ("Stat'ia No. 362"). Though the change was motivated by practicality, what could be more symbolic of the USSR's status as the harbinger of the future? It was rolled back in the Russian Federation in the mid-1980s, only to be restored just one month after the December accords that wiped the Soviet Union from the face of the earth ("Postanovlenie Sovmina"; "Postanovlenie Pravitel'stva RF"). The Soviet Union also had daylight saving time, which was made permanent in Russia in 2011 (i.e., the country sprang forward without falling back), and then abolished in 2014 (falling back, never to spring forward again) ("Russian Clocks Go Back for Last Time").

From an outsider's perspective, time in the USSR was never straightforward. Even setting aside the five-year plans (and the calls to fulfill them in four) or the early Soviet emphasis on speed (Valentin Kataev's 1933 novel, *Time, Forward!*, starts with "Chapter 1: The first chapter is omitted for the time being" [2]), experiments with the everyday experience of time were a recurring feature of Soviet life. In 1929, the USSR instituted the *nepreryvka*, the endless workweek with no set days off for the weekend. (Workers were assigned to different shifts with different days of rest) (Henkin 4). An unsurprising failure, the practice was revised into a six-day week in 1931, and the country reverted to a five-day week in 1940. Another innovation, working a twenty-four-hour shift every three days, has remained a fixture of many Russians' schedules (Tiapukhin).

In some areas, the centrality of Moscow led to a time frame that completely ignored conditions on the ground. Until 2018, all train schedules in the Russian Federation (and, previously, in the Soviet Union) indicated arrival and departure in Moscow time (Shadrina). Never mind that the country has eleven time zones. On vacation in Lithuania in 1992, I realized that I could not be sure what time my return train was actually scheduled to depart: the ticketing seemed exactly the same as the old tickets, but Vilnius and Moscow were now in different time zones. For the time being, it turned out that Moscow time still reigned. In preparation to fly back to Moscow from Tomsk in 1993, I was surprised to find that the moment I passed security and entered into the waiting area for my flight, I was on Moscow time; the clocks were four hours behind the ones on the other side of the gate.

Other aspects of the Soviet, and now Russian, calendar are also inflexible. The official first day of school is September 1, even if that date falls on a Saturday or a Sunday—the exact opposite of the often-confounding American custom of scheduling certain holidays, such as Thanksgiving, by day of the week, rather than date.[1] Flexibility is instead the province of the religious holidays that have become more prominent since the Soviet collapse: the Russian Orthodox Church, like many other religious traditions, has a number of movable feasts.

Post-Soviet Russia had its share of calendrical decisions to make, beyond the aforementioned reforms of decree time and daylight savings. Holidays were renamed: "Soviet Army and Navy Day" became "Defender of the Fatherland Day," and "International Workers' Day" became "The Day of Spring and Labor." The Russian Federation made June 12, the date that the Russian Parliament declared sovereignty in 1991, a national holiday in 1992. Initially "Day of the Adoption of Sovereignty of the Russian Federation," it became "Russia Day" in 2002. In 2005, the country adopted November 4 as "Unity Day," an old imperial holiday commemorating the 1612 expulsion of Polish invaders. Clearly meant to displace the

---

1. This difference between American and Soviet/Russian approaches to time was noted by Stephen Hanson in *Time and Revolution*, a book that has been invaluable as background research for this project. For more on the standardization of time in the modern West, see Vanessa Ogle's *Global Transformation of Time*.

Soviet holiday of October Revolution Day (November 7), it has an additional significance to which we will return shortly.

The real disruption to the normal flow of time, however, was less about formal measurements and work schedules than it was about the country's relationship to its past, its understanding of the present, and the ability to imagine a future.

Russia had come unstuck in time.

Time of Troubles, or, the Trouble with Time

In the prologue to his classic utopian novel *Red Mars* (1992), Kim Stanley Robinson describes the adjustment human colonists have made to the clocks on their new world:

> And then it was ringing midnight, and they were in the Martian time slip, the thirty-nine-and-a-half-minute gap between 12:00:00 and 12:00:01, when all the clocks went blank or stopped moving. This was how [the colonists] had decided to reconcile Mars's slightly longer day with the twenty-four-hour clock, and the solution had proved oddly satisfactory. Every night to step for a while out of the flicking numbers, out of the remorseless sweep of the second hand—[2]

The Martian time slip was a way of stepping outside of ordinary time while also acknowledging its passing. Within this gap, it felt as if they had slipped loose from time entirely, even though some mechanism was clearly keeping track of those thirty-nine and a half minutes in order to resume the ordinary chronology once the slip elapsed. The Martian time slip is a temporal state of exception, an exclusion that helps constitute the (counting) system from which it purports to be absent.

Human experience is filled with such times, moments that are counted and uncounted simultaneously—whether they be the sacred time of sabbaths and cyclical holidays; the timeless encounters with the numinous facilitated by meditation, prayer, or hallucinogens; or the fuzzy semiconsciousness of sleep. Then there are historical periods defined primarily by their absence of definition, epistemological chaos, and general sense of falling outside of ordinary history. This is the interregnum.

In his *Prison Notebooks*, Antonio Gramsci extrapolated from the dictionary definition of interregnum to define it as the period when the existing social

---

2. *Martian Time-Slip* was the title of a 1964 novel by Philip K. Dick; Robinson (and his colonists) are engaging in an in-joke.

order is no longer functional, but its replacement has yet to materialize (276). Zygmunt Bauman ("Times of Interregnum") and Carlo Bordoni (*Interregnum*) have extended the concept further, applying it to the economic, environmental, and governance crises that characterize the first decades of the twenty-first century. While both of these reinterpretations of interregnum have undeniable value, for the Russian Federation in the immediate aftermath of the Soviet collapse, it is nonetheless worth retaining at least some of the term's literal meaning. Not only does it work retrospectively for the period between 1991 and Putin's revival of supreme central authority, but it also corresponds with the earlier Russian historical era that has provided a metaphorical model for periods of chaos and confusion: the Time of Troubles.

The Time of Troubles began in 1598, when the tsar died without an heir, leading to a succession crisis complete with famine, two imposters claiming to be the tsar's dead son, war with Poland, and foreign occupation by Poland-Lithuania. It ended in 1613 with the election of Mikhail Romanov as tsar and the inauguration of the dynasty that shared his last name. Memorialized most notably in Pushkin's (and Mussorgsky's) *Boris Godunov*, the Time of Troubles has remained current, both as an available phrase and a point of reference, and its application to the chaotic, impoverished, crime-ridden 1990s was inevitable. As Russian scholars and media figures have begun to reexamine the Nineties, the appropriateness of this comparison has been (rightfully) called into question.[3] As I argued in *Plots against Russia*, the framing of the Nineties as a decade of hell has been a cornerstone of the myth of Vladimir Putin as the country's savior (107–10).

But there is a difference between calling the decade a Time of Troubles retrospectively and calling it by that name while the "Troubles" are still unfolding. In addition to the everyday struggles arising from economic and social breakdown, the true horror of living in such an interregnum is the collapse of teleology. When is all this going to end, and how? Soviet ideology, while it remained current, justified any number of sacrifices in the name of the promised radiant future, either draining the present of all meaning or imbuing it with significance based entirely on what was supposed to come. Perestroika promised improvement (reform) and eventually the replacement of an old system with a new one. But the 1990s offered only vague talk of democracy and markets, peppered with incomprehensible imported jargon that failed to obscure the extent to which the overwhelming majority of the population was getting railroaded. Instead of

---

3. See Gulnaz Sharafutdinova's *Red Mirror* for a particularly convincing analysis of the Time of Troubles metaphor for the 1990s. Also see Adrian Selin's "Uroki smutnogo vremeni."

a grand narrative with a goal in sight, the 1990s offered endless iterations of meaningless misery.

When pressed to imagine a possible end to chaos, the media and culture industry repeatedly returned to two familiar historical models: total civil war and the dictatorship of the "firm hand." In the 1990s, Sergei Norka produced a trilogy of novels that, after explaining just who was behind Russia's problems (the usual suspects), imagined a way out thanks to a "Russian Inquisition" that would bring an authoritarian nicknamed the "Dark Horse" to power (Borenstein, *Plots against Russia* 83–88). The best outcome was a replay of history, whether Russian or more generally European.

The very metaphor of the Time of Troubles presupposes that chaos ends only through the reinstitution of strong central rule. In that regard, the outcome is a foregone conclusion. But the fact that the Yeltsin Era would officially end with the last moments of 1999 was by no means guaranteed. While this is one of those rare instances when the calendar and the popular sense of the period prove to be in near-perfect alignment, the inauguration of what would eventually be seen as the Putin Era came as a complete surprise to the families gathered around their televisions for the traditional new year's greetings from the country's leader. Nor did Yeltsin's statement, "I'm leaving. I've done all I could," sound particularly momentous—let alone the phrase as it is misremembered in the popular consciousness and Internet memes: "I'm tired. I'm leaving") (Bormatova).

Thus the Time of Troubles works for the 1990s both because of the retrospective ability to see it as a distinct historical era and the contemporary experience during the 1990s of an unstructured time with no end in sight. As an interregnum, it is a discrete period with a beginning and end that nonetheless describe a time marked by a sense of total timelessness. The 1990s were the Moscow time slip.

Time out of Joint

Like the book you are currently reading, Kurt Vonnegut's 1969 novel *Slaughterhouse-Five* contains multiple beginnings, as if the author is not quite ready to get started. According to the end of chapter 1, the book starts in chapter 2, with this:

> **Listen:**
> Billy Pilgrim has come unstuck in time.
>
> Billy has gone to sleep a senile widower and awakened on his wedding day. He has walked through a door in 1955 and come out another one

in 1941. He has gone back through that door to find himself in 1963. He has seen his birth and death many times, he says, and pays random visits to all the events in between.

According to the novel, Billy Pilgrim died in 1976. Had he lived ten more years, he could have encountered his fictional heir, Jon Osterman, the physicist in Alan Moore and Dave Gibbon's *Watchmen* (1987) who, after being transformed into the godlike Dr. Manhattan, moved back and forth along his personal timeline in much the same way Billy did. Both Billy Pilgrim and Dr. Manhattan are jolted out of linearity by a catastrophic event: Billy in response to his experience of the bombing of Dresden, and Dr. Manhattan through his complete disintegration and self-reconstruction in a freak lab accident. In other words, they have each been displaced by trauma. Certainly, Billy's frequent returns to his time in World War II resemble the flashbacks that plague veterans suffering from Post-Traumatic Stress Disorder, while Dr. Manhattan's flat affect and indifference to humanity might, in a less science fictional mode, suggest its own variation on shell shock.

Recognizing the risk of straining the metaphor beyond its breaking point, I nonetheless submit that the Soviet collapse loosed Russia from the bonds of linear time. Not literally, of course; as all the discussion of clocks a few pages ago demonstrates, empirical time continued to be tracked. Years followed one another in the customary sequence, and human bodies continued to age (in the cases of the most vulnerable, they probably aged precipitously). But the 1990s was a temporal derailment, one that sent pundits racing for historical precedent: the Time of Troubles, obviously, but also the Russian Civil War, the New Economic Policy, and the fall of Rome, among many others. Experienced as a time out of time, it would retroactively be cordoned off as a strictly delimited period of timelessness to which no one would wish to return. Its end, however, was not entirely a return to linear time.

Much of Russia's cultural production in the twenty-first century suggests that, even if it put an end to the Time of Troubles that preceded it, the Putin Era has not been a straightforward return to linearity. Certainly, the long-standing tendency to connect the current moment with a historical precedent has been intensified. The commemoration of the Sixtieth Anniversary of the Soviet victory in World War II seemed designed to make the Great Patriotic War feel contemporary. Where the fiftieth anniversary in 1995 had numerous living veterans to celebrate and congratulate, the sad truth was that, with the passage of time, the commemorations would eventually be taking place in their absence. Thanks to the initiative of three journalists, the 2012 commemorations in Tomsk featured a parade of younger people displaying pictures of relatives who had served in the war. They called themselves the "Immortal Regiment," and by the next year, similar demonstrations were mounted throughout the Russian Federation. As it happened, the spread of the Immortal Regiment coincided with the outbreak of war in Ukraine (the fighting in Donbas began a little more than a month before Victory Day 2014), facilitating the government's propaganda campaign to frame the fighting as a replay of World War II.[4] Ukrainian nationalists were "Banderites" (the name of the anti-Soviet Ukrainian nationalist forces who fought on the side of the Germans), as if Ukraine had somehow kept Nazis in reserve, to be awakened in an emergency by breaking their glass container. The following year, 2015, Russian motorists proudly displayed bumper stickers saying "1945—we can do it again." By the time the coronavirus hit Russia in 2020, Putin's habitual invocation of Russia's historical triumphs had turned into a self-parody: "Everything passes, and this will pass. Our country has gone through many serious challenges: When tormented by the Pechenegs and the Polovtsians Russia has handled them all. We will defeat this coronavirus contagion" ("Putin Sets Off Meme Storm").[5]

Just a few years later, Putin would appeal to a much more common historical touchstone to justify a catastrophe of his own making. When the Russian Federation invaded Ukraine on February 24, 2022, the president made a televised address to his country's citizens in order to explain his decision: "If history is any guide, we know that in 1940 and early 1941 the Soviet Union went to great lengths to prevent war or at least delay its outbreak. To this end, the USSR sought not to provoke the potential aggressor until the very end by refraining or postponing the most urgent and obvious preparations it had to make to defend itself from an imminent attack. When it finally acted, it was too late . . . We will not make this mistake the second time. We have no right to do so" (Putin). Thus a criminal act that took place without any immediate provocation becomes justified as a defense against repeating the tragic losses of World War II.

The manipulation of Russian historical precedent for present-day political gain is rather clear-cut, as is the prominence of nostalgia in post-Soviet Russia. Indeed, the study of Russian nostalgia is something of a scholarly cottage industry, producing stellar work by Birgit Beumers, Otto Boele, Svetlana Boym, Tatiana Efremova, Lioudmila Fedorova, Ilyak Kalinin, Ilya Kukulin, Maya Nadkarni, Boris Noordenbos, Sergei Oushakine, and Olga Shevchenko, among others.

---

4. See Maxim Hanukai's "Resurrection by Surrogation" for a thorough and insightful discussion of the Immortal Regiment.

5. The translation of Putin's remarks in this article renders "Polovtsy" as "Cumans." This is an acceptable translation, but, given that all the word play involves "Polovtsian," it is confusing. I have replaced "Cumans" with "Polovtsians" in this particular quote. For more on the memetic afterlife of Putin and Polovtsians, see my *Meanwhile, in Russia* (99–122).

Mark Lipovetsky's "post-sots" paradigm for art that uses the tropes of socialist realism without necessarily importing the ideological content, is also an important framework for understanding post-Soviet reappropriations of the past (Lipovetsky, *Postmodern Crises* 169–94). But I propose something a bit different.

Circle Games

The limitations of nostalgia and, to a lesser extent, post-sots are tied to suppositions about affect: nostalgia presupposes a set of emotional responses, however complex.[6] Focusing exclusively on the political uses of the past is also a bit narrow: even if the deployment of World War II tropes is useful to Putin, Putinism cannot explain everything. Instead, if we take a distant, bird's eye view of all these phenomena (Putinist propaganda, nostalgia, post-sots, and contemporary Russian literature's preference for the past over the present as identified by Lipovetsky, Kirill Kobrin, and Alexander Etkind), we see a contemporary Russia that, like Billy Pilgrim, is unstuck in time, hopping back and forth in the timeline of its past.[7]

But what about the future? The question is raised in the song I chose for the present study's epigraph: Alexander Elin's 2012 "Our Nuthouse Is Voting for Putin" (Nash durdom golosuet za Putina), performed by Rabfak: "Why is today yesterday and not tomorrow?" (*Pochemu vmesto zavtra segodnia vchera?*).

On the most obvious political level, Elin's lyrics are targeting a backward-looking political system whose best attempts at articulating a vision of the future amount to primitive nostalgic revanchism. Not to mention the fact that the song came out during an election year, when voting Putin back into the presidency (after his interim stint as prime minister) made the equation between past and future more literal. The past was Putin, the immediate future was Putin, and after Putin? The media and the political class have proven unable to think beyond Vladımır Vladımırovich; and in any case, it looks more than likely that he will remain in office for the rest of his life. The protesters in 2011 called for a "Russia without Putin," but his most zealous public surrogates would insist that Putin and Russia are one, and that a Russia without Putin is inconceivable. Perhaps we can chalk this up to what Timothy Snyder calls the "politics of eternity," the insistence that nothing will ever change, but it does run up against the obvious barrier of Putin's own mortality (8–17).

---

6. Hence Sergeui Alex. Oushakine's wonderful article title, "'We're Nostalgic, but We're Not Crazy.'"
7. See Kobrin and Lipovetskii; Kobrin, "Eternally Wonderful Present"; and Lipovetskii and Etkind.

Fictional attempts to depict Russia in the future have been hampered not by political censorship but by the inability to conceive of the country in concrete, novel terms. According to Frederic Jameson, this is precisely the situation that can and should be resolved through utopian thinking: "The Utopian form itself is the answer to the universal ideological conviction that no alternative is possible, that there is no alternative to the system. But it asserts this by forcing us to think the break itself, and not by offering a more traditional picture of what things would be like after the break" (232).

But with the exception of a few relatively marginal movements I discuss in chapter 5, this is not the path taken by post-Soviet Russian speculative fiction. Quite the contrary: while much of the science fiction set in the far future has generic heroes and settings, when the focus is on Russia in particular, the future ends up looking like the past. Whether the postapocalyptic feudalism of Tatyana Tolstaya's *Slynx* (2003) or the neo-medievalisms of Mikhail Yuriev's *The Third Empire* (2006) and Vladimir Sorokin's *Day of the Oprichnik* (2006), a future Russia seems doomed to travel back and forth along its own personal timeline. At best, the future is a dead end, a notion that is sometimes expressed in space as much as it is in time. When the post-Soviet era was just beginning, Vladimir Makanin imagined a war-ravaged, near-future city where intellectuals survived by hiding in an underground bunker (*Escape Hatch* [Laz'], 1991); just fourteen years later, *Metro 2033*, Dmitry Glukhovsky's transmedia postapocalyptic juggernaut, had all of Moscow's human survivors living in the subway, with many of the stations strangely recapitulating nations and movements from the past: the Hanseatic League, the Nazis, the Reds.[8]

The architecture of Glukhovsky's nightmare civilization is inadvertently instructive. By committing to the Moscow Metro as humanity's last redoubt in Russia, he is beholden to the unique structure of the city's underground transportation system. The map of the Moscow Metro is a variety of zigzagging, intersecting lines, as one would expect from a subway, but they are all united by the circle they intersect: the Ring Line. This combination of convoluted linearity with an endless circle could also map out the temporality of the postsocialist Russian imaginary.

Our story of postsocialist Russia's complicated relationship with time begins with the most popular subgenre of Russian science fiction, which doesn't even have a name in English: *popadantsy*. The word actually describes the heroes rather than the genre, but the heroes' name has become the genre's default nomenclature. Derived from the verb *popast'* (in this case, to "end up somewhere" or "find

---

8. On *Metro 2033*, see Griffiths (494–504); Hoet, Howanitz, and Sokolova.

yourself somewhere"), a *popadanets* (the singular of *popadantsy*) is someone who, usually through a completely mysterious or underexplained fantastic or science fictional plot device, ends up in another world, another dimension, or most often, another time. These sorts of stories have been and continue to be written by English and American authors as well, from Mark Twain's 1889 *A Connecticut Yankee in King Arthur's Court* to Octavia E. Butler's 1979 *Kindred* to the 1980s American television show *Quantum Leap*. But they are neither numerous nor popular enough to have coalesced into an identifiable genre. By "genre" I do not mean simply a set of familiar tropes (the Anglo-American stories certainly have those), but rather a set of expectations of narrative pleasures that a given exemplar of the genre should rightly fulfill.

Finding a satisfying English term for rendering *popadantsy* has been a challenge; the title of chapter 2 characterizes them as "accidental historical tourists," an awkward phrase that gives me no sense of translator's pride. I've toyed with borrowing from the title of a 1960s *Doctor Who* serial and calling them "time meddlers" but find it unsatisfactory. It suggests more agency than is often appropriate. *Doctor Who* nonetheless came to my rescue (as it usually does), thanks to the title of a 2007 eight-minute "mini-episode" starring the actors who played the fifth and tenth Doctors. An accidental collision between their two TARDISes throws them together, a rare event given that they are from different eras. The episode's title? "Time Crash." I propose calling *popadantsy* "Time Crashers"; the phrase highlights the accidental nature of the travel and fits with the Russian term's etymology: *popadat'/popast'* has the root used for a variety of verbs involving falling, while the Russian equivalent of "being hit by a car" is to *popadat'/popast' pod mashinu* ("to end up/fall under a car"). To crash something in English is also to arrive uninvited, which certainly characterizes the journey of the average *popadanets*. So Time Crashers they shall be.

Time Crasher stories play out on the cusp of two more familiar fantasy and science fiction subgenres: time travel and alternate history. Certainly, these are time travel stories, but they tend to be about visiting (and often staying at) only one particular point in history and are almost always the result of an accident. Few of the most familiar pleasures of hard-core time travel tales are to be found—no one is at all bothered by the idea of paradoxes resulting from the deaths of butterflies, grandfathers, or Hitlers. There is little or no reflection on the philosophy of time or causality, and the general preference for points in the national history is almost as distinctive as the lack of interest in the future.[9]

---

9. Oleksandr Zabirko discusses the Time Crashers' cavalier relationship with changing the past in "Magic Spell of Revanchism" (289), as does Ian Garner in "From Stalingrad to the Stars."

One could, perhaps, look at Time Crashers as the fulfillment of an unconscious bias built in to the (nonparadoxical) grandfather of all modern time travel stories, H. G. Wells's *The Time Machine* (1895). As Wells's traveler goes farther and farther into the future, he is presumably telling us what happens to our world, but geographically his machine never goes much beyond the London basement where it was constructed. *The Time Machine* literalizes the trope of British "insularity," projecting it across the ages through its absolute conviction that a few hundred square meters of English soil are representative of the world at large. The most popular Time Crasher stories dispense with the pretense of speaking for the entire globe, though their chosen arena is much greater than the footprint of even the wealthiest English home: their world is Russia.

By the same token, Time Crashers cannot be simply assimilated to the category of alternate history, despite the genre's popularity around the world and in Russia in particular. While alternate history certainly *can* involve time travel, it does not have to. Look no farther than the genre's foundational work, Philip K. Dick's *The Man in the High Castle* (1962), in which the Axis wins World War II. Dick's novel speculates about the fictionality of its own scenario but does not move back and forth between timelines (a possibility raised by the finale of the television adaptation's first season). Instead, Time Crashers are a variation of what Farah Mendelsohn calls "portal quest fantasy," where characters find doorways to other worlds (Narnia, Oz); only here the other worlds are almost always the historical past. They are portal quest historical fiction, like Diana Gabaldon's *Outlander* series, whose goal is often the *creation* of an alternate history. They are the subject of chapters 1 and 2.

Tomorrow's Soviet Union Today

In the early 1990s, one of the Russian Federation's national evening news programs wrapped up its broadcast each night with the weather forecast. Names of cities would scroll across the screen, accompanied by an instrumental cover of The Beatles' classic song, "Yesterday." Apparently, no one at the station was troubled by the fact that their predictions for tomorrow were set to a melody about the previous day. While this mismatch might not have bolstered confidence in meteorology, it did inadvertently presage the wave of nostalgia that would start washing over the country by the decade's end. Why couldn't tomorrow look more like yesterday? For that matter, couldn't we get started on this today?

Once again, as with the Time Crashers, popular entertainment's response involves something adjacent to alternate history. The Time Crasher stories are also not exactly alternate history, but one of the more popular plot lines featuring them is about making an alternate imperial history possible: going back in time and preventing the collapse of the Soviet Union. In such stories, a thriving twenty-first-century USSR is a fairy-tale happily-ever-after; it need not be described in detail but merely has to happen.

This does not mean that a healthy Soviet Union that has lived to see its centenary has not captured some part of the Russian artistic imagination. Like the now established steampunk genre, which can include a present-day or future quasi-Victorian or Edwardian world extrapolated from mechanical rather than digital technology, Russia has begun producing imagery and stories about a USSR whose continued existence is based on the digital technology that barely had a chance to take off before the Soviet collapse. For years now, the hashtag #SovPunk (and its variations, #sovpunk and #sovPunk and #SovietPunk) has popped up intermittently on both the English- and Russian-language Internet (on Twitter and Pinterest as well as a tag on Flickr), often attached to retro-Soviet objects and styles, though it has not coalesced into a significant movement.

The aesthetic appeal of the SovPunk idea is clear, as are the parallels to steampunk's fetishization of analog technology. The comparison has its limits, however. In steampunk, the reappropriation of the nineteenth century is largely a matter of aesthetics and adventure; to the extent that there is nostalgia, it is at a great remove from the implied reader's experience or ideological framework. Coined by analogy to the much more politically charged genre of cyberpunk, the inherently backward-looking steampunk lacks its parent genre's critique of capitalism and speculation about the nature of the posthuman. In steampunk, the coolness is the message.

This is one of the weaknesses of the "SovPunk" coinage. While the imaginary Soviet present (and, occasionally, Soviet future) certainly look to the past for inspiration, the guiding principle is not primarily aesthetic. The USSR in the twenty-first century can serve a variety of ideological and artistic purposes: it can compensate for the lingering sense of defeat and loss stemming from the Soviet collapse; it can serve as a utopian or dystopian alternative to the current order of things; and, perhaps most important, it can estrange the reader and viewer from the actual world around them, making our world seem somehow off thanks to the sheer ordinariness of the constructed alternative Soviet present.

The present-day Soviet Union is not all that common in Russian fiction; Elena Chizhova's 2017 novel *The China Expert* (Kitaist) comes close, and even this book derives much of its power from its position within the "Hitler wins" category of alternate history. In the novel, the prewar territory of the USSR is divided between an independent, communist Soviet Union and a Nazi-dominated Russia. Moreover, *The China Expert* seems to take place in the 1980s, which leaves the USSR's continued survival an open question. Rather, the present-day Soviet

Union featured prominently in two of the most popular television series of the last decade: *The Dark Side of the Moon* (Obratnaia storona luny, 2012–2018), a Russian remake of the British TV series *Life on Mars* (2006–2007), and *Chernobyl: The Exclusion Zone* (Chernobyl': Zona otchuzhdeniia; 2014–2017; feature film, 2019). The uses of the alternative present-day USSR are the focus of chapter 4.

Fantasies about a Soviet Union that never collapsed are an extended exercise in the conditional subjunctive, what the world would be (or would have been) like in this scenario. As fantasies, they can be immersive—no one in the story is aware that they are a different or imaginary world—or they can be portal/quest fantasies, like *The Dark Side of the Moon* and *Chernobyl: The Exclusion Zone*, in which one or more characters from our reality travel to an alternate present-day USSR, and these characters' alienation from their new surroundings is part of the story. Either framework can serve as an exercise in wish fulfillment, even when the new Soviet "reality" proves less than enticing.

But science fiction and fantasy are not the only paths to a Soviet present, or even to visiting a Soviet past. The Soviet conditional subjunctive can also be the result of a collective act of will on the part of people who know that they are deviating from post-Soviet reality or rejecting it all together. Chapters 3 and 4 look at a wide range of attempts, both in fiction and in real life, to revive or maintain the fallen Soviet Union in the present day. The most obvious form is the theme park, as in the 2006 film *Park of the Soviet Period* (Park sovetskogo perioda) and the brief public event at Gorky Park under the same name. More evocative and controversial is Ilya Khrzhanovsky's years-long film series, exhibits, and experiment in communal living called *DAU*, which immersed all of its participants (and, eventually, visitors) in the reconstruction of a lost Soviet world. Dogged by accusations of cult-like behavior and sexual violence, *DAU* would be an object lesson in going overboard.

On a less sinister but potentially more politically disruptive note is the movement of people scattered throughout the former Soviet space who insist that the dismantling of the USSR was illegal and invalid, refuse to pay taxes, and use "Soviet" identity documents. They are the apotheosis of the nation as imagined community: they refuse to see the Russian Federation as a real legal entity, insisting on the existence of the Soviet Union as an act of sheer collective will.

When Russia's president compares viruses to the vaguely remembered barbarian invaders of yore, and when the first post-Soviet decade is continually framed in terms of an early seventeenth-century crisis, should we really be surprised that so many visions of Russia's future resemble popular conceptions of the Middle Ages? The medieval future is, of course, a familiar trope in the history of science fiction, most notably in Walter M. Miller Jr.'s classic *A Canticle for Leibowitz* (1959), which features generations of monks trying to recreate civilization after a nuclear holocaust. Though a postapocalyptic setting makes a medieval future seem more plausible, it is not a requirement, as Frank Herbert's *Dune* novels (1965–) certainly show. Medieval settings can also be projected onto other, less "advanced" planets, as in the Strugatsky brothers' *Hard to Be a God* (1964). The medieval trappings of epic fantasy (and the rise of the Russian genre known as "slavic *fentezi*") have certainly kept the Middle Ages alive in speculative literature, as have the numerous medieval-themed video games.

The most common Western medieval futures tend to be not merely postapocalyptic but postnational: the very idea of the preapocalyptic nation is as distant as nuclear fission. (Here the insistent Americanness of *A Canticle for Leibowitz* is an exception rather than the rule.) While there are plenty of Russian science fiction stories that feature a more generic, supranational future, I would argue that they are fighting against internal ideological trends in the post-Soviet space. The Putin Era's emphasis on sovereignty above all else, combined with the prominence of crackpot theories of ethnicity and nation inspired by the work of Lev Gumilev, renders a world without national borders dystopian by definition.

Russian medieval futurism, by contrast, is insistently *Russian*. The futuristic medieval setting is within some iteration of Russian territory. And the medieval future, far from being always dystopian, might not even be that bad. Mikhail Yuriev and Vladimir Sorokin are two authors who look to a particular moment in Russian medieval history, Ivan the Terrible's *oprichnina* (1565–1572), which they project onto the Russian near future. Yuriev's *Third Empire* is fiction, to the extent that it describes events that haven't happened (yet), but is much more in the tradition of the early works of utopian literature that dispense with plot and character in favor of chronicle and travelogue. If *The Third Empire* is a blueprint for a Russian imperial revival modeled on a sixteenth-century reign of terror, Sorokin's *Day of the Oprichnik*, *Sugar Kremlin* (Sakharnyi Kreml'), and, to a lesser extent, *Telluria* turn Yuriev's fantasy into the stuff of nightmare.

The Post-Soviet Uncanny

The subtitle of this book is "On the Post-Soviet Uncanny." Where, you might ask, does the Uncanny fit in? The vast literature on the subject follows from Freud's classic 1919 essay, "The Uncanny," which establishes a compelling argument about the nature of the phenomenon, albeit through a less than convincing etymological sleight of hand. Noting that the German term *unheimlich* (uncanny) contains within it the word *heimlich* (homey), Freud uses examples from literature and case studies to assert that the uncanny is that which was once familiar, subsequently repressed, and then brought back to create the "uncanny" effect. Never mind that this etymology doesn't work in most other languages (the English word "uncanny," for example, has nothing to do with any word for "home")—if it's in German, it must be true.

If Freud's approach is persuasive, however, it is not because of his shaky linguistics. If anything, *un/heimlich* serves as a useful mnemonic for the dynamic he identifies, rather than as evidence. The tension between the familiar and its frightening, distorted counterpart explains the eeriness associated with statues and dolls (which don't move . . . but what if they could?), or animated human representations that try their best to be realistic rather than cartoony (and end up trapped in the "uncanny valley" to which hyperreal animation is prone).

Alternate Soviet Unions, trips to the national past, and representations of a medieval Russian future are also prone to an uncanny effect but not the one that might be expected. A twenty-first-century USSR is both familiar and strange, but the uncanniness lies elsewhere. It is the uncanny effect that immersive fantasy can have on our perceptions of the world in which we live.

When I was around eight years old, one of my older brothers and my future sister-in-law took me and another brother to a marathon showing of all five of the original *Planet of the Apes* movies. According to IMDB, that comes to a total, back-to-back runtime of eight hours and six minutes; with breaks, it must have amounted to about nine hours. It was morning when the marathon started, and night when we came out. But the biggest shock came when we looked around at all the people on the street: where were all the apes? Seeing nothing but human faces should have been the most ordinary thing in the world, but at that moment, it seemed thoroughly bizarre. The familiar human form became briefly uncanny.

Though simians may be underrepresented in modern Russian entertainment, the result of immersion in post-Soviet alt-Russia fantasies is not that different. These stories start out as side trips into a conditional-subjunctive existence, but their overall effect is to create estrangement from the real post-Soviet existence. The uncanny lies not in the strange familiarity of the fantastic scenario but in the revelation of the uncanny strangeness in the reader's or viewer's everyday reality.

1

WORLD WAR ME

Hello, Stalin!

It's 1940, and a young Pioneer named Vitya Solnyshkin has been given the rare honor of meeting with Joseph Stalin in the general secretary's Kremlin office. Vitya quickly explains that he is not what he seems. He is, in fact, Viktor Egorovich Petrov, a sixty-four-year-old retired construction worker whose consciousness abandoned his dying body in 2017 and somehow found itself housed in the form of a little boy three years before Petrov was born.

Curiously, Stalin is not at all surprised. When Vitya warns him of the impending German attack and advises him to execute such future traitors as young Borya Yeltsin and little Misha Gorbachev, Stalin is unmoved ("You really don't like third-graders, do you, Pioneer Solnyshkin?") (Lukianenko 394). It's not that Stalin doesn't believe him; quite the contrary, he's heard it all before: "What do you think, that you're the only one? That you're unique? No one else has come to the past from the future before?" (Lukianenko 394).

Whether they found a time machine, were mysteriously transported due to a cataclysm or transmigrated like Vitya, time travelers have been giving Stalin advice for years now. And not just Stalin: as far back as Ivan the Terrible, records suggest that emissaries from the future have been paying visits to Russia's leaders. Stalin assumes his contemporaries Adolf Hitler and Franklin Delano Roosevelt are getting their fair share of self-appointed twenty-first-century advisers, but none of it amounts to anything actionable. Everyone seems to have their own version of the historical timeline, and all their advice is conflicting. Stalin will send Vitya to join other travelers in a special research group in the Urals, but he is not planning on altering his decisions based on their input.

This story ("Vitya Solnyshkin and Joseph Stalin") is, of course, a parody of countless other tales of its kind: the stories of the Time Crashers, the accidental tourists who find themselves in another time, space, or dimension, usually for no apparent reason. Stalin is a popular figure in this genre, but here he plays an unusual role. Ordinarily, the traveler (most often, from our time) is the primary point of reader identification, but here it is Stalin who is the reader's stand-in. He's heard too many of these stories before, and it's going to take more than an encounter with a prepubescent time-traveling senior citizen to impress him.

"Vitya Solnyshkin and Joseph Stalin" does its best to demystify the genre while still invoking its usual mystical hand waving (Viktor Petrovich ends up in Vitya's body by unexplained magic). The point is not that such travel is impossible, since the genre has never depended on convincing readers that such stories could happen. Instead, "Vitya Solnyshkin" demonstrates that the trip simply isn't worth taking. History has happened, and no amount of narcissistic fantasy about the hero's intervention is going to change anything. Nor is any individual story going to add much to the genre. We've seen it all before.

The Time Crashers are easy to parody, and "Vitya Solnyshkin" would be unlikely to stand out from the crowd were it not for its author, Sergey Lukyanenko.[1] One of the few Russian-language genre writers to gain global fame, Sergey Lukyanenko is best known for his *Night Watch* series of novels and stories, which inspired two films by Timur Bekmambetov: *Night Watch* (2004), which was an international hit; and *Day Watch* (2008), which was not. Lukyanenko's work in English translation consists of few entries besides the *Night Watch* series, which could lead readers to believe that the author deals exclusively in urban fantasy. But his vast Russian catalog tells a different story. Lukyanenko has tried his hand at virtually every subgenre of Russian fantasy and science fiction (F&SF), except for one: the author is vehement in his disdain for historical Time Crasher stories.

Lukyanenko has no objection to sending characters to other worlds or dimensions by accident or through alien intervention, but he finds the historical tales derivative and unrelentingly conservative, if not quasi-fascist. Yet he cannot ignore them. Time Crasher stories appear to be the fastest growing variety of F&SF in Russia. Even excluding accidental travel to nonhistorical

---

1. Lukyanenko's story was first published in the collection *Lost Watch* (Zateriannyi dozor). Though the book contains sixteen different stories, it is Lukyanenko's name that is put in bold on the cover, along with an announcement of a new *Night Watch* story (Lukyanenko made two contributions to the collection).

destinations, the genre is too large to keep track of. The twenty-fourth edition of the online *Complete Encyclopedia of Popadantsy to the Past* (Viazovskii and Garik, *Polnaia entsiklopediia*, 24th ed.) has 2,100 entries, including 222 works that were not listed in the previous edition posted only five months earlier. No surprise that Stalin is weary of these time-traveling guests! The real shock is that Pioneer Solnyshkin was able to get a private conversation with the general secretary. By rights, his office should have been jam-packed with Time Crashers, nattering on about how to save the Soviet Union from enemies foreign and domestic.

Lukyanenko's story is not the most likely gateway into the Time Crasher genre; characterized by bemused exhaustion rather than a sense of wonder, "Vitya Solnyshkin" reads more like a farewell. Given the backward-looking nature of the genre, however, "Vitya Solnyshkin" proves quite appropriate. Imagine Time Crasher stories as a brand-new genre, with Lukyanenko dropping in from the future in order to, if not save it, then at least nudge it in the direction of self-awareness.

This leads us to one more thing worth noting about the story: "Vitya Solnyshkin" reflects not just a generic reader's impatience with the Time Crashers but that of the story's author. No fan of Stalin, Lukyanenko nonetheless uses the Soviet dictator as a point of authorial identification. Stalin's presence sums up the critique of the genre Lukyanenko already made elsewhere under his own name ("Popadantsy"). This kind of authorial self-insertion can be found in any genre but is particularly characteristic of fan fiction (fic) (Bacon-Smith 154–56; Jamison). Perhaps inadvertently, Lukyanenko shows how much fan fiction and the Time Crashers have in common. The Time Crashers may be accidental tourists, but their creators are essentially writers of fic. Their fandom is history.

What looks like simple nostalgia proves to be much more complicated; the accidental time traveler's relationship with both his home time period and the world in which he arrives is one of profound estrangement. Both in the present and in the means by which he travels to the past, he exerts little agency over his own life. Only in the historical fantasyland that greets him does he get to play the hero. If the circumstances of the present are beyond his control, those of the past are not.

After some consideration, I have chosen to use the masculine pronoun to refer to the typical Time Crasher, not only because the character really is almost always male (women show up more often as part of a group that does the traveling) but to highlight the way in which historical estrangement becomes gendered. Some of the more interesting examples of Time Crashers involve the implantation of a present-day man's mind into the body of a young girl. Others use the hero's personal timeline to represent the problem of historical origins. Time travel stories often flirt with the grandfather paradox (going back in time and accidentally killing your grandfather so that you are never born), but Time Crashers prefer the other variant, familiar to viewers of *Back to the Future*: the possibility of either incest (a sexual encounter with the mother in the past) or disturbing age gaps hidden by discrepancies between the hero's old mind and his young body.

Traveling in time is usually a life-changing event for the traveler, but the fate of the world is not always at stake. This chapter takes a look at the Time Crasher stories in which the hero's agency is critical: he is to perform a task that will alter or preserve history, either saving or improving himself along the way. Such stories both construct and rely on the near-total identification of personal history with the history of the world or, more often, the nation. This is, of course, flattering to the hero and to the readers/viewers encouraged to identify with him, but it also encourages an affective attachment to the country's history that is easily assimilated by nationalist or imperialist agendas. The plots are about the restoration or affirmation of a "natural" historical order with Russia at the center, an order that, while under threat, can still be saved through the dedication and possible self-sacrifice of the patriotic Time Crasher. Unsurprisingly, World War II (to which Vitya Solnyshkin found himself drawn in Lukyanenko's parody) is a frequent, but not exclusive, setting. The next chapter examines the lower-stakes stories in which the drama is almost entirely personal.

But first, we need to take a look at the origins of the genre itself.

In Search of Lost Time Travelers

As James Gleick demonstrates in *Time Travel*, fictional characters have been traveling to the future and the past for centuries, but time travel as a distinct notion is surprisingly new (28–43). It was H. G. Wells who shifted the concept from pure fantasy into the realm of "scientific romance" when he published *The Time Machine* in 1895. The fact that the book's title now seems so generic underscores just how influential Wells's work was—apparently, no one before him had ever thought to put "time" and "machine" together.

The result was not only the eventual proliferation of time travel stories but a particular framework rooted in science and logic: time travel can create paradoxes, and therefore becomes an irresistible logical puzzle. Ask the average person what trappings they associate with science fiction, and they will probably mention robots, spaceships, and time machines. Within the science fictional framework, time travel stories are an ideal testing ground for theories about determinism and free will, the importance of individual people or events, and even the makeup of the cosmos. And, of course, time travel provides endless possibility for adventure.

With the exception of adventure, most of these concerns are irrelevant to the Time Crasher phenomenon. Not only do these stories rarely bother with mechanical or pseudoscientific contrivances, but they also tend not to care at all about the method of travel. As for the possibility of paradox, their concern is selective and sporadic at best. They lack a fundamental feature of science fictional time travel stories: an implicit or explicit theory of time. Despite the enduring centrality of Wells to the Russian understanding of *fantastika*, most Time Crasher stories are composed as if decades of science fictional time travel tales had never been written. We should recall that the Russian equivalent of "science fiction" is *nauchnaia fantastika*—"scientific fantasy." The Time Crasher genre jettisons the scientific in favor of the fantasy, instead following in the tradition of Mark Twain's *A Connecticut Yankee in King Arthur's Court*. The titular Yankee ends up in Arthurian England after a blow to the head knocks him unconscious. When he wakes up, he is in a different time. How does this work? The correct answer is crucial to appreciating the story: it doesn't matter.

Readers of Time Crasher stories have no particular reason to believe that a head injury, a mysterious fog, or lying on one's deathbed are feasible means of time travel. Rather, readers make different demands of the text. In this, Time Crasher stories differ from other hard-core F&SF genre entertainments, whose devoted fans often derive satisfaction from expanding and interrogating a particular text's or franchise's lore. This holds true for fantasy as well as for science fiction, as even a cursory familiarity with *Harry Potter* fandom demonstrates. These fans find as much pleasure in the mechanics of the imaginary tale as they do in the tale itself. All Time Crasher readers require is for the players to get where they are supposed to be.

Generally, in both fantasy and science fiction time travel is expected to be replicable, but Time Crashers primarily travel by means that are idiosyncratic and personal. A pre-teen science fiction reader might dream of building a time machine, but they are unlikely to induce a head injury in order to kill baby Hitler. This underscores the frequent status of the hero as an authorial stand-in: it is the author's sensibility (and ideological agenda) that propels the trip to another time.

The ubiquity of the hero as author's mouthpiece helps explain why so many Time Crashers travel in mind but not body. The hero's knowledge from the future and of the past's future are what matters. When bodies do travel backward in time, they are often accompanied by useful artifacts, particularly laptop computers, the material embodiment of information from the future. Mikhail Koroliuk's *Save the USSR!* (*Spasti SSSR!*) splits the difference by having the adult hero's mind end up in the body of his fourteen-year-old self, which has magically gained the power of "brain surfing," allowing him to call up information as if he had the entire Internet downloaded into his adolescent head.

On a superficial level, psychic time travel avoids some of the more obvious potentials for paradox. When Marty McFly meets his future parents in the 1950s in *Back to the Future*, that means that, as teenagers, they always knew someone who would happen to look like the teenage son they would have decades later. But the implantation of the adult mind into the child's or adolescent's body turns out to be fraught with perils not unlike Marty's near-incestuous encounter with his future mother.

Trying to fix world or national history by hijacking one's own personal history is the assertion of a particular type of cosmos, in which the micro is a synecdoche for the macro. The personal is not just political; it is integral to the fate of the nation. This is narcissism on a cosmic scale, beyond even the "great man" theory of history. The hero/authorial stand-in (often an office or IT worker, both of which are common day jobs for F&SF writers) just happens to be the person who can save everything. Office drones to the rescue!

Psychic time travel lays bare the device of post-Soviet nostalgia and historical fandom. Watching or reading stories of the Soviet past can be a form of escapism, sending the audience back to an idealized time. The psychic Time Crasher moves the audience out of the role of passive spectator and into something more like a gamer in a first-person shooter. These stories emplot the phenomenon Svetlana Boym calls "restorative nostalgia," which "reconstruct[s] emblems and rituals of home and homeland in an attempt to conquer and specialize time" (49). In terms of fandom, these stories combine the "curatorial" ethos (guarding the canon against heresy) and the "transformational" impulse (in fixing history, the Time Crashers are improving on a beloved storyworld) (obsession_inc 2009).

By necessity, psychic travel along one's personal timeline reduces the scope of time travel to the length of the hero's life span. Pensioners go back to World War II, while members of the last Soviet generations end up somewhere in the Brezhnev era. In each case, the connection between the personal and historical is far stronger than any jaunt to the age of Ivan the Terrible might be. The Soviet Union, we should recall, lasted for just under seventy-four years (if we count from the October Revolution), which was only a few years longer than the average Soviet male life span in 1991 (68.47 years). The USSR's life cycle is easily comprehensible in human terms, all the more so for people whose lives began in the Soviet Union. In trying to correct the moments where their country went wrong, these Time Crashers are rebooting their own lives.

Portrait of a Grandpa as a Young Girl

In the introduction, I noted that the genre's inherent dissatisfaction with the present creates an uncanny effect: something about the present simply does not feel right. Even more, in the Time Crasher stories the present day is uncanny: the hero has a continual sense of not quite fitting into his own time and place. In its combination of familiarity and wrongness, the uncanny becomes internalized: what could be more *unheimlich* than the suspicion that the problem resides in one's very sense of self? One particularly unusual set of Time Crasher narratives intensifies the sense of the uncanny by attaching it to the hero's body as gender dysphoria. In the novel that gives the collection *Student, Komsomol Girl, Athlete* its title, the male author's stand-in is reborn in the past as a girl (Arsen'ev, Studentka).[2]

Student, Komsomol Girl, Athlete is narrated by an old man who, sometime in the 2040s, has reached the end of a life marked by disappointments and tragedy. His son died defending his motherland (now renamed the "Democratic Republic of Muscovy," abbreviated as "SHIT" in Russian), his daughter died in a nuclear blast in the "Baltic Republic," and his young granddaughter was tortured and murdered. He drops dead of a heart attack and wakes up in the body of an infant girl named Natasha on December 31, 1960. He has all of his memories and mental capacities as an adult man, which allow him to become a child prodigy. Continuing to use the masculine pronoun and verb forms in his first-person narration, Natasha excels in organizational work at his elementary school, joins the Pioneers at an early age, has a brief, successful film career while still a teenager, and then becomes an athlete who eventually specializes in marksmanship.[3] This is all part of his master plan, which succeeds when, in 1980, Natasha is presented to the leadership of the Soviet Union at the opening of the Moscow Olympics, whereupon he shoots and kills Andropov, Gorbachev, and Yeltsin, saving the Soviet Union from collapse. He dies happy, knowing that he has created a new timeline, one whose further history is explored (and again rewritten) in the other two stories collected in the volume.

The author, Sergei Vladimirovich Arsenyev, appears to be an elderly man who got his start writing online. Most of his work is hosted by Samizdat (samlib.ru), a self-publishing portal ironically reappropriating the Soviet term used for writing disseminated unofficially. *Student, Komsomol Girl, Athlete* was posted in November 2011, then picked up by EKSMO—one of Russia's largest publishers—for commercial publication the following year. (It seems to be the only one of

---

2. The Komsomol is the abbreviation for the Communist Youth League, while the book's title comes from Leonid Gaidai's immensely popular film *Kidnapping, Caucasian Style* (Kavkazskaia plennitsa, 1967). It has become the standard humorous description of a girl who is held up as a model of good behavior.

3. Though he would be unlikely to use such terminology, Natasha's preferred pronouns are masculine (at least in the privacy of his own thoughts). I am following his example.

his works to make this sort of crossover.) In addition to other Time Crasher stories, Arsenyev has written in numerous other F&SF subgenres, as well as in historical realism.

Imputing psychological motivations to an author is always a tricky business, all the more so when information is so sparse. But Arsenyev's Samizdat page contains a brief manifesto titled "Sergei Arsenyev on His Work" ("Sergei Arsen'ev o svoem tvorchestve," 2010). It consists of ten points, including condemnations of capitalism and democracy, praise for Stalin and denial that the Terror happened, calls for qualified tolerance of national minorities ("as long as the migrant behaves like a person, and not like an ape that's escaped from the circus"), belief that the collapse of the USSR was one of the greatest catastrophes in history, disdain for the "opportunists" in the Communist Party of the Russian Federation, and a declaration that Hitler was "not an idiot" but rather a leader who did a great deal for his country in the 1930s (even if by 1945 he had degenerated into "a total shit"). This is fairly standard stuff for both contemporary Russian science fiction and fan fiction, but there is one more point that stands out: "6. I hate homos" (*Nenavizhu gomosekov*). This, too, is hardly unusual, but its placement in the middle of the manifesto, as the shortest and therefore presumably least complicated proposition is intriguing. Especially when one considers that his favorite trope is the transmigration of an old man's mind into a little girl's body.

While I may not be comfortable psychoanalyzing Arsenyev from a distance, commenters online have no qualms about offering an armchair diagnosis. A self-identified gay man writing under the username Skepsis on March 5, 2021, asks how it is possible to "seriously" espouse an ideology combining homophobia, tolerance of ethnic minorities, and an admiration for Hitler:

> It's extremely sad, Arsenyev, that you are a man-hater who is disgusted with his own body. Because only such clinical abnormalities can explain the SIMULTANEOUS presence of the red thread running throughout your entire work—the transfer of an adult man's consciousness into the body of a little girl while maintaining a sexual orientation toward girls that is normal for a man but not normal for a girl. Moreover, you manage to describe this along with straightforward disgust for intimacy with a man and a declaration of your hatred of homosexuals. But, alas, I must remind you that female homosexuality, which is clearly found in your novels, is ALSO homosexuality and eroticism, characteristic of "homos." (Skepsis)

Skepsis's take on Arsenyev isn't quite a model of progressive critique. His attack on the author's homophobia is predicated on a notion of the "normal," and his characterization of the book's same-sex eroticism manages to combine trans erasure with outright transphobia. But the tension he finds between Arsenyev's homophobia and his predilection for magical trans narratives is undeniable. The temptation to attribute stealth trans longing to the author's own psychological makeup is all the stronger given the near-perfection of the hypercompetent heroines who had once been old men of the author's generation.

We cannot know for sure if Arsenyev's own personal gender dysphoria is finding its way into his texts like some repressed Freudian symptom, with the author's militant homophobia serving as cover for his own trans desire. What we can do, however, is ask what role the text's explicit gender dysphoria might play in this particular strain of Time Crasher narrative. Just as Solovyov's Oedipal crisis points to the regressive character of Time Crasher nostalgia in *Dark Side of the Moon* (see chapter 2), the gender dysphoria in Arsenyev's work highlights the sociopolitical estrangement of the post-Soviet subject and the uncanny ontology of this subject in both the present day and the imagined past.

I Enjoy Being a Girl

In the prologue, the man who will be Natasha is taking stock of his life in the moments before the heart attack that kills him, and the picture is not pretty. In the decades since the Soviet collapse, the world has become a hostile, alien environment even as his body has begun to betray him. The first page is a litany of complaints that are the familiar lot of the elderly: his body can no longer handle the cold, nor can he walk without a cane. But not all of his dissatisfaction is the inevitable result of old age. He has to rely on humanitarian aid (expired dog food and stale bread), because after he pays his rent and utilities, his pension is almost exhausted. It is when he mentions money that we begin to see the strangeness of his world, as all the prices are calculated in euros rather than rubles.

He has the classically masculine instincts of a protector, sheltering a seventy-year-old widowed neighbor who has been evicted from her apartment, though she dies in her sleep just three months later. But overall, he has been a failure as a protector and provider, albeit through no fault of his own. Both his children are dead, and his young granddaughter has been murdered. When he dies, he leaves behind a world that could not let him succeed as a man.

The protagonist's gender swap allows him to redeem both himself and his country, rewriting the literal past of the Soviet Union while symbolically reversing the biggest tragedies of his own life. On one hand, everything bad that happened to him in the original timeline can be attributed at least indirectly to the collapse of the USSR; on the other hand, his losses are also experienced as the personal failures of a father, husband, and grandfather. The USSR fell apart due to incompetent or treacherous leadership, leading to destruction of the narrator's family as a failure of his husbandry. Reborn as Natasha, he becomes both a hyper-competent caretaker (no one will die on his watch now, with one key exception) and the world's least likely but most successful political assassin. In so doing, he exchanges helplessness for agency.

Young Natasha immediately distinguishes himself on the domestic front. Natasha's mother dies suddenly, not long after giving birth to twin boys, on her daughter's eighth birthday, leaving behind a husband who is incapable of running their home. (He goes out on a drinking spree for three days before Natasha whips him back into shape.) With the help of a girlfriend his age, Natasha takes over the cooking and the cleaning, along with the care of his infant brothers. He is, of course, exhausted, but he does not let his new burdens impede his efforts to build a new book collection for his school and assume a leadership position among his peers.

As he grows older, Natasha moves from triumph to triumph, even starring in a movie that was one of his (original) childhood favorites. His never-ending success, along with the constant praise he receives from all those who surround him, are the hallmarks of authorial self-insertion in fan fiction. Yet the story's wish-fulfillment fantasy is always complicated by Natasha's own complicated gender identity. In his mind and in his narration, Natasha remains stubbornly male, using masculine pronouns and maintaining a sense of continuity with his previous life as a man. In his daily interactions, however, he functions as female, using feminine pronouns and grammatical forms. If *Student, Komsomol Girl, Athlete* is the author's fantasy of trans rebirth, it is certainly idiosyncratic. Taking the narrator's words at face value, the novel creates rather than solves gender dysphoria. According to the logic of the novel itself, *Student* is not the story of a trans woman reborn as a cisgender girl, but of a cisgender man reborn as a transgender boy who never comes out to those around him.

If we follow the argument of the hostile samizdat.ru commentator discussed earlier, we have before us a Freudian return of the repressed. Rather than confront what Skepsis assumes is the assigned-male writer's forbidden fantasy of being a girl, Arsenyev addresses his dysphoria by reversing it: his hero must live life as a girl while knowing he is a man. But if we refrain from imputing motive and desire to Arsenyev himself, we are left with an even more intriguing statement about the Time Crasher fantasy. In such a reading, gender dysphoria is the Time Crasher's price of entry, the burden he must bear if he is to travel to the past and rewrite history for the better.

Once Natasha has arrived in 1960, gender dysphoria is the only true conflict in the novel. Otherwise, nearly everything goes according to plan. The real flaw the book struggles with is the idealization not of the protagonist but of the setting. Brezhnev-era Russia is overwhelmingly wonderful, a utopian alternative to the dystopian 2040s. By having Natasha live in the "wrong" body, Arsenyev unites both time periods in a shared discomfort, amplifying the uncanny effect of a familiar malaise throughout the novel. Contrary to the reading that imputes trans desire to the author, the saving grace of *Student, Komsomol Girl, Athlete* is its refusal to be a perfect fulfillment of a fantasy. Natasha can be a girl saving his beloved homeland from its degradation into a neoliberal hellscape, or he can reside in said hellscape as a man. Natasha cannot "have it all."

As a child, Natasha resists his mother's efforts to get him to wear bows, eventually managing to have his hair cut short. He checks himself for signs of sexual interest in boys but finds none. This does not mean he has resolved never to have sex. If sleeping with a man will get him closer to his goal, then he'll do it. Instead, he is interested in girls, even kissing a German girl in public: "When it comes right down to it, why do Brezhnev and Honneker get to do it, but not Elsa and me, huh?" (213).

Still, the book suggests that gender dysphoria is a small price for Natasha to pay in exchange for a better world. When he was an old man in the 2040s, Natasha's focus was on his family and friends and all the misery they endured; the sociopolitical situation that caused their troubles was always in the background but far beyond his ability to affect. In his own time, "everyone understood that they had lost. Fighting on was impossible. No one believed in victory" (147). The 1970s were another matter: "People believe in the future. In the future of themselves and their children" (147).

In the hands of a more subtle writer, we might identify productive irony and ambiguity in a declaration about "belief in the future" made by a time traveler to the past. Natasha, who has seen the terrible future, is the last person who should have any optimism. As an eleven-year-old girl in 1972, he can soberly assess the world he came from and the world in which he now lives: "Now this country is perhaps at the peak of its might. And no one can see that we are heading toward the abyss, and in literally a decade and a half it will all end in a grandiose Catastrophe" (145).

On their own, the optimists of the 1970s cannot create the future in which they believe. It will take the machinations of a visitor from a terrible future to make the bright future that ordinary people expect.[4] He will never be able to live in the world that he creates, but that does not matter. In the scheme of things, his first death meant nothing, just as the deaths of all his loved ones were pointless.

---

4. In "My popali," Leonid Fishman sees the *popodanets* as the heir to the Strugatsky Brothers' progressors: when he ends up in the past, he is a modernizer by default.

Now he can choose to make a sacrifice. In an inversion of the Stalinist slogan, Natasha dies and is reborn to bring a fairy tale to life.

To Natasha, saving the USSR from collapse means preventing the deaths of his loved ones in the future (never mind the time paradoxes involved). His impending Christ-like sacrifice is preceded by a brief digression into a Gethsemane of doubt:

> I could just stop, to hell with the Plan. Live the life of a normal Soviet person. Or go into business. Or even government. I could try to get into Yeltsin's inner circle (even if it means sleeping my way there) and get towed along into the Kremlin. . . . And watch my Motherland die. . . . No! I'm not going to stop. Ninochka! I remember you and I'll save you! (223)

Right before the assassination, he reminds himself of his purpose: "For my Vovka, killed by NATO. For my old, sick neighbor Sergei Kuz'mich, mugged at the drugstore. For my only granddaughter Nina, raped and tortured to death. For the impoverished, half-starved existence of old people who worked all their lives" (235).

The whole point of Natasha's second life is to right wrongs. Post-Soviet Russia was never really his home, because it was the corrupt wreckage of a once great country. Natasha's rebirth as a girl works because it helps prevent him from ever being truly comfortable in the world that he needs to save, thereby helping him resist the temptation to remain behind. For him, the 1970s will always meet both of Freud's etymological definitions of the uncanny: it is familiar (homely), but he can never forget its strangeness as the world in which he finds himself. Granted, his discomfort manifests itself rather rarely once Natasha is no longer an infant, perhaps supporting the reading of the book as the author's forbidden transgender fantasy. Either way, the resulting world that lives on after Natasha's (second) death is a restoration of a lost era, a projection of a vibrant Soviet Union into the post-1991 future. What was broken is now whole, and this new integrity is reinforced by a minor plot point from the middle of the book. Teenage Natasha encounters his original mother as she is taking her baby out for a stroll: "The baby in her carriage was named . . . Natasha! Now that was something I never expected. . . . It's me. But in this world I was born a girl! So it's either the "butterfly effect," or HE has a truly outstanding sense of humor" (143).

We are on unusual Oedipal ground, with just a hint of the time paradox of Robert Heinlein's classic short story, "All You Zombies," in which every character turns out to be a version of the narrator from a different moment in time, including the protagonist's mother and father. No matter who his parents are, Natasha will now always be Natasha. Natasha-the-narrator and Natasha-the-baby might best be seen as two different transgender fantasies. The narrator, by retaining his memories of himself as a man, is either newly dysphoric (because he was fine in a male body before) or a fulfillment of a fantasy of existing in an assigned-female boy while maintaining continuity of consciousness with his previous self. In the second scenario, Natasha-the-narrator remains a trans character in a new body. Natasha-the-baby, who will never have had the life experiences of Natasha-the-narrator, has the chance to grow up as a cisgender girl. Just as the citizens of the twenty-first-century Soviet Union will have no memory of the Soviet collapse, the new Natasha will have no memory of having lived in the world as an adult man. The promised land not only undoes all rupture and dysphoria but hides the traces that they ever existed. If Arsenyev really is working through his own gender troubles in his fiction without acknowledging them, then he has landed on the perfect fantasy—a Soviet Union that lives up to ideals and a rebirth as a girl that amounts to a kind of trans erasure.

This erasure carries over to the short stories that serve as sequels to the novel proper. Each is narrated by a girl with a distant connection to Natasha but with virtually no tonal or stylistic distinction from the narration of Natasha herself. They benefit from Natasha's sacrifice, born in the world Natasha created, experiencing lives free of both the general malaise of the previous, post-Soviet iteration of reality and the gender dysphoria that haunts the novel. They are just like Natasha, except that they are girls living with no contradiction to the gender assigned to them at birth. One of them even manages to repeat Natasha's heroic rewriting of history. Accidentally finding herself in Nazi Germany in 1941, she befriends Hitler, prevents World War II and the Holocaust, becomes the first cosmonaut (even appropriating Yuri Gagarin's famous catchphrase), founds a new world order based on a Nazi/Soviet alliance, and takes over for Hitler as the Führer of the Third Reich.[5] Arsenyev's fictional world is now several steps removed not just from our reality but from the dystopian future imagined in the collection's first pages. Through the efforts of multiple Time Crashers, Arsenyev has erased all trace of both the original sin of our reality (the collapse of the USSR) and the complicated gender issues that the initial novel could not ignore. It is the perfect utopian move, erasing all traces of the unpleasant history that led up to it in order to create a perfect, self-contained world whose past, present, and future all form an idealized closed loop immune to the profane misery of actual history.

---

5. Within the Time Crasher genre, such a scenario is not all that surprising. Many fascist-leaning "patriotic" Russian writers have imagined a persistent Soviet/Nazi alliance as the best of all possible pasts.

War and Remembrance

When Arsenyev sends another young girl named Natasha back to 1941, it is decidedly *not* to fight in World War II. Certainly, her age and gender make her an unlikely combatant, but that is presumably not the only reason she isn't sent to the front lines. Her purpose is to prevent war rather than wage it, and her journey depends on the efficiency of the "great man" school of history: all she need do is influence one key figure (in this case, Hitler), and Natasha's mission is accomplished.

Natasha is far from the only hero(ine) whose travels through time bring her face-to-face with one of the key figures of World War II, as Lukyanenko's Stalin informs the young Pioneer in the story with which the present chapter opened. But such meetings are not the most common feature of a 1940s setting. On the whole, Time Crashers who end up in World War II are there to wage war rather than prevent it, whether as infantry on the front, as drivers of time-traveling tanks, or as fighter pilots defending the motherland. World War II is the site of *action*.

Given the human toll suffered by the Soviet Union, along with the justifiable pride in the defeat of the Nazi invaders, this should come as no surprise. It is also consistent with one of the functions of World War II in Soviet postwar mass culture: the Great Patriotic War was one of the few settings that justified the representation of action, violence, and bloodshed. As such, it was a rare outlet for narrative heroic fantasy, while also reinforcing the general militarization of adventure tales in Soviet times. In the absence of superhero or vigilante stories and the scarcity of espionage films and novels, the military played an outsize role in male-oriented entertainment. Moreover, service in the armed forces was technically mandatory for all adult Soviet men (even if many of the privileged found ways around it), which meant that the military formed the basis of a kind of masculine lingua franca. Since the Soviet collapse, adventure stories, like other entertainments, have significantly diversified, but the role of the military remains pronounced.

So when men are sent back to the Great Patriotic War, they fight. And, for the most part, they fight well, which in itself is an important point. Dropping men from present-day Russia onto the battlefields of World War II could yield a variety of results, but it is worth thinking about what these stories are *not* doing. It would be no stretch to imagine a masculinist morality tale about out-of-shape, effete office drones rediscovering their manhood while saving the motherland. The perennial anxieties about Soviet or Russian masculinity could easily express themselves through such a story, whether they be the Brezhnev-era "crisis of manhood" analyzed by Mark Dumancic in *Men out of Focus* or the 1990s compensatory masculinity I discuss in *Overkill*. By the twenty-first century, the discursive work of propping up Russian masculinity has been done. When contemporary Russian men end up in World War II, they are quite capable of fighting. Instead, they have other lessons to learn.

In addition to the hundreds of novels about time travel to World War II, there are also two series of films for the big and small screen: *We Are from the Future* (2008) and its sequel, *We Are from the Future 2* (2010); and *The Fog* (2010) and *The Fog 2* (2012). The first *We Are from the Future* had a theatrical release before its expanded version appeared on television, while *The Fog* is effectively two four-episode seasons of a single television drama. Each tells the tale of a group of young men who inexplicably find themselves thrown back in time to World War II, and each delivers a patriotic message that is as far from subtlety as their protagonists are from home.

In the crowded field of World War II time travel narratives, these two stand out by virtue of the size of their audience. Popular as Time Crasher novels are, they are still a small niche in comparison to television and film viewership. Over a million people saw the first *We Are from the Future* in theaters. Obviously, film and television are more expensive propositions than prose fiction, so the filmmakers would take care to ensure their work has mass appeal. Sending attractive young men to fight and die in the past makes a lot more box office sense that filming the adventures of a septuagenarian man in the body of a schoolgirl.

Mental time travel is not enough for these films; their heroes must be corporeally transported back to the 1940s. It is their bodies that must endure the very real physical dangers they encounter; indeed, in some cases, those bodies even die (if only temporarily). But just as the films are a vehicle for patriotic propaganda, their bodies are vehicles for the stories' true subjects, their inner selves. Though it is not merely their consciousness that travels to the past, it is their consciousness that must undergo the greatest transformation. By the end of the story, it will have been raised.

The age and experience of the young men would suggest that their time in World War II is a rite of passage from youth into maturity. In fact, the films enact two parallel life-cycle rituals: one for the men, the other for the country itself. *The Fog* starts its present-day story line in the run-up to Victory Day (May 9), the official commemoration of the defeat of Nazi Germany. This holiday had long been the cornerstone of Soviet mythology. Pride in this victory was justifiable and understandable; more important, it was framed as universal. Talk of the repression of entire nationalities during the war as suspected potential enemy collaborators was discouraged until perestroika, and the extent of collaboration with the Nazi occupiers in the western parts of the USSR was downplayed. Everyone alive owed the Soviet military a great debt, including citizens of the rest of the world, who had the USSR to thank for crushing Hitler's forces. War memorials were treated as objects of reverence, and proud, medal-bedecked veterans marching in the annual parades were accorded respect.

The annual ritual of remembrance took on new poignancy after 1991. The country that defeated the Nazis was no more, and the public condemnation of Stalin's crimes was an uncomfortable fit with the long-held idea that Stalin's military brilliance and the country's huge economic growth in the 1930s were responsible for the victory. Meanwhile, the veterans were obviously getting older and, more to the point, fewer. The huge celebration of the fiftieth anniversary of the Soviet victory in 1995 made sense because of the significance of the date but was also a kind of last hurrah: one could not help but be aware that the men and women marching in the fiftieth anniversary parade were unlikely to make it to the sixtieth.

This helps explain the Immortal Regiment procession discussed in the introduction. The absence of the veterans themselves is at least partly compensated by the photos of the dead, whose status in the processions resembles that Russian Orthodox icon. The phenomenon grew quickly after its 2011 introduction, to the point where it has now been thoroughly coopted by the state as a manifestation of official patriotism. But the practice associated with the Immortal Regiment was not new; similar events took place as far back as 1968, recurring at different times and places over the next few decades with a randomness that suggests multiple people coming up with the same idea independently. With the passage of time, the practice is the logical next step after parades of living veterans cease to be a viable option.

Replacing the combatants with their photos changes the entire notion of participation in the celebration of Victory Day. Victory becomes not just a legacy but an inheritance experienced both individually and collectively. In the absence of actual participants, their descendants must take up the mantle of the fallen warriors. With the Immortal Regiment, Victory Day becomes a ritual like the Passover Seder: Jews are taught to talk of the time when "we" were slaves in Egypt, not "our ancestors." Historical time and present time collapse through the willful engagement of empathy.

Millennials vs. Nazis

Or at least they should. Both *The Fog* and *We Are from the Future* are premised on the breakdown of this transhistorical empathy, due to the current young generation's lack of historical consciousness. The protagonists of *The Fog* and its sequel are a small group of Russian soldiers who are by no means bad people. To the contrary, they are almost relentlessly ordinary. True, one of them seems to be a born leader, while another, nicknamed Yandex after the popular Russian search engine, is the resident brainiac whose endless font of knowledge will be invaluable to them when they find themselves on the front lines.

Their story unfolds according to the logic of allegory, with their movements in space and time doubling as a representation of their moral development. Before they travel in time, they take part in a training exercise requiring them to hike across a vast terrain. Instead, they choose a short cut, and when they are lost and in danger of missing their deadline, they actually seize a bus full of World War II veterans who are on their way to a commemoration. In their desire to cut corners, they disgrace not only themselves but the men who came before them (now, briefly, their prisoners). The punishment imposed on them by their commander pales in comparison to the punishment inflicted on them by karma: when they march through a thick fog, they end up in World War II.

Once they arrive, the story plods ahead with an uninspired predictability that nevertheless reinforces the overall sense of historical inevitability. After an initial period of confusion, the young men throw in with the Red Army and fight the German invaders. Their twenty-first-century cynicism is replaced by a 1940s' Sense of Purpose. Though they have no idea if they can ever make it back to their home time, they realize that part of their mission has to be to make sure that the futuristic weaponry they have brought with them does not remain in Nazi hands, or else they will have inadvertently changed the course of the war. In the last episode of the first season, several of them die heroically, only to be miraculously resurrected when the whole group has returned back to its proper time. They have arrived at precisely the right moment to watch the victory parade, with special attention to the proud veterans whom they had so deeply offended in the first episode. The camera pans across the faces of our heroes as they try in vain to restrain the tears that well up in their eyes.[6]

We Are from the Future teaches similar lessons but from a different point of departure.[7] The film's four protagonists have much further to go in order to redeem themselves. Rather than soldiers, they are unscrupulous treasure hunters who comb World War II battle sites in search of medals and memorabilia.[8] They

---

6. As for the second season, they basically do it all over again. Television repeats itself, first as melodrama, then as a naked ratings grab.

7. Not that these films are otherwise all that different from each other. As Ilya Kalinin puts it in "Future-in-the-past," "they are all basically the same film, and there is no need to talk about each one separately."

8. In Russian, such people are referred to as *chernye kopateli*, which literally means "black diggers." In English, the film is occasionally titled *Black Hunters*, which would be unlikely to make sense to the uninitiated.

are led by Sergei Filatov, a former St. Petersburg University history student whose nickname (Borman) refers to a top official in Hitler's Reich, and among their ranks is a neo-Nazi skinhead called Skull (Cherep) who has a swastika tattoo on his shoulder. Where the heroes of *The Fog* are merely jaded and disrespectful, the men in *We Are from the Future* start out as repulsively cynical.

At a dig outside of St. Petersburg, they are approached by an old woman who lost her son at this site during the war. She begs them to find his silver cigar case. They humor her and promise to give it back to her if they come across it, even though they have no intention of doing so. Inside a dugout, they stumble across a set of military IDs with their names and photos on them, an uncanny shock that convinces them they must be on drugs. Naturally, they run to skinny dip in a nearby lake in order to sober up, but once they are in the water, they find themselves back in 1942.

Naked but still in possession of the mysterious ID papers they found in the dugout, the men are presumed shell-shocked and incorporated into a local Soviet military unit. Slowly they become part of the team, though taking part in actual warfare is still a shock. Along the way, they meet an orderly named Nina with whom Borman falls in love. They even stumble upon Sokolov, the old lady's lost son and possessor of the mysterious silver cigar case. A dying Sokolov asks them to take his cigar case and bring it to his mother. By the end, our heroes have become thoroughly dedicated to the Soviet cause; Nina is presumed dead; one of the men is mortally wounded; and all four go back to the lake, this time successfully returning to the present. The wounded man is miraculously healed, but that is only an external manifestation of the changes to their hearts. The film ends with Skull trying to scrape the swastika tattoo off his skin.

Their moral transformation is now complete—so complete, in fact, that in the sequel Skull has grown his hair out, and Borman is played by an entirely different actor (the other two members of the original group are absent). All the same, *We Are from the Future 2* actually adds to the franchise's message, unlike the sequel to *The Fog*, which simply sends the guys back again for another iteration of the premise.[9] Borman and Skull have completely turned their lives around, becoming real archeologists rather than unscrupulous treasure hunters. Their official work is doubled in the film by their newfound moral purpose: they will teach other cynical young men that the Soviet victory is sacred.

---

9. In *The Fog 2*, the men accidentally cause the near-death of Mikhail Yegorov, the soldier who would go on to raise the Soviet flag over the Reichstag. They spend four episodes trying to undo this rather dubious damage; a brief appeal to the Butterfly Effect explains why this change in history is important, but it is worth noting that, at this point, what is at stake seems only symbolic. Given the tenor of World War II commemorations during the 2010s, this seems entirely appropriate.

In the first film, our heroes had to overcome their own immaturity and lack of respect, but now they have a more complicated task: combatting the forces of Russophobia and Ukrainian nationalism that would not only complicate the narrative of the war as pure good vs. pure evil but resurrect pro-Nazi sentiment as part of the Ukrainian nation-building project. The film came out in 2010, three years before the Euromaidan protests and four before the outbreak of armed conflict, but five years after the Orange Revolution in Kyiv unleashed growing anti-Ukrainian sentiment in the Russian state media. Borman and Skull are supposed to take part in a reenactment of the 1944 Brody Cauldron battle that was key to the Red Army offensive against the Germans. Appalled at the local Ukrainians' enthusiasm for Nazi regalia and their hostility toward all things Russian, they try to make the best of things. But they quickly find themselves the object of ridicule on the part of two young Ukrainian men, the nationalist Taras and his friend Seryi (the pampered son of a Ukrainian parliamentarian). As a prank, Taras and Seryi throw an old World War II bomb into the ruins where Borman and Skull are standing, assuming it is a dud. The bomb goes off, sending all four men back to 1944.

We Are from the Future 2 is a dutiful sequel in terms of both plot and theme. Now it is Taras and Seryi who have to learn the lesson that the Russian heroes mastered in the previous film, while Borman and Skull continue the soap opera plot halfheartedly developed during their previous journey. Confronted by the villainous Ukrainians who fought on the side of the Nazis, the twenty-first-century Ukrainians refuse to take part in the fascists' slaughter of innocent villagers. By the time they are back in the present, they have completely internalized the cult of the Soviet Victory, while also experiencing an object lesson in the virtues of solidarity between Russians and Ukrainians.[10]

Meanwhile, the Russians discover that Borman's beloved Nina is not dead but in her ninth month of pregnancy by her soldier husband. Nina gives birth, but she and her husband heroically die during a bombing, leaving the now-penitent Taras to save their baby. Borman will nonetheless find happiness on his return to the present, when he meets Nina's granddaughter, who looks exactly like her. It's a cheap twist but a consistent one: only by dedicating himself to the motherland's heroic history can he create for himself a happy future, making the present and the future into felicitous iterations of the past.

Were it not for the simplicity of the film's ideological message and the studio's commitment to straightforward entertainment, this sequel could have pushed

---

10. Oleksandr Zabirko argues that the film establishes the Nazis as "the ideological forerunners of the contemporary Ukrainian state" (291).

the franchise in a more self-aware, reflective direction. Its iterative function (We Are from the Future 2!), its pointed references to post-Soviet disunity, and in particular the choice of a twenty-first-century setting all point back to a contemporary Russian preoccupation with the reframing of history. In the first film, the protagonists are on a mission to loot the past; their transformation involves the recognition of the primacy of sentimental and historical value over the potential economic rewards of cashing in on World War II artifacts. In the second, we move from archeological dig to historical reenactment, from grave-robbing to voluntarist resurrection.

In a historical reenactment (or "reconstruction," the Russian term for it), contemporary participants strive for verisimilitude as they simulate a historic battle while obviously aware that they have not traveled in time. The Time Crashers of *We Are from the Future 2*, having just been transported from a reenactment, are initially unable to recognize the real thing, mistaking it for the deliberate, ludic fraud they have just left. Verisimilitude is not enough; they must experience actual danger to know that they are far from the realm of play. And yet, have they really stopped playing? We see them suffer, we see the danger, but they will, of course, survive. Time Crashing, like historical reenactments, requires a compromise between seriousness and gaming. In each case, the young men involved are using the past to either learn about or remind themselves of the solemnity of the Victory, but even as they are led to identify with the combatants in the Great Patriotic War, they remain aware that there is someplace outside the game (or the war) for them to return to.

The Time Crasher narratives discussed in this chapter are, of course, about history, but history here should be understood as a subset of a larger philosophical concept: the cosmos. By "cosmos" I mean the ancient belief system that presumes homologies between the universe and the individual, that imagines the universe as organized along human principles. The alignments of the stars determine the fates of people on earth, and when all is working well, there is harmony between earth and sky. Both the films about traveling to World War II and Arsenyev's stories of Natasha and her descendants are tales about the restoration of order and harmony in a time of collapse. In the case of the war films, post-Soviet cynicism and Ukrainian nationalism (presented as anti-Russian by definition) have produced a generation of young men without a moral compass (indeed, they literally go off course before ending up in the past). Joining the fight to save the motherland against the fascists sparks their spiritual rebirth, and they return to the present as better people than they were before they left. Of course, the viewers have no such opportunity, no matter how much World War II-focused entertainment and propaganda are thrown at them, but the heroes' experience is clearly meant to be inspirational.

Arsenyev's stories are both more transformational and more pessimistic than the World War II films: they result in the total reconfiguration of history, beginning with preventing the collapse of the USSR and ending with a thousand-year joint Soviet-German Reich. But unlike the films, they do not have a mechanism for returning the Time Crasher to his point of origin, reborn by the experience. To the contrary, the man who would be Natasha has to die for the plot to begin. No doubt this is a function of age, not just of the protagonists (young men in the army vs. a desperate pensioner) but of its producers. The heroes of the films (and their target audience) have their whole lives ahead of them and can use their experience to help build a better world. Arsenyev's protagonist had no future left before he woke up in the past. Yet, even though it would be impossible for a reader to follow in Natasha's footsteps, the worldview it offers is largely the same as that of the World War II films: Russians today are fundamentally linked to their country's history and fate, and it is only by living consciously in accordance with this truth that their lives acquire meaning.

2
HISTORY'S ACCIDENTAL TOURISTS

Time Travel and the Rejection of Politics

Revisiting history is inherently political. No choice made about representation, characterization, and plot contributes to a vision of the past that can be considered neutral. But the politics at stake are almost always about the author's present day rather than about the time to which the heroes travel, as the World War II Time Crasher films clearly show. But just as every utopia contains an implicit anthropology ("humans are X who need Y to be happy"), every Time Crasher story embodies theories of history, politics, and human agency.

There are reasons why so many Time Crashers end up on the battlefield, reasons beyond both questions of entertainment and the crucial role wars have played in modern Russian history. For all their complexity, wars are particularly conducive to a simplistic model of cause and effect; for the Time Crasher, they are, at best, Gordian knots waiting for a sword to slice them in two. The fantasy of traveling back to a historical war rests on the identification of specific turning points when a single intervention can change the course of history.[1] But how does this work in peacetime?

---

1. See, for example, Oleksandr Zabirko: "The typical Russian popadanets is usually preoccupied with saving and strengthening a metaphysical Russian statehood, which may appear in any of its historical incarnations. The dominant theme and most frequently applied historical setting is the Second World War, which resonates with the Soviet concept of the 'Great Patriotic War' as the main legitimizing narrative of the Soviet Union."

It seems to work for the Soviet Union—or, rather, the authors of Time Crasher stories have little trouble making it work. The Soviet government portrayed in these stories is top-heavy, hierarchical, and, most importantly, devoid of modern politics. What passes for politics is more like palace intrigue: who is plotting against whom, who can come out ahead. The extent to which this is an oversimplification of actual Soviet governmental structures is a question I'm happy to leave to historians, but at the very least it is worth noting how easily the Soviet Union gets represented in such a fashion. All it takes to right the wrongs of history is to assassinate the appropriate target.

When I try to imagine going back to the second half of the twentieth century to steer the United States on a path that parallels my own political leanings, it is hard to come up with a reasonable agenda. Prevent Ronald Reagan from being elected, perhaps, but how would I do that? Get the Federal Communications Commission not to cease enforcing the Fairness Doctrine in 1987 in order to prevent the rise of Fox News? Even Arsenyev's favorite device, political assassination, would have problems beyond the crucial question of morality. What would the electoral and political consequences have been if John Hinckley had succeeded in his 1981 attempt on Reagan's life? Liberal procedural democracy, for all its many flaws, does not provide many obvious levers for a Time Crasher to pull.

Successful Time Crasher interventions have a built-in bias against political complexity, one that suspiciously reflects the ideological leanings of the genre's most prominent practitioners. The authors of Time Crasher stories tend to prefer an illiberal, hierarchical, centralized form of government, one that is easy to project onto the Soviet past. Procedural politics is replaced by conspiratorial scheming, whether by the evil (often liberal) cabals that must be defeated, or the guardians of righteousness who know better than to let legal formalities or ethical scruples prevent them from doing what is best for the country.

This disdain for complexity points back to the central premise of the genre itself. Time Crasher stories have no patience for internally consistent, plausible explanations for time travel, just as they have no interest in procedural politics. The broader time travel genre, by contrast, uses detail and nuance as part of the appeal ("Just how does time travel work here?" "What are the possible unintended consequences?"). The complexity of the time travel posited by a story is in direct proportion to the complexity of its view of politics.

That politics is usually one of a romantic, organic conception of the nation or state. The stories that have Time Crashers personally intervene in pivotal moments of history encourage identification between the individual and the nation, recapitulating a model of heroism that is familiar from Soviet socialist realism. The story needs a hero, a man whose personal qualities help him save the day, but along the way the hero either learns or confirms his own lesser individual importance in comparison with the greater good. Any rugged individualism he might have is properly subsumed into the ideology of patriotism that justifies the individual's existence.

But when the Time Crasher's destination is not of grand historical import, and when his presence in the past (or, very occasionally, the future) is either not connected to any particular salvational mission or, as in the case of the *Save the USSR!* series, so drawn out over a series of novels as to retain only the slenderest thread of a mission statement at a given moment, the relationship between the individual and the nation is less clear-cut, and possibly open to renegotiation. Instead, the hero's story comments on both the nation's past and the present day's preoccupation with that past metaphorically. The hero's personal travails, and particularly his relations with loved ones, highlight the regressive nature of both contemporary nostalgia for the Soviet past and the Time Crasher genre itself—particularly when the Time Crasher is mentally traveling backward along his own personal timeline.

How I Met My Mother: *The Dark Side of the Moon*

Physically traveling back in time is a much less direct rebuke to the very idea of either progress or entropy, because awakening in a younger body is an obvious regressive fantasy. Lukyanenko's Solnyshkin/Petrov is a dying old man rewarded with a literal second childhood, while the protagonist of *Save the USSR!* gets to relive his teenage years with the confidence, maturity, and foreknowledge of his adult self. This adds an uncomfortable element to the fantasy, since now we find ourselves witnessing the seduction of teenage girls by a middle-aged man effectively disguised as an adolescent.

The sexual transgressions, whether teased or realized, are revealing. Consider Claude Lévi-Strauss's classic reinterpretation of the Oedipus story in "The Structural Study of Myth." In nearly every aspect of the story, from the parricide and the incest on the one hand to the riddle of the Sphynx on the other, Lévi-Strauss sees the centrality of kinship, whether overemphasized (incest) or underemphasized (parricide), resulting in a mythic investigation of the drama of origins: the strange mystery of biological reproduction (the child is the product of the mother and father) and the confrontation with the opposing myth of autochthony (creatures like the Sphynx arise from the earth without parent or precursor). The attempt to answer the question "where did my country go wrong?" (and subsequently remedy the error through personal extrahistorical intervention) is bound up with the problem of individual human origin and development (how did I get this way, and how can I be better?).

An Oedipal undercurrent flows throughout the first season of the hit series *The Dark Side of the Moon* (2012). It is so Oedipal, in fact, that it satisfies the criteria for Freud, Levi-Strauss, and even Sophocles. *Dark Side of the Moon* is one of the many international remakes of the British series *Life on Mars* (2006–2007), about a Manchester police officer who gets into a car accident in 2006 and wakes up in 1973 (North American, Spanish, Czech, and South Korean versions aired in 2008, 2009, 2017, and 2018, respectively, and a Chinese series is said to be in the works).[2] Part of the fun in *Life on Mars* is vicariously experiencing the hero's culture shock as he is confronted by the crude and racist police tactics of the 1970s. Imagine how much greater the contrast is for the Russian (and, presumably, the Czech) remake. The years represent a catastrophic rupture, with the hero traveling not only in time but from a relatively new country to the collapsed empire from which it emerged.

The drama inherent in the Soviet collapse could have been enough of a hook, but the producers of the Russian remake added a significant personal complication. Where Sam Tyler, the hero of *Life on Mars*, goes back to 1973 as himself, Moscow Police Captain Mikhail Mikhailovich Solovyov wakes up in the body of his father, Moscow Militia Captain Mikhail Ivanovich Solovyov. This is particularly poignant, since the show begins with Solovyov and his mother sitting in a hospital corridor after Mikhail Ivanovich, the estranged husband and father, has just died. Mikhail Ivanovich has always been a mystery to his son, one he will never have a chance to solve. Or will he?

This mystery, it turns out, is as Oedipal as can be. Oedipus, we recall, had to solve the riddle of the Sphynx ("What goes on four feet in the morning, two feet at noon, and three feet in the evening?"), the answer to which is "man." As a man, Oedipus is a subset of the riddle's solution, but also a particularly exemplary one, since, as Lévi-Strauss points out, his biography acts out wordplay based on his name. "Oedipus" means "swollen foot," an apt description based on the result of his foot being tied to a stake when he was exposed on a hilltop as an infant. As a result, he walks an errant path, which is true in every sense: he runs into his unknown father (and kills him) and marries his own mother. The answer to the Riddle of the Sphynx is not just "man," but the human life cycle itself, and Oedipus is the human life cycle as twisted tragedy.[3]

---

2. On the successes and failures of some of these adaptations, see Bonaut and Ojer; Lavery; and Mills.

3. The fact that the young Solovyov has his father's first name makes the connection between their identities all the stronger.

Solovyov, now in his father's body, has an uncanny relationship with mirrors: when he looks in them, he sees himself in his own adult body. Somehow, the mirror displays the "real" Solovyov trapped inside his father's body, even though logic would tell us that he should see his father's face. Solovyov cannot see himself in the mirror as his father; like Oedipus, he does not recognize his sire. His mother thinks of him as her husband, and Solovyov's horrified rejections of his mother/wife's affections only increase his parents' estrangement. Even worse, Mikhail Mikhailovich Solovyov is already alive in 1979, as a small boy who finds his father's behavior baffling. In the first episode, Solovyov frantically tries to stuff his childhood self's head with useful knowledge about the future, only to confuse him completely ("Buy dollars before the ruble collapses!"). He tells his son not to get involved with Svetka, who will give him the "hussar's drip" (*gusarskii nasmork*), slang for gonorrhea. When little Misha asks his mother about Dad's case of "hussar's drip," she draws the logical conclusion, and soon Solovyov is kicked out of the house.

Solovyov's interference in his own timeline is tantamount to the destruction of his parents' marriage, a combination of both Oedipal wish fulfillment as nightmare (taking the father's place) and the child of divorced parents' guilty fantasy (that the child is responsible for the parents' separation). Every encounter Solovyov has in 1979 with an adult woman, no matter how innocent, puts another nail in the coffin of his parents' marriage. When Lyuda, his mother/wife, sees him talking with the nurse who helped him at the hospital, she tells him that their son (little Misha) will never be like him (Misha's father, or adult Misha in Misha's father's body). In fact, she says, "I'll make sure of that" (*Ia postaraius'*). Yet Misha does grow up to be like his father, following in his figurative footsteps as cop before literally filling his shoes by taking over Mikhail Ivanovich's body in the past.

Solovyov's possession of his father's body makes all his interactions with Lyuda impossible. The Oedipal taboo has taken firm hold of his adult consciousness precisely at the point when his physicality and living situation would make breaking the taboo conventional and expected. Meanwhile, his meetings with Lena, young Misha's teacher, are complicated by the same dynamic but with the valences reversed: as he himself informs her, little Misha has (had) a crush on her, and we can see that those feelings live on in the adult Solovyov. Lena, of course, could harbor no such romantic sentiments for a prepubescent boy but finds Solovyov's father irresistible.

The tragedy of *Oedipus Rex* is famously structured on the interplay between knowledge and ignorance, brought to the forefront at moments of revelation: when Oedipus realizes the man he killed was his father, and the woman he married was his mother, he puts out his eyes. When Jocasta realizes she has been sleeping with her son, she hangs herself. In the failure to recognize what in other contexts would be familiar, not to mention "homey" (*heimlich*), *Oedipus* is a tragedy stemming from the heroes' inability to recognize the uncanny scenario they inhabit. Mother is Mother, but also something else at the same time. Solovyov does not have the luxury of blindness, whether literal or figurative: he knows that he has returned to the scene of his childhood but in a world that, for him, is now askew. His is what Time Crasher stories posit as the essential post-Soviet condition: living somewhere between two equally familiar and equally strange worlds.

Let us dispense with the niceties that Oedipal language affords us—the Solovyov family is fucked up when we meet them, and *The Dark Side of the Moon*'s first season, in the guise of a time-traveling police procedural about catching a crazed killer, is the story of how Solovyov himself fucks up his family (the metaphor works in both English and Russian, if somewhat differently). *The Dark Side of the Moon* is a remake, but the incestuous, dysfunctional family drama is entirely the invention of the Russian series' creators. What does it add, and what does it have to do with the historical drama that the time-traveling metaphor affords?

Surely, it is about more than mere paradox. Time travel paradoxes are a dime a dozen, as are cautionary tales about leaving history alone. In any case, the radical indeterminacy of time travel as a plot device in *The Dark Side of the Moon* does not make the series a compelling vehicle for such messages. As in *Life on Mars*, the show never lets the viewer be sure just how real the past in which the hero has found himself actually is; repeated attempts by doctors to contact a comatose Solovyov in 2011 could mean that the entire series is nothing but a hallucination. And if it is not a hallucination, what is the point in highlighting the dangers of temporal interference if the hero has no control of his comings and goings?

That Seventies Show

The stakes of the Solovyov family drama lie outside the science fiction genre, because the problem is fantasy itself. Here I am deliberately conflating "fantasy" in the Freudian sense (a desire that is entertained and perhaps simultaneously suppressed) and in terms of genre (stories with a fantastic premise). Solovyov the adult is forced to act out the fantasies of Solovyov the child and, as a result, puts the grown-up Solovyov in a strangely childlike position (it doesn't help that the actor is constantly contorting his face into bug-eyed confusion). By going back in time, Solovyov is enacting inherently regressive fantasies (about his mother, his father, his teacher). Technically an adult, he becomes a child's projection of an adult's behavior ("When I grow up, I'm going to be a militia captain and date my teacher"). In the *Odyssey*, Telemachus remarks that "it is a wise child that knows his own father." Little Misha never understood Mikhail Ivanovich, and now that the child has become the father (to the man?), he gains practical knowledge of the events of his family's rupture but remains in the dark about his father's inner life. Even when trapped within Mikhail Ivanovich's head, Solovyov is just as far from understanding his father as he always had been. His father's actual thoughts and feelings will always be a mystery. This is what makes his encounters with mirrors so poignant. When he looks in the mirror, it is his own reflection that looks back at him: he literally cannot see his father.

This is all well and good, but to care about Solovyov's time-displaced Oedipal angst might require that we care about Solovyov, or at lease to argue for the psychological complexity of the show's characters or the depth and nuance of its writing and direction. On those terms, *The Dark Side of the Moon* provides too weak a foundation to support a theory-heavy exegesis. It stands out as one of the better serials produced in the beginning of the 2010s, but as police dramas go, it's not exactly Russia's answer to *The Wire*.

What, then, do Solovyov and his family tell us about the show's central conceit—that is, about the immersion of a present, post-Soviet consciousness into the Soviet past? If the time travel is viewed as a metaphor (where it certainly functions better than as an actual science fictional trope), any possible cautionary tale would be about a particular kind of *preoccupation* with the past, an interrogation of the nostalgic impulses that dominated so much of Russian mass culture in the first Putinist decade.

On that level, *The Dark Side of the Moon* is deceptively seductive. Many episodes include a moment when Solovyov happens to run into a future luminary under humorous circumstances. Whether it's meeting the future shlock pop star Filipp Kirkorov, as a little boy expressing contempt for the pop diva Alla Pugacheva (whom he will grow up to marry), or interrupting the filming of a Soviet adaptation of Astrid Lindgren's *Karlson on the Roof* series (a beloved children's franchise so ubiquitous in the Soviet Union and its successor states that it may as well be Russian), *The Dark Side of the Moon* provides a steady supply of just the sort of nostalgia-tinged easter eggs to satisfy the tourist/viewer's demand for recognizably dated realia.

But one of the best easter eggs appearing in the second episode mixes humor and politics in a fashion that should give the viewer pause. Solovyov stands by as a young woman breaks up with her boyfriend, who protests that one day, he will accomplish great things. In fact, it immediately becomes clear to both Solovyov and the viewers that this young man will grow up to be the exiled oligarch Mikhail Khodorkovsky. Khodorkovsky spent a decade in prison on what are widely considered politically motivated bribery charges. Upon his release in 2013, he devoted himself to funding opposition and civil society initiatives in the Russian Federation.

When the episode aired, Khodorkovsky was still incarcerated, and at the time when the story takes place, he would have been sixteen, with no legitimate reason to imagine himself as either a rich man or a political prisoner. Only Solovyov (and the viewer) can see the future oligarch and convict in the form of the gangly boy. Trying to reassure a heartbroken Khodorkovsky, Solovyov tells him, "Everything is going to work out fine for you. [Beat.] Well, almost everything."

It's clever and funny, but it is also ethically complicated. As a joke in 2011, Solovyov's remark is a perfect example of the way something that could be a hot-button political issue gets addressed on state television. The moment relies on our knowledge of Khodorkovsky's career without in any way commenting on either the validity of the prosecution against him or the legality with which he (and all the other oligarchs) amassed their fortunes. Between 1979 and 2011, things just happen to Khodorkovsky; his wealth and incarceration, like Kirkorov's marriage to Pugacheva, are simply recognizable milestones on the road from the Brezhnev era to the Medvedev years.

There is nothing that Solovyov could reasonably have been expected to do in order to change Khodorkovsky's fate (assuming that this would be a desirable goal), so this scene is simply one of many in which Solovyov as the viewer's stand-in is not faced with any real-time ethical dilemma. The fact that the show refrains from taking any kind of stand on Khodorkovsky at all is, in itself, a decision with ethical ramifications: is this a matter on which one can really simply be "neutral"? The reasonable fear of political repercussions for taking such a stand in 2011 in many ways gets the creators of the show off the hook. Who would really expect to turn on Channel One and watch a fantastical police procedural defend the country's most famous political prisoner?

But there is another aspect of this scene that must be kept in mind: Solovyov's role here is simply that of random observer. He is not operating in his professional capacity as an officer of the Moscow militia. Elsewhere, however, his encounters with potentially loaded historical moments unfold as part of his job. This raises a question that the show studiously avoids: what does it mean to enforce the law under a completely different political system? And are these the laws that should be enforced?

Who Watches the Watchmen?

First broadcast in 2012, *The Dark Side of the Moon* nevertheless chooses 2011 as its setting. This might simply be an artifact of the production process, but the year 2011 could not be more significant for a Russian police drama. On March 1 of that year, the federal government implemented a sweeping reform of the

Russian policing systems, aimed at, among other things, addressing corruption, clarifying the rights of detainees, and improving the force's image. Not only was the system completely federalized but its very name was changed, from militia (*militsiia*) to police (*politsiia*) (Semukhina 1–2). Solovyov is specifically a police officer, so the action has to take place after March 1. The change in nomenclature helps intensify the alienation effect of the hero's travel to 1979, since he has to get used to being a militiaman again (even if he could not have been "police" for more than a few months before the show started). Even without the 2011 reform, the contrasts with the 1979 militia would have been stark. Adding in the reform might make the show feel more contemporary to 2012 viewers, who have just gotten used to the new name. More important, however, is that starting out in postreform Moscow further *historicizes* the police.[4] As much as the proponents of strict law and order might prefer to act as though police organizations are apolitical entities that simply enforce the laws of the land, the dual settings of *The Dark Side of the Moon* remind us (and, perhaps, Solovyov) just how historically and politically contingent police activity actually is.

When one of Solovyov's cases involves black marketeers illegally trading in Western rock records, Solovyov's knowledge of Pink Floyd allows him to pose as a buyer, just as his fluency in English (a rarity in the USSR in 1979) helps him communicate with an American journalist accused of spying. In the first case, both Solovyov and the contemporary viewer cannot be expected to see these activities as truly criminal, but Solovyov seems to have no compunction about simply doing his job (to be fair, he's also trying to solve a murder). In the second, the journalist does turn out to be involved in espionage, so simple patriotism is enough of a justification, but the question still remains that in stopping the spy, what exactly is Solovyov defending? Particularly in 1979, the year that the Soviet Union invaded Afghanistan?[5] Or, on a far more prosaic note, in Episode 6, as part of a murder investigation, he confronts a saleswoman in an electronics store about her illegal purchase of . . . Polish lipstick. She bursts into tears and begs him not to send her to prison. He doesn't, but the question remains: if Solovyov could put a woman in prison for buying imported black-market cosmetics from a Polish visitor, is there any justice in his work?

---

4. The original *Life on Mars* also contrasts 1970s' police practices with their contemporary counterparts. Andy Willis (57–62) argues that, despite the numerous instances of corruption featured in the show, the depiction of late twentieth-century policing in *Life on Mars* reinforces a conservative framework for the failings of the police in today's United Kingdom.

5. Solovyov's foreknowledge of the invasion becomes a plot point in the first season when he wins a large amount of money betting that the Taraki government in Afghanistan will be toppled. This event occurred on September 16; the invasion itself took place on December 24, after the events of Season 1.

Solovyov's double consciousness as a Time Crasher creates as many problems as it solves. Early on, we see that the 1979 Solovyov accidentally causes the scar that will set the adult Red, his antagonist in both time periods, on the path that leads to their time loop. Solovyov, with his foreknowledge and confusion, inadvertently ruins his parents' marriage. But the pleasures of the show are based precisely on the viewers' privileged twenty-first-century position as they gaze upon (or, in Solovyov's case, act upon) a nostalgia-tinged late Soviet Moscow. If Solovyov turns out to be culpable for much of what happens in his own twisted timeline, what does that say about the viewers?

When Solovyov returns to 1979, he is back in the seemingly innocent world of his childhood, both discovering and ensuring that it is actually not all that innocent. The Seventies are a popular destination for Time Crashers, but for a very different type of story from the adventures that heroes encounter when traveling back to World War II (the most popular destination of all). Heroism in the 1970s is hard to find, and that may well be the attraction. This is the height of what the perestroika era called the "Period of Stagnation," now viewed through rose-tinted glasses as a time of enviable stability. And, indeed, *The Dark Side of the Moon*, by placing Solovyov right before the invasion of Afghanistan, lets the viewers visit the Soviet Union during the peak of Stagnation. Meanwhile, the contemporary viewer turns out to be living in the last days of true Putinist stability (while the series was produced, Putin and Medvedev announced their plan for Putin's return to the presidency; the economy was plummeting, and Russia was about to experience a wave of protests unlike anything it had seen in years).

The plot of *The Dark Side of the Moon* brings together two eras that were already linked discursively, and, thanks to Solovyov's interference, draws them into something approaching quantum entanglement. Just as Solovyov is obliged to rethink his parents' marriage and his place in their family, the viewers are confronted with the inconsistencies in their own nostalgia: they may appreciate the 1970s' law and order, but what about the time spent chasing down purveyors of Pink Floyd, a group now so beloved and mainstream that its most famous album is used as the series' title?[6]

The Soviet nostalgia encouraged by the early Putin years was a libidinal investment on the population's part, focused on most of the citizens' childhood or youth. The end of the first season of *The Dark Side of the Moon* shows what

---

6. As Amanda Lerner notes, changing the series title from a Bowie song ("Life on Mars") to a Pink Floyd album makes sense, since the latter group had a much bigger following in the Soviet Union in the 1970s. This also brings *Dark Side* closer to one of the elements that made the British original a success: its deployment of beloved, period-appropriate music, something the North American version failed to do (88).

happens when historical passions turn incestuous. It is not just Solovyov's family that has been irrevocably broken but, thanks to his own actions in 1979, when Solovyov wakes up again in 2011, he is in a completely new world, one in which the Soviet Union still exists. For many, this would be the perfect nostalgic wish fulfillment, but the second season might make them reconsider. Life might not be better on the dark side of the moon.

A Hero of Someone Else's Time

Perhaps due to its roots in the original *Life on Mars*, *The Dark Side of the Moon* stands out not just for the close attention to family dynamics but for the relatively low stakes of the entire first season. By "low stakes" I do not mean that the events of the series are inconsequential. Far from it. After all, Solovyov's interference in his own timeline creates the alternate reality that is the setting of Season 2. But this is an accident unrelated to the overall plot of Season 1. In fact, it is a rather arbitrary consequence of the plot. Unlike so many other Time Crashers, Solovyov is not on a mission of historical import. He is not intervening in a battle, preventing a war, averting a catastrophe, or advising a leader. Arguably, this is a more appropriate use of the Brezhnev-era setting than turning it into the last chance to save the USSR. To the extent that this Period of Stagnation has taken a nostalgic hold in the popular consciousness, it is precisely as a time when an ordinary, uneventful life was possible. Where dissidents were stymied by the near impossibility of inciting any kind of meaningful change, many post-Soviet Russians find real comfort.

The low stakes are also a function of the show's generic hybridity. Like its prototype, *The Dark Side of the Moon* slowly advances its fantastic premise over the course of a season, the individual episodes of which function primarily according to the conventions of the police procedural. For many Time Crashers, the trip to the past is the moment when they trade in their dull, everyday lives for a heroic role that could previously only have been the stuff of daydreams: the office worker becomes an action hero. But Solovyov is a police detective; he already *is* an action hero. The series continually highlights the differences between Soviet-era militia practices and twenty-first-century police work, but the comparison rests on the fact that, by and large, Solovyov is doing the same job in each time period.[7]

---

7. Coming from 2011, Solovyov is almost *too much* of an action hero for 1979. As Lerner notes, "One of the markers of the first episode of *Dark Side of the Moon* is Solov'ev's hurriedness, his inability to take things slowly... Those around him—particularly the doctors and nurses he encounters in the halls of the hospital—seem perturbed by his instinctive urge to rush" (105).

The Dark Side of the Moon continually teases the viewers with the possibility that the whole time-displacement story line takes place entirely in his head. In 1979, Solovyov gets brief communications from doctors and friends sitting by his comatose body in 2011. It is no stretch to imagine the show as an expression of Solovyov's fantasy. But the fantasy is primarily personal, centered around his childhood and his parents. More often than not, Time Crasher tales are personal in an entirely different way, functioning as heroic fantasy projections involving an authorial stand-in. If, as I suggested earlier, Time Crasher stories are fan fiction whose fandom is history, their heroes often resemble a familiar fan fiction type known as the "Mary Sue."

Mary Sue is the teenage protagonist of the 1973 *Star Trek* fan fiction parody "A Trekkie's Tale," written by the fanzine editor Paula Smith (1974). The youngest officer in Starfleet, Mary Sue solves every problem she faces over the course of the ten-paragraph story, even taking over the bridge from Captain Kirk while he runs out to get them coffee. When she dies, she is surrounded by all the show's protagonists, "all weeping unashamedly at the loss of her beautiful youth and youthful beauty, intelligence, capability and all-around niceness. Even to this day her birthday is a national holiday on the Enterprise." Smith came up with Mary Sue in response to the countless story submissions she received featuring protagonists who were idealized self-insertions of the author into a beloved fan universe. The name quickly became a term for this type of character, with fans simultaneously embracing it as the recognition of a familiar, widely loathed trope while also expressing concern that it could easily be used for the sexist dismissal of any competent female character.

Time Crashers rarely match the classic Mary Sue in sheer insufferability (though Arsenyev's heroines come close), probably because their effectiveness under their new circumstances owes less to their innate superiority than to the power granted by hindsight. Coming from the future, they have the advantage thanks to knowledge of the past and, occasionally, either a greater facility with technology or the assistance of the near-magical laptops that somehow keep working in their new, inhospitable environments. Their superiority is almost democratic. Virtually anyone who stayed awake during history class and is also handy with tools could do just as well.

The classic Mary Sue is, as her name suggests, female, reflecting fan fiction's largely female demographic; Time Crashers, by contrast, skew male. There are, of course, plenty of male Mary Sues (referred to by various masculine names, such as "Gary Stu"). But the self-insertion practiced by Time Crasher authors need not be a matter of self-aggrandizement; the protagonists of *Save the USSR!* and its ilk are more like the passive heroes of Russian fairy tales, who need magical helpers in order to save the day. As heroes, they represent the triumph of a particular kind of male mediocrity.

In these Time Crasher stories, the protagonist can be both authorial stand-in and cypher, since the true hero is more setting than person. The protagonist exists in order to allow the reader's consciousness to move back in time with him, looking at the past from the privileged vantage point of the present in the hopes of intervening in the course of history. *The Dark Side of the Moon* frames its hero's involvement in history as more than simply the solution of an intellectual puzzle, downplaying the historical questions in favor of a personal, Oedipal soap opera that, in turn, comments on the historical machinations of the Time Crasher narrative. Rewriting the past is tantamount to rewriting the self, hence the prevalence of the grandfather paradox in more traditional time travel stories.

Time Crashers and the Hidden Hand of History

Dark Side of the Moon does its best to frame its (and Solovyov's) interventions in Soviet history as apolitical. True, the second season is set in an alternate future Solovyov accidentally created while still in the 1970s, but, as we see in chapter 4, this seems to have been a late addition to the show's trajectory. Instead, the first season insists on treating politically loaded topics as entirely neutral (Khodorkovsky, the petty "crimes" that would now be an ordinary part of capitalism). The show seems to withhold judgment and encourage the viewers to do this same. This is not only an inherently political gesture; it is also a hallmark of early to mid-Putinism (the Medvedev years), whose unofficial motto was, "Let's not talk about politics."

Nonetheless, politics and ideology are inevitably implicated. Time travel stories are generally wrapped up in the question of free will, either by suggesting that the future is set in stone or by stressing the importance of even the most seemingly insignificant action on the course of history (the Butterfly Effect). Time Crasher stories can do this as well, but they add a layer of uncertainty about basic human agency. Time Crashers rarely embark on their journey intentionally, and almost never do they (or the reader) understand how the trip is happening. Time Crashers are puppets with visible strings that lead nowhere.

Who, after all, is pulling the strings? The obvious, extradiegetic answer is the author or authors, who know that the genre conventions allow them to leave the process unexplained. But the resulting uncertainly makes Time Crashers a particularly noteworthy post-Soviet genre. As I have argued in *Plots against Russia*, the media and chattering classes are always looking to assign intent and blame to malign, shadowy forces (99–132). Consumers of Time Crasher tales, in contrast, are tacitly encouraged to accept a cosmos that, at first glance, is either random or mechanistic, with nary a satanic schemer in sight. They have heeded the advice of the Wizard of Oz and pay no attention to the man behind the curtain.

But sometimes the plot device that sends the hero on his cross-time journey gives a glimpse behind the scenes, because, like the fabled Wizard, that plot device is actually a person. This is the case in Valery Rozhnov's four-part miniseries *Back to the USSR* (Nazad v SSSR [2010]). Like most of our examples so far, *Back to the USSR* is unlikely to be celebrated as a cinematic masterpiece, even if multiple creators are at pains to claim authorship.[8] A cliché-ridden melodrama about Anton Rodimov, a thirty-something, hard-partying oligarch who can no longer bear the emptiness of his consumption-driven existence, *Back to the USSR* offers its hero the standard alternative afforded the protagonists of the Time Crasher genre: the opportunity to go back to a simpler, purer time. His best friend sends him to an AA meeting, where he meets a man called Stalker, whose offer of the adventure of a lifetime turns out to include time travel. Beaten in an alley by thugs, Anton wakes up in 1975.

The usual hijinks ensue. Anton doesn't believe he's really in the past but is quickly befriended by a beautiful young woman named Natasha, with whom he, of course, falls in love. He spends some time in a mental hospital but escapes, and even finds himself mistaken for the son of a local party official destined for great things. Along the way, Anton discovers the joys of a simpler life in a simpler time, before a second head injury sends him back to the present.

There is only one thing that distinguishes *Back to the USSR* from the many stories it resembles: Anton discovers that it was all a lie. He never traveled in time. The entire scenario was arranged by the Stalker at the behest of Anton's best friend, who was desperate to shake him out of his alcoholic torpor. The people he met, Natasha included, were actors hired to make the illusion seem real. Anton eventually tracks down Natasha while she is performing on stage and discovers that the one thing that proves to have been real was their love.

So *Back to the USSR* turns out not to be a Time Crasher story at all. Instead, it is the story of people pretending to be in a Time Crasher story, placing *Back to the USSR* in the generic company of other quasi-therapeutic mind games set against the backdrop of late capitalist anomie, such as *The Game* and *Fight Club*, not to mention the total simulation of an American retrograde utopia that deceived the eponymous hero of *The Truman Show*.[9] Besides the lack of actual time travel,

---

8. Valerii Rozhnov wrote and directed the film, but Oleg Ulanov claims that the studio plagiarized his then-unpublished novel *Unusual Travel Agent* (Agenty nestandartnogo otdykha, eventually released along with a sequel). Rozhnov not only denied the allegation but produced his own novel based on his screenplay (Rudenko).

9. See Fedotov.

this very different genre has much more stringent requirements for verisimilitude and explanation. Audiences might accept some vague nonsense involving fog, head injuries, or explosions to justify actual time travel but could not be expected to accept a scenario in which a trip to the past somehow fakes itself. There has to be a somewhat plausible mechanism, as well as a reason to bother.

Curiously, the revelation of the miniseries' prosaic nature only highlights the story's resemblance to a more fantastic genre—namely, the fairy tale. The Stalker is a variation on one of the most common folkloric tropes identified by Vladimir Propp in *Morphology of the Folk Tale*: the magical helper without whom the hero could never solve his problem. In *Back to the USSR*, the helper role is doubled, since the Stalker is merely the agent of Anton's true helper, his friend. At the same time, the magical helper's function might seem less benign on a meta-level: he is the reason we have spent nearly four hours being deceived about the actual plot. We are also forced to reevaluate our assessment of the accuracy with which the series recreates 1975, since now it no longer has to completely convince the audience at the same time it convinces the hero. Any anachronisms committed by the filmmakers can be chalked up to the inadequacy of the Stalker as a reenactor.

In pretending to be a Time Crasher tale, *Back to the USSR* ends up using the idea of time travel as a moral and psychological justification for the historical reenactments that have become increasingly popular since the Soviet collapse. The simple fact of occupying the role of Soviet subject is an antidote to the spiritual rot of neoliberal Russia. The plight of the alienated individual (here, Anton) is one of context and relations; in placing himself in a world beyond the cash nexus and interacting with people who are supposedly motivated by something other than money, he can become a better version of himself. Never mind the fact that the people he meets are actually actors doing work for hire; he experiences them as people who are not at all mercenary, and Natasha's love for him turns out to be more than a mere act. Even Soviet faux-sincerity, though purchased with money, is better than what the real world has to offer.

If, by the end, Anton has found true love through fake time travel, then the Stalker and the best friend are more than just magical helpers; they are practically fairy godmothers. Like Cinderella, Anton meets his prince(ss) under false pretenses but manages to rescue a happy ending from the wreckage of fantasy. Is *Back to the USSR* anomalous not just for its plot twist but for the visibility of the fairy godmother's magic wand?

Propp's structuralist approach to fairy tales, which supplied us with the term "magical helper," may turn out to be a magical helper in its own right. Propp identified the various functions that make up the basis of a given fairy tale but may be absent from a given iteration of the story. Cinderella might have two sisters in one telling, and three in another; one of them might hack away at her oversized foot to try to fit it into the slipper, while others may not. The Time Crasher genre is a hybrid of both "legitimately" authored fiction (published by presses or produced by film studios) and a vast amount of online amateur fan fiction that occasionally crosses over into the mainstream and is, in any case, highly formulaic—a bit of structuralism (in carefully measured doses) might be illuminating.

And this is why *Back to the USSR* is so valuable. Who would be more cognizant of the underlying formula than authors who are essentially parodying it? There are actual Time Crasher stories that have a magical helper figure like the Stalker. *Save the USSR!*, for example, has a mysterious figure who sends the hero back to the 1970s and then disappears from the novel. Boris Akunin's play *The Mirror of St. Germain*, in contrast, involves swapping two men from New Year's Eve 1900 and New Year's Eve 2000 and has the titular St. Germain (among others) playing a similar role. Continuing in our formalist/structuralist vein, these stories *lay bare the device* behind the time travel in this genre. The magical helper figure is in the deep structure of the Time Crasher narrative.

Even in Time Crasher stories with minimal or no explanation for time travel, the magical helper is implicit, in that the trip to the past is usually beneficial both to the traveler and to the world. The Time Crasher, as we have seen, tends to become a better person through his experience, attaining a moral clarity that his home time period would obscure. While in the past, he either ensures that history moves along its proper course or changes it in order to create a better future.

Thus the apparent randomness of the travel as experienced by the Time Crasher must be understood as evidence not of the arbitrary nature of the universe but of a benevolent (fictional) cosmos striving for improvement. More than that, though, it is the cosmos's way of negating the evils of our present. Whether that present is understood as a harsh, meaningless world of late capitalist savagery or (as is more often the case) the result of the concerted efforts of evil forces, the implied magical helper is acting in the best interest of both his hero and his world. As the instrument of the author's often tendentious worldview, the helper's ability to right all wrongs is a wish-fulfillment fantasy familiar from fan fiction: the magical helper is the hidden hand of Mary Sue.

Sleep to the Future

As fantasies go, the majority of Time Crasher stories are regressive. In sending the hero back through history, they combine nostalgia for a simpler or more heroic time with an implied or explicit critique of the present day. Kirill Kobrin and Mark Lipovetsky ("Strakh nastoiashchego") have pointed out that even the present has been an unpopular setting for much of post-Soviet literature, which seems to prefer the recent and distant historical past.

There are other reasons for their appeal, of course. A narrative sandwich of historical and science fiction, they hit an intergeneric sweet spot. The world building required by the author has the advantage of clarity. Doing research on World War II might be daunting, but it does not require coming up with a whole new world from scratch. More to the point, the first few post-Soviet decades have not made imagining the future easy. This is particularly a problem for the near future. What does it mean to project Russia into the 2030s or 2040s when it's all but impossible to imagine the simple fact of presidential succession, which always threatens to turn a political process into an existential question?

For whatever reasons, Time Crashers rarely end up in the future. Perhaps this is because they do not have a well-defined role to play in imagining the world to come. What possible mission could they be asked to accomplish that would be comparable to their typical role in stories based in the past?

Western science fiction has long provided an answer to this question, but it is usually based on a dystopian scenario. John Barlow, the protagonist of Cyril M. Kornbluth's 1951 "The Marching Morons," is a con man thawed out in a future world overrun by idiots who force the few intelligent people left to work on their behalf. Barlow uses his public relations (PR) wiles to launch a scheme that tricks the morons into voluntarily signing up for mass extermination. The 1973 film *Sleeper* features Woody Allen as a jazz musician awakened to a tyrannical police state two hundred years in the future, so that he can help launch a revolution. And, of course, Mike Judge's 2006 *Idiocracy*, whose hero wakes up from a five-hundred-year nap to discover a vapid and stupid America run by President Dwayne Elizondo Mountain Dew Herbert Camacho, took only a decade to start looking prophetic.

There is an appealing symmetry here with the Russian Time Crasher genre. Just as the Time Crashers endlessly recycle the conceit of *A Connecticut Yankee in King Arthur's Court*, the accidental freezing and defrosting of a man from "our" time in the future recalls both Rip van Winkle and Edward Bellamy's classic 1888 utopia novel, *Looking Backward*. Contemporary Russian science fiction rarely avails itself of this trope, at least for tales set in the future.[10] Yuri Burnosov's "Moscow 22" is an exception, but its hero needs only an eight-year coma to awaken to a "nightmare" world in which everyone is forced to be gay.[11]

---

10. Vladimir Voinovich brings the protagonist forward in time in his 1986 satire, *Moscow 2042*, with the help of a West German trans-temporal travel agency, although he does include a thinly veiled parody of a cryogenically preserved Alexander Solzhenitsyn, revived in 2042 in order to try to bring back tsarism.

11. I describe this story in more detail in *Plots against Russia* (174).

Burnosov's vision of compulsory homosexuality is instructive, though perhaps not in the way the author intended. Utopias so often are created to reflect the particular concerns of the times in which they were written. In the wake of the British enclosure laws, Thomas More's *Utopia* spends more time talking about the allocation of agricultural lands than the average urban twenty-first-century reader might care to read. Burnosov needs the reaction of a "normal" contemporary to express outrage at what he clearly wants the reader to see as the inevitable outcome of tolerance run wild.[12] A Time Crasher ends up in the future because he bears a value or has an ability that will be lost, whether it be the rugged heroism of Buck Rogers or the unscrupulous genius of a Fifties' con man.[13] There is a peculiar kind of positivity to these seemingly pessimistic scenarios, since they are predicated on the idea that our present has something to offer the future. This is the antithesis of the moral logic that catapults the protagonist out of the morally compromised present into the past for the purpose of spiritual improvement. Yet it is not the sort of imaginative leap that comes naturally to post-Soviet writers of fantasy and science fiction.

Flyover Country

Dystopian futures, like the utopias that originally inspired the genre, descend from the tradition of satire, often exaggerating a contemporary trend or vice as a comment or cautionary tale. Usually, the object of satire is clear enough to a contemporary reader without any need for a fictional stand-in. Time travel becomes much more valuable as a device if the satire is focused on the present day. In that case, bringing someone from our past to their future (i.e., our present) provides endless opportunity for defamiliarization, wry commentary, and metaphysical speculation.

Bellamy's *Looking Backward* provides the structural model for these sorts of tales, even as it differs from them in two important respects: (1) though the book

---

12. A similar conceit can be found in two pro-Putin online commercials. In 2018, a middle-aged man dreams that, because people like him didn't bother to vote in the upcoming election, now families like his are required to host unattached gay men and even share their beds with them. Two years later, another commercial shows a near future in which a young orphan boy is adopted by a gay male couple, one of whom says to call him "mama" before presenting him with a dress and makeup.

13. Occasionally a writer will split the difference, sending someone from our past into our future. In his discussion of Stalingrad in contemporary Russian science fiction, Ian Garner highlights Oleg Tarugin and Aleksei Ivakin's novel duology *The Shtrafbat's Constellation*, in which the "best soldiers in history" are brought from the 1940s to 2297, where they can bring the experience and spirit of Stalingrad to bear on the struggle against the lizard people who threaten to wipe out human civilization.

functions as a satire of Bellamy's present, it is deadly earnest about the world in which his hero arrives; and (2) Bellamy's hero ends up in the reader's future, while the works that borrow from it deposit the traveler in the present day.

The classic Soviet example of this kind of story exists in two versions that tell basically the same story. In Mikhail Bulgakov's 1935–1936 play *Ivan Vasilievich*, a faulty time machine swaps a Soviet building superintendent with Ivan the Terrible (both men are named Ivan Vasilievich). After the legendary Russian tyrant gets over his initial shock, it turns out that he is perfectly equipped for navigating Stalinist reality. In 1973, the director Leonid Gaidai adapted the play into a film called *Ivan Vasilievich Changes His Profession* (sometimes called *Ivan Vasilievich: Back to the Future* in English), performing an additional feat of time travel by moving the action from the 1930s to the 1970s.

The visitor from the past forces us to look at the present with new eyes: our time turns out to truly be a "brave new world," in both the original Shakespearean sense and Huxley's ironic, dystopian spin on the phrase. The present is both magical and horrible, in a manner that rarely fails to be instructive.

The Rip van Winkle scenario is the point of departure for one of the most celebrated Russian novels of the early twenty-first century: Eugene Vodolazkin's *The Aviator*. The novel's premise is simple: born in 1900, Innokenty Petrovich Platonov is frozen as part of a life-extension experiment in the Gulag in the 1930s, only to be defrosted and revived in 1999. After suffering from amnesia, he slowly acclimates himself to his new environment, with the help of his physician, Dr. Geiger, and, eventually, his young wife, Nastya, the granddaughter of the now-nonagenarian love of his life, Anastasia. By the end of the novel, he is beset by the symptoms of a terminal post-thaw mental decline, and when last we see him, he may be facing death in a plane crash.

A powerful novel in its own right, *The Aviator* looks even better in comparison to the works it superficially resembles. Not just the Time Crasher genre, though we will certainly get to that, but also its older utopian and dystopian precursors. Bellamy's *Looking Backward*, for example, not only shares the same basic premise but even involves a similar jump in time. It also features an incredibly simplistic trope that is developed, if not entirely redeemed, by *The Aviator*. When Julian West awakens in the year 2000, he is forever separated from his fiancée, Edith Bartlett, but finds solace in the arms of her great-granddaughter, Edith Leete. Where Bellamy seems perfectly happy to render the two Ediths entirely fungible (as if they were just another commodity to be found in the socialist Costcos Julian so admires), Vodolazkin (and Innokenty) is careful to recognize them as distinct individuals. In its depiction of the slow return of Innokenty's memories followed by his cognitive decline, *The Aviator* also resembles Daniel Keyes's *Flowers for Algernon* (with which it shares its diary format).

The diary (which also includes notes by Nastya and Geiger) is the formal manifestation of the primary distinction between *The Aviator* and the works we examined the previous chapter. Time Crasher stories often privilege the big events, the turning points in history, subsuming everyday life into the project of righting historical wrongs. *The Aviator*, too, is concerned with history (history being one of the primary preoccupations of nearly all of Vodolazkin's work), and the choice of the Gulag as the site of Innokenty's cryogenic suspension firmly roots the story in one of the most important, and shameful, moments in the Soviet era. But the Gulag does not make up the majority of Innokenty's reminiscences (which tend to be about the years prior to his arrest). Even more important, Innokenty firmly and consistently rejects any attempt to frame his life within the grand narratives of history. When people ask him to describe the past, he argues that they already know about the big events; what he can describe is how it felt to live during that time. He focuses on the sounds, the smells, and all the things that words on paper could not have preserved. His interest in reproducing the sheer dailyness of the past is perfectly mirrored in his descriptions of everything novel he finds in the dailiness of 1999.

The Aviator, unlike the Time Crasher stories, paints a picture of sudden, involuntary time travel as disruptive rather than restorative. As Innokenty writes early in the novel: "A person is not a cat and cannot land on four paws wherever thrown. A person is placed in a certain historical time for some reason. What happens when someone loses that?" (86). Time Crashers are heroic, but Innokenty, once he has had the chance to brush up on the last seven decades of history, causes a small stir at a public event when he rejects the Russian president's comparison of his travel in time to Gagarin's orbit in space: "I'm afraid I do not deserve the comparison with Gagarin . . . because my courage was forced. It is probably more akin to the courage of Belka and Strelka, who also had no other choice" (258).

In rejecting the heroic paradigm, Vodolazkin (via Innokenty) puts the maximum distance between his own work and the historical wish-fulfillment fantasies that have come to prominence in the first decades of the twenty-first century. Innokenty is no Mary Sue, and *The Aviator* is not historical fan fiction. When it comes to twentieth-century history, neither Innokenty nor Vodolazkin could be called a fan. By the same token, the novel resists using Innokenty to become the equivalent of the grumpy old man complaining about today's world. Yes, Innokenty cannot help but notice the tackiness of contemporary society, particularly the media, nor is he blind to the younger Nastya's materialistic streak. But Innokenty is not interested in rendering judgment on post-Soviet Russia; instead, he subjects it to the same keen powers of observation he deploys when writing about the past.

In *The Aviator*, Vodolazkin employs the tropes of the Time Crasher tale much as a trial lawyer questions a hostile witness. The tropes are essential for building his case (his novel), primarily because their own inherent weaknesses make his points for him. There is nothing heroic about Innokenty's survival, just as there is no particular reason to expect the average Time Crasher to be able to save the world simply because he has traveled in time. The fact that, of all the test subjects, he is the one to survive is a happy accident, and it does not give him any particular mission to fulfill once he is awakened in the twenty-first century. What Innokenty does have (and what most Time Crashers sorely lack) is a personal sensibility whose collision with a new time period is rewarding to observe. And even that sensibility (which is the heart of the novel) is fragile, threatened with total deterioration in the novel's last pages.

The Aviator is not the Time Crasher novel to end all Time Crasher novels. For one thing, like the dystopias written by mainstream authors who otherwise disdain science fiction, it is not engaged in a conscious dialogue with a genre that I can only assume would hold little appeal for a sophisticated writer of literary fiction like Vodolazkin. Even the audience that makes up the Venn diagram of the intersection between Time Crasher fans and Vodolazkin readers might not make the connection, since *The Aviator* is not designed to provide the pleasures readers of Vodolazkin are likely to seek when they pick up a hard-core Time Crasher novel. Instead, *The Aviator* builds an inadvertent critique of Time Crashers by interrogating the naïve conceptions of history underlying both the smaller phenomenon of the Time Crasher genre and the larger forces that help ensure the genre's popularity.

Post-Soviet nostalgia, the cult of World War II, the rehabilitation of Brezhnev's Stagnation years, and even the endless discussion of Russia's "historical mission" all share the same defective reasoning. They all reduce historical eras to hyperreal simulacra of themselves, in which one or two broad features define virtually everything. They all assume that history is guided by a teleological impulse, whether it be God's plan, national destiny, or simple determinism. There are no accidents, and any pattern we can see in history is evidence that it follows laws that can be known and explained. This determinism is facilitated by what might seem to be its opposite: the crucial role played by the heroic individual in the right place at the right time. The "great man" and determinism prove to be dialectical, easily mapped onto the spontaneity/consciousness dialectic of socialist realism. The individual's intervention in history serves only to underscore the extent to which he and history shape each other, ultimately reinforcing the individual's identification with his country's historical past and future destiny.

Vodolazkin, of course, is having none of this. When his protagonist moves forward in time, it is hugely disruptive, but it does not change the nature of his relationship to historical events, whether they are now in the past or are unfolding in the present day. As a child, he dreamed of being an aviator, but he is, instead, what most people are when they are on an airplane: a passenger, albeit one whose powers of observation make all his journeys intriguing to follow. By the end of the novel, when he is literally on a plane, he may be about to crash. Or he may not. Either way, there is nothing he can do about it.

3

THE EMPIRE NEVER ENDED

The USSR Is Hiding in Plain Sight

In 1974, Philip K. Dick had an experience that was either a psychotic break or a mystical epiphany (or perhaps both at once): history had actually ceased in the first century c.e., which meant that the Roman Empire never really ended. Still drugged after a visit to the dentist, he saw the fish symbol a delivery girl was wearing around her neck and came to realize that the empire (which he also called the "Black Iron Prison") had stopped the flow of time. Both he and the girl were actually secret Christians avoiding persecution by a hostile, heathen Rome.

However one characterizes Dick's new outlook on the world, it was undeniably productive for his writing. He had already single-handedly sparked an entire subgenre of science fiction in 1962 with *The Man in the High Castle*, the first modern example of alternate history, as well as the forerunner of the speculative plot that can be boiled down into the two words "Hitler wins."

For Dick, the continued existence of the Roman Empire was not alternate history but history itself, and he never wrote a story about an alternate twentieth-century Imperial Rome. Instead, he explored this and other ideas in the thousands of pages of the *Exegesis* of his vision that he wrote from 1974 until his death in 1982, as well as bringing the never-toppled empire into his novels *Radio Free Albemuth* and *Valis*.

In the sort of alternate universe that Dick himself might have admired, one can imagine him living a few decades longer, but as a man who had spent most of his life in the now-defunct USSR. Picture him, decades after 1991, writing a never-ending tract in Russian rather than English, arguing (among many other things) that the Soviet Union still existed all around us, if only we could see it.

Or perhaps one might imagine Dick's post-Soviet counterparts mining a similar vein, but even Victor Pelevin, whose work comes close to the American science fiction writer's psychedelically inflected metaphysics, has not postulated that he still lives in the Soviet Union. Nevertheless, the notion of a persistent USSR endures. The forms it takes are less gnostic than Dick's Eternal Rome, but they do have much wider cultural currency.

Other Russias

Imagining the Soviet Union after 1991 is not restricted to people living or born in the post-Soviet space. Allegations that Vladimir Putin wants to revive the USSR have been a common neocon talking point for decades and have received a new lease on life thanks to the 2022 invasion of Ukraine. Within the Russian Federation, one might chalk up fantasies of a contemporary Soviet Union as nostalgia, but there is more to it than that. The continued Soviet Union can be seen as one of many manifestations of a wish for, if not change, then something *different*. From 2006 to 2010, opposition leaders as diverse as the chess grandmaster Garry Kasparov and the National Bolshevik writer Eduard Limonov were part of a coalition called "Drugaia Rossiia" (the name was subsequently taken by the party Limonov founded in 2010). The most accurate translation of the name would be "A Different Russia," but the firmly entrenched English rendering is "Another Russia." The aspiration is obviously not geographical. Rather, it is the somewhat utopian aspiration that a different kind of Russia could take root on the land where Russia now exists.

To the extent that they can be said to (fictionally) exist, all of these Other Russias can be experienced only in a kind of double consciousness, not unlike Dick's ability to see both the default world and the Black Iron Prison at the same time. Even when the Other Russia is described within the confines of immersive fantasy (i.e., without any diegetic connection to our "real" world), their function for the reader or audience depends on the two worlds' complementarity: each functions as a comment on the other. This makes these Other Russias uncanny by definition, in that each world, in relation to the other, seems both "off" and familiar, rendering them not entirely hospitable.

Their complementarity recalls the premise of China Miéville's novel *The City and the City*, which takes place in two metropoles, Beszel and Ul Qoma, that exist in overlapping geographical space but are kept separate by the requirement that the residents of one city "unsee" the residents and the buildings of the other. Those who actually see the other city commit the violation called "breaching," which is as much phenomenological as it is criminal: in seeing what has always been around them, they are acknowledging the uncanny nature of their everyday existence.

The residents of Miéville's two fictional cities must pretend that something real is not there. By contrast, those who partake in the narratives of Other Russias are willing something into existence rather than out of it. Through the sheer force of their imagination, they are undoing a loss or closing a wound. This imaginative work, then, is usually an example of what Svetlana Boym called "restorative nostalgia, which does not think of itself as nostalgia, but rather as truth and tradition . . . Restorative nostalgia protects the absolute truth, while reflective nostalgia calls it into doubt" (xviii). Or, in the more populist vein that I mined in *Soviet-Self-Hatred*, it is an instance of curatorial fandom, the protective, rearguard impulse to maintain a beloved cultural object according to a rigid set of received terms, rather than the more fluid and playful transformative fandom. To go back to the example from the 2010s, transformative fandom wants a "Different Russia," while curatorial fandom wants to revive a "Russia That We Have Lost." Both activities are inherently creative, but the former celebrates this creativity while the latter wants to cover up all traces of it to maintain the pretense that its proponents are practicing archaeology rather than fan fiction.

Soviet Antiquity

In this reading, the Soviet Union becomes a lost civilization that can be rebuilt from its ruins, cloned, *Jurassic Park*-style, from its amber-preserved DNA, or perceived as always present but barely visible, like one of Miéville's unseen overlapping cities. The *Jurassic Park* metaphor is particularly powerful, giving rise to wordplay used by the film and Soviet Park, a public art project. The coinage works much better in Russian: "Jurassic Park" is, literally, the "Park of the Jurassic Period," which gives rise to "Park of the Soviet Period," and, subsequently, the original Russian edition of Sergei Medvedev's *The Return of the Russian Leviathan* ("Park of the Crimean Period").

"Jurassic Park" may be the most dramatic of the temporal metaphors for the lost Soviet Union, but it still has a lot of company. Recent discussions of Soviet neoclassical architecture refer to a "Soviet antiquity," while the notion of the Soviet Union as a variation on ancient Atlantis can be found across the political spectrum.[1] Eduard Limonov even published a poem and collection called "The

---

1. Ilya Kalinin's analysis of an underwater Soviet statue park is particularly evocative ("Soviet Atlantis").

USSR Is Our Ancient Rome." Yet the most remarkable thing about these metaphors is how unremarkable they seem. The Soviet Union was barely a decade gone before it started to be discussed as if it were Pompeii or the lost continent of Mu. Meanwhile, Anatoly Fomenko and the followers of his New Chronology were taking the opposite approach to history, arguing that ancient Greece and ancient Egypt occurred during the Middle Ages.[2]

What unites Soviet antiquity, the New Chronology, Other Russias, and the varieties of nostalgia and fandom is a voluntarist approach to nation, time, and geography. This is also the common thread to nearly all varieties of Time Crasher stories, including the travels to the past discussed in the previous chapters. For the Time Crasher, every wardrobe is a potential portal to Narnia, every train station conceals a platform for the Hogwarts Express, and every nap could lead to awakening from a century-long slumber. Those Time Crashers who don't end up fighting Nazis or preventing perestroika often find themselves in better worlds, or at least intriguingly different ones. One of the most popular fantasy series of the post-Soviet era, Max Frei's *Labryinths of Echo* series, chronicles the light-hearted adventures of an unremarkable man (named Max Frei) who becomes a detective in an alternate world. Despite its propensity to spark just enough crime to keep Max's department busy, the land of Echo stands out for its self-satisfied hedonism. Max escapes to a world where good food, good company, and an inordinate number of bathrooms per private home are the norm. The hero of Lukyanenko's *Rough Draft* (Chistovik) novels finds himself erased from his everyday Moscow existence, only to learn that he can travel to parallel earths, eventually taking on the task of interdimensional customs agent. Escapism is more than a description of the pleasures such books offer their readers; it is their literal subject matter.

Given such a wide range of alternatives, imagining a never-fallen or somehow restored Soviet Union might seem downright pedestrian. Yet the "reality" (such as it is) turns out to be much more complicated, both because the stakes are higher and because the imaginary world in question is so much closer to people's lived experience. The demands for verisimilitude are that much greater, while the political implications are far more immediately obvious than those of, say, an alternative Russia where vampires and werewolves are real. A persistent USSR does not *necessarily* contravene the laws of physics, or even contradict the "laws" of history (as opposed to contradicting actual historical events). Just five years before the Soviet collapse, the end of the USSR seemed unthinkable rather than inevitable, and if opinion polls over the last two decades are any indication, to a

---

2. The New Chronology project claims that all of antiquity actually took place during the Middle Ages, a truth that has been hidden from humanity by various sinister cabals (Sheiko and Brown 65–98).

large majority of Russian citizens, it now looks regrettable. Brezhnev's Period of Stagnation, now reconceived as a lost age of harmony and economic health, was haunted by the unavailable temptations of Western consumerism (blue jeans, rock music, and so on). Why not imagine a twenty-first-century Soviet Union that made room for the Internet and smartphones, while still retaining the glory of a world-class superpower?

A Dream of a Thousand Cats

In the eighteenth issue of *Sandman*, Neil Gaiman's acclaimed comic about storytelling and dreams, Gaiman and the artist Kelley Jones detour from the series' main plot, handing the narrative reins to an abused female Siamese cat. Traumatized by her owners' drowning of her newborn kittens, she falls asleep and meets the Cat of Dreams, who reveals to her that the world used to be completely different. In the past, giant cats ruled the earth, with tiny humans as their playthings. But one day, the humans realized that if they all dreamed the same dream of a world in which humans ruled and cats were pets, they could transform reality. When she wakes, the Siamese realizes that she has a mission: to travel the world and convince every cat to share the dream of undoing human domination and restoring the golden age of kitty supremacy.

The cats' and humans' collective rewriting of the world raises questions about the nature of reality, questions that could be addressed through the discourse of philosophy or through its less reputable cousin, the gauzy syncretism of New Age "thought." But the cats' dilemma is as much political as it is metaphysical. Who gets the right to define the world? While it is unlikely that even the most outré political activists in Russia are plotting feline restoration, *A Dream of a Thousand Cats* inadvertently models voluntarist wish-fulfillment fantasies about power, nationhood, and consent in the aftermath of the Soviet collapse.

Thanks to Benedict Anderson, scholars in the West have long been accustomed to understanding the nation as an imagined community: nations, countries, and all social collectivities are not natural phenomena that must be accepted as given. Meanwhile, in the wake of the influential writings of Lev Gumilev and his theory of ethnogenesis, Russian social science and public discourse has become increasingly dominated by precisely the opposite notion: the framing of the ethnos as a virtually biological entity with origins and an existence that are close to independent from historical and political contingencies. Ironically, the same historical circumstances that have enhanced the appeal of Gumilev's theories of ethnos have also exacerbated a long-standing historical tendency to imagine Russia and the Soviet Union as entities that can be redefined through sheer force of will.

Examples include Peter the Great's radical transformations of Russian society and the construction of a new capital in a fetid swamp, the Bolsheviks' restructure of the empire along Leninist lines, Stalin's revolution from above, and Gorbachev's perestroika. The end of the Soviet Union followed hurried, ultimately fruitless debates about redefining the relationship of the Union republics with the central government and renaming the country—which, for a while, seemed on the verge of becoming the Union of Sovereign States—with the USSR itself wiped from the map with the stroke of a pen. The last fifteen years of the twentieth century posed a serious challenge to geographic object permanence.

Contrary to the Putinist fetishization of the sovereign state while still relying on the very feelings of patriotism and attachment that the current government so exalts, it is not so difficult for many within Russia to act as though any given iteration of either the empire or nation-state were not just socially constructed but the product of collective, consensual delusion. The end of the Soviet Union was both a cataclysmic, once-in-a-lifetime event and an abstract, bureaucratic action bordering on conceptual art. On December 8, 1991, the day when the USSR was first declared defunct, no bloodthirsty foreign invaders were breaching any borders, no revolution was brewing in the streets. It was a Sunday, and the accords were signed by the leaders of the three Slavic republics (Russia, Ukraine, and Belarus) in secret. The three Baltic republics had seceded in August, and eleven of the twelve remaining republics confirmed the December 8 declaration on December 21. Gorbachev announced his resignation on December 25, and the next day, the Supreme Soviet of the USSR voted itself out of existence.

But what did all of this mean immediately for ordinary citizens in the newly constituted Russian Federation? On a material level, probably little, at least for those who were not directly employed by the Soviet government or military apparatus. The economic transformations were wrenching, of course, but no more on those particular days than the ones immediately preceding or following them. I was living in Moscow at the time and remember a paradoxical sense of both the momentous and the immaterial, of something and nothing happening at the same time. What could be a greater confirmation of the state as consensual fantasy than the fact that its dismantling was, like some underproduced Soviet commodity, unevenly distributed?

The state's collapse should have been a Zen koan: if you live in a small village with little contact with the outside world, did the Soviet Union ever really end? Or did you ever really live in it? In the absence of pervasive state violence and surveillance, much of the individual subject's connection to the state is affective, conceptual, and therefore potentially independent of the facts on the ground (at least for women and for men beyond conscription age). One needs a set of strong reasons, intellectual or emotional, to identify with a political structure that extends so much farther than one's immediately accessible environment. My own personal investment in American federalism is rooted in rootless cosmopolitanism rather than patriotism. My country is more appealing to me as a large, fungible space where my rights are everywhere the same, and I have little interest in (and significant distrust of) local, parochial political formations. But I also recognize that mine is a minority position.

A voluntarist conception of Russian and Soviet statehood is not just an academic exercise, nor is it merely the stuff of fiction (though rest assured, this is fictional stuff to which we will return). Since 2010, the activities of several groups throughout the Russian Federation have been the object of increasing state and media attention precisely because of their insistence that the Russian Federation does not, in fact, exist. The Russian Federation, they argue, is itself a fiction, with no legal basis for its existence. Instead, they claim citizenship in the Union of Soviet Socialist Republics, a country that is very much alive. The empire, it turns out, never really ended. Or at least, this is the dream that thousands of post-Soviet cats would very much like to see as their own reality.

My Address Is the Soviet Union

How do you prove that the USSR no longer exists? The obvious route would be to point out that, by the end of 1991, all the former Soviet republics had declared their independence and been accepted as sovereign states by the international community, with embassies, UN seats, recognized national borders, armed forces, national governments, international agreements, and all the other accoutrements of sovereignty. When the constituent republics declared the Soviet state defunct, and in the absence of any resistance on the part of military or governmental forces representing the USSR, the relocation of the Soviet Union from the present to the past tense became part of consensual reality. The USSR ceased to exist because there was no one with any authority left to declare otherwise.

The many former Soviet citizens who lamented their country's collapse were left with few options: impotent nostalgia and obsessive melancholia, membership in increasingly marginal communist parties, agitation for a new form of empire, or a disenchanted retreat from the public sphere. It took two decades for some ex-Soviets to develop the most straightforward response to their collapse—denial.

The various groups that espouse the continued existence of the USSR do not agree on everything, but they do share a familiar point of departure. As many anti-liberals have said since 1991, the people who declared the Soviet Union dead had no legal standing to do so. Not only did 77.85 percent of respondents to a March 17, 1991, referendum vote in favor of preserving the Soviet Union, but the subsequent actions that nullified the USSR were not provided for in the Soviet constitution. Boris Yeltsin, president of the Russian Soviet Federative Socialist Republic (RSFSR), should not have had the authority to rename it the Russian Federation, since the republic was still under the jurisdiction of the USSR's Supreme Soviet. More important, the leaders of the three Slavic republics did not have the constitutional authority to declare the Soviet Union defunct.

Three decades on, these all sound like moot points, or at least purely theoretical ones. Giorgio Agamben famously called into question our received notions of sovereignty when, building on the work of Carl Schmitt, he argued that the power of the sovereign rests precisely on his ability to suspend due process under the law. The sovereign is the sovereign by virtue of his capacity to legally do away with legality. But by what right can the sovereign declare the state itself to have ceased to exist? It is one thing to suspend the constitution, but it is another to declare both the constitution and one's own office to be null and void.

In *Plots against Russia*, I argued that the Putinist obsession with what I called "bare sovereignty" is a reaction to the traumatic failure of Soviet statehood and the concomitant fear that statehood could fail (or be undermined) in the future (112–15). But it is also a rejection of both the very idea of regime change and the possibility that the current iteration of the state could be supplanted by a new one. Putinist sovereignty is built on a paradox: the assertion that the collapse of the USSR was a tragic error that should have been avoided while simultaneously insisting on the legitimacy of the forms of statehood that emerged from it. Nostalgia for lost great-power status is one thing, but Western observers are often oblivious to the delicate balance on which Putinist rhetoric rests. Putinist sovereignty gains nothing from an ideology that is tantamount to sawing off the branch on which it stands. And this is why the constant Western drumbeat that Putin wants to restore the USSR is a misreading of something that is actually much more complicated.

When it comes to Putinist geopolitics and post-Soviet nostalgia, Western pundits make a rookie semiotic mistake: they confuse the Symbolic with the Imaginary, and assume a simple, linear connection to the Real. Rather than striving to resurrect the Soviet Union, the Putinist state peddles "Sovietness," cherry-picking the attributes of great power, empire, and purpose without activating either the ideology or the bureaucratic structures that underlay them. Even if we were to accept that a restored Soviet Union is the goal of Putinism, it would be a goal dependent on infinite deferral. Like the arrival of the messiah for rabbinical Judaism, it would be an outcome that is theoretically desired but never really expected. Instead, the current, technically ad hoc structures are meant to endure in the perpetuity of our profane time. What from the outside might appear millenarian is actually a quite comfortable fit with the current state of affairs.

Actual millenarianism is a threat to the status quo. Just as many mainstream Jews have little patience for the Lubavitcher Hasidim who (displaying a strangely unself-conscious lack of originality) insist that their dead Rebbe is going to come back as the messiah, Putinism cannot tolerate actual Soviet restorationists. Nor can it abide those who claim that the USSR still exists and the Russian Federation is a fiction. Such groups are a problem not just because of allegations of fraud, brainwashing, and terrorism, but because they reflect badly on a regime that has used Soviet nostalgia as a cornerstone.

Though the movement to reaffirm Soviet sovereignty dates back to 2010, it took a few years for the media and the state to pay it much attention. Like so many other countries, the Russian Federation has no shortage of crackpots and cranks. When Sergei Taraskin, an ethnic Russian dentist who had moved from Tajikistan to the outskirts of Moscow to open an initially successful clinic, announced in 2010 that he was the "acting president of the USSR," there was no reason to assume he was anything other than a novelty. Taraskin founded the Union of Slavic Forces of Rus, a group that managed to sound both ethnonationalist and retro-Soviet at the same time (in Russian, its initials are CCCP, the same as those of the USSR).

Indeed, Taraskin's announcement looked like little more than a desperate attempt to avoid his financial responsibilities. One of his clinic's investors had pulled out, and he was faced with eviction. In the Moscow Court of Arbitration, instead of declaring, say, bankruptcy, he declared himself the Soviet president ("Samoprovozglashennogo 'prezidenta SSSR' Sergeia Taraskina"). As he explained at the time, the office of the Soviet presidency had been "vacant for more than eighteen years," since the "deserter" Gorbachev stepped down. "None of the soldiers and officers of the Soviet army, who were supposed to carry out their military oath, had filled the position" (Klimova). Where Taraskin allegedly fit in the Soviet military chain of command is an open question, but against the backdrop of the "president's" increasingly outlandish claims, it can be considered moot.

Taraskin gathered a following both in person and on YouTube. By some metrics, his movement has been a great success. Unlike so many anti-government groups of the past two decades, his Union of Slavic Forces of Rus (and the various offshoots and affiliates) is not confined to the capitals. The sheer geographic breadth of the criminal cases brought against Taraskin and his fellow travelers attests to the wide reach of his ideas. Like Philip K. Dick's secret Christians subverting the Roman Empire in Berkeley, California, Taraskin's people were creating a shadow Soviet Union in opposition to the illegitimate authorities who refused to acknowledge the USSR's continued existence.

This success is, of course, fraught with irony. Despite Taraskin's own origins in the Soviet Tajik Republic, his followers and epigones were marking their territory primarily within the bounds of the very entity whose legal existence they rejected: the Russian Federation. Even more troublesome (if entirely predictable) were the centrifugal forces that would threaten to tear their restorationist movement apart. Contrary to the early post-Soviet fears that the Russian Federation might, like its predecessor, collapse into its constituent parts, the Russian state has proved quite powerful and stable, while Taraskin's organization has been unable to match the centralized dominance of Putin's power vertical. Taraskin's undead USSR has demonstrated its vulnerability to separatism.

Thus Taraskin is the center of attention in media coverage of the Union of Slavic Forces of Rus, but not when the story is about one of the many offshoots that do not recognize his authority. Even if we accept for the moment that the USSR never fell, there is no escaping the fact that this shadow state has yet to develop its own TASS, Pravda, or Channel One that can speak for the country with one voice. The head of the "State Registration Chamber of the USSR in Ekaterinburg" told his followers on social media in late 2019 that if they did not immediately register with his office after watching his video, this could be considered a "renunciation of USSR citizenship" (Zhilova, "Sekta grazhdan SSSR"). In the Siberian city of Surgut, Anton Bulgakov heads a group called Living People (a Russian variation on the American "sovereign citizens" movement) whose belief system is so syncretic that the insistence that the USSR still functions is among the least bizarre elements of their doctrines. Valentina Reunova, the head of the "Supreme Soviet of the USSR," not only issues passports but also excommunicates enemies. Thanks to her, both Putin and Medvedev have been deprived of Soviet citizenship (whether or not they know or care is beside the point).

In 2014, Sergei Torgunkov, another financial wizard who had fallen on hard times, followed up his earlier book about Christ's impending second coming in 2012 and proclaimed himself the acting president of the USSR's Novosibirsk regional branch. On November 23 of the following year, he paid a visit to the Novosibirsk police in order to give them his latest presidential decrees, only to find himself involuntarily committed to a psychiatric hospital (Merlizkin).

In some cases, Taraskin's rivals are outright imitators. Chief among them is Sergei Demkin, a St. Petersburg businessman whose resume is more suggestive of "would-be titan of industry" than "die-hard communist revanchist." After serving in the army in the 1990s, he became an oil trader, construction company director, and electrical services company owner. In 2016, he "realized that something wasn't quite right"; everything he had could be taken from him in an instant, leaving his family with nothing. As he puts it, he could have either emigrated or stayed and taken action. He met with Taraskin, only to decide that an organization consisting of "grandmas selling documents" was not the way forward.

He thought about Soviet history and about how "Lenin and Stalin relied on labor unions." Concluding that Russia needs a "revolution of consciousness" rather than a political revolution, he formed an organization called the Union of the SSR Labor Union (profsoiuz "Soiuz SSR" [Zhegulev]). It is easy to conflate Demkin's group with Taraskin's, since both are built on a very specific economic appeal. But where Taraskin (and Bulgakov) use their economic policies as a starting point for much more baroque ideologies, Demkin's approach is more technocratic.

Demkin's Labor Union has distilled the movement down to those features that have always attracted the most attention. Like Taraskin, Bulgakov, and the rest of this fractious paranoid politburo, Demkin offers would-be Soviet citizens a set of very practical incentives. Since the Russian Federation (RF) is an illegal entity, squatting on a large chunk of Soviet territory, Soviet citizens are under no obligation to pay any bills they might owe to the RF. In other words, Soviet citizens are on an extended utilities strike. The economic appeal is straightforward, especially when considering how many of these citizens are senior. Utility bills can be particularly burdensome to people on a fixed income.

Of course, these same senior citizens have no qualms about receiving their RF pensions. Nor do the contradictions end there. The leaders of the various "Citizens of the USSR" groups claim that Russian money is not legal tender, with some of them even issuing Soviet rubles as a replacement. But, again, these groups accept payment for membership and services in supposedly fictitious Russian rubles. Their rates are not necessarily high, unless we continue to keep in mind the limited resources of their elderly target audience. The most noteworthy (or notorious) Citizens of the USSR product costs anywhere from two thousand to four thousand rubles (twenty-five to fifty dollars): a Soviet passport.

Ode to a Soviet Passport

Is it possible to be sentimental about a passport? Apparently, it is. In 1929, Vladimir Mayakovsky wrote *Verses on My Soviet Passport* (Stikhi o sovetskom pasporte), one of the many late works that helped generations of Soviet schoolchildren learn to loathe this great and complicated poet. For readers who were not obliged to declaim these verses by heart while proudly wearing their Young Pioneers kerchief, here is a brief summary. Mayakovsky begins the poem by affirming his long-standing hostility to bureaucrats and nearly all their hateful works but reserves special *affection* for one particular document as he sets a scene that would be familiar to those privileged few who, like Mayakovsky himself, traveled outside of the Soviet Union during a time when this country was none too popular with its neighbors. Such intrepid voyagers knew that not all passports are created equal: "At some passports / the mouth smiles. / At others / it spits" (K odnim pasportam— / ulybka u rta. / K drugin— / otnoshenie plevoe). Border guards accept American passports "like tips," but when they come to the poet's red-skinned booklet, they hold it gingerly, like a poisonous snake. But Mayakovsky, being Mayakovsky, responds to contempt with proud defiance: "From my wide pants / I / take out / a copy / of my priceless cargo / Read it / Envy it / I / am a citizen of the Soviet Union" (Ia / dostaiu / iz shirokikh shtanin / dublikatom / bestsennnogo gruza. / Chitaite, zaviduite, / ia— / grazhdanin Sovetskogo Soiuza) (Maiakovskii 594–97).

In Mayakovsky's poem, the passport is the physical manifestation of the speaker's pride in his country; it is the pride of citizenship. But the passport he describes is not one that would have been available to all his fellow Soviets. The poem is about his *zagranpasport*, his foreign travel documents that were in no way an inalienable right. The Citizens of the USSR cannot pretend to make such passports, because they would run up against the fundamental flaw in their model of Soviet sovereignty: a foreign passport can function as such only if countries *other* than one's own recognize them as legitimate, but the entire world has accepted that the Soviet Union no longer exists. In the twenty-first century, a Soviet foreign passport is no more valid than an invitation to Hogwarts.

And so the Citizens of the USSR must confine themselves to making (or forging) passports that are not actually designed to facilitate border crossings. In both the former Soviet Union and the Russian Federation, the identification documents issued to every citizen aged fourteen and over are called "passports," with a design to match. Like most passports, these internal documents are in a booklet format that is unfriendly to both wallets and lanyards. Consisting of twenty pages and containing information about marriages, divorces, children, domicile, and conscription status, the latest (2007) version of the Russian internal passport is an awkwardly portable compendium of all the biometric data that the state deems essential for moving through daily life.

The Citizens of the USSR's objections to the Russian passport are multiple, reflecting a range of attitudes toward documentation from paranoid skepticism to something akin to idolatry. Numerous commentators have demonstrated the ideological links between the Citizens of the USSR in the post-Soviet space, the Reichsbürger (Reich Citizens) movement in Germany, and the various Sovereign Citizens groups active throughout the United States. All three reject the generally recognized statehood of their respective countries in favor of a previous constitution or legal framework that they claim has never been invalidated. Since 1985, the Reichsbürger have insisted that the 1919 Weimar Constitution is still in effect, rendering the current Federal Republic of Germany an illegal entity (often said to be controlled by the World Zionist Conspiracy, of course). They refuse to pay taxes and issue their own documents (for a fee).

In the United States, the Sovereign Citizens movement, rooted in the Christofascist Posse Comitatus movement, argues that the Fourteenth Amendment of the US Constitution disrupted the citizenship regime that had existed up to that point, obliging "sovereign citizens" to assume the status of "federal citizens" and subject themselves to the tyranny of the US central government. Given the overt white nationalism of most of the Sovereign Citizens groups, the fact that the Fourteenth Amendment was the mechanism for granting citizenship to previously enslaved Black people is hardly coincidental.

As much as these three movements have in common, however, their approach to documents, while superficially similar, shows a divergent attitude toward bureaucratic modernity and the modern state. The Sovereign Citizens have developed in a country with a long-standing suspicion of central power; unlike Germany, the Soviet Union, and the Russian Federation, the United States has never issued or required national IDs (hence the disputes over requiring identification for voting, which would be a non-issue if all citizens carried such documentation as a matter of course). Also important is the Sovereign Citizens' selection of the ratification of the Fourteenth Amendment as a historical turning point. Adopted in 1868, the Fourteenth Amendment precedes the Weimar Constitution by fifty-one years and the Soviet collapse by more than a century, representing for Americans a much more significant rupture with modernity than 1919 or 1991.

Where the Sovereign Citizens can display unalloyed contempt for the very idea of federal documentation, the Citizens of the USSR find themselves engaged in a balancing act. As their very name suggests, their identity is based on the concept of a powerful central state. The Sovereign Citizens look back to a time when the federal government left them alone, while the Citizens of the USSR long for the days of a lost great power. If we think of the state as a figurative parent, the Sovereign Citizens are playing at parricide, while the Citizens of the USSR demand the return of the Prodigal Dad.

Hence the movement's insistence on their own documents' necessity while denouncing all the instruments of Russian Federation data collection as instruments of oppression. Again and again, Citizens of the USSR exhort their skeptical family members to withhold their personal information: "Yesterday I told a relative that my Sberbank card is finally ready, and I can pick it up tomorrow. Him: Did you give your biometric information? Me: When I get the card. Him: Don't even think about it. It's all the work of Satan. When I ask why, and where biometrics and Satan come in, there's no real answer" (Zhilova, "Muzh sestry").

As another frustrated relative puts it: "Mama answered that we don't actually live in Russia but in the USSR, and that we're all being zombified [brainwashed] and that they want to harvest our organs. She stated that all the information about us is known by our enemies, because we give our biometric data when we get our passports" (Zhilova, "Muzh sestry").

But when it comes to the documents forged by the movement's leadership, all hostility to the collection of biometric data vanishes. The Citizens of the USSR love paper documents; they cannot get enough of them. Of course, issuing their own documentation is a significant source of income (as it is for the Sovereign Citizens and the Reichsbürger), but that does not explain the emotional attachment displayed by rank-and-file citizens, whose zeal for their passports is positively Mayakovskian. But it is also a manifestation of the binary thinking so common to conspiracy theorists and moralizers. Soviet (and pseudo-Soviet) documentation is heroic, if not holy, while the corresponding papers issued by the Russian Federation are, at least in the opinion of some Citizens of the USSR, literally the work of Satan himself.

The fixation on Soviet documentation makes sense primarily in the context of Soviet absence. Anything that works to establish the existence of this long-gone, abstract entity is a net positive. For the Citizens of the USSR, Soviet documents are a guarantee of object permanence, providing reassurance that the object of their love is not actually lost. It is telling that the documents in question are almost always internal passports, because the reassurance has a circular character: as long as the Soviet Union still exists, the Citizens of the USSR have a country to call home, and as long as people have Soviet passports, the Soviet Union remains with them. Usually, when we talk of people identifying with a group or a country, we are speaking figuratively, but in this case, the Soviet Union establishes both its own identity and that of the Citizens of the USSR themselves. Like Narcissus enchanted by his own reflection, the Citizens of the USSR cannot risk looking away.

The Citizens of the USSR's belief system should allow them to reject RF documents as a matter of course, just as the Sovereign Citizens and Reichsbürger do in response to their own governments. If the state is illegitimate, how could its documents be anything else? But the Citizens of the USSR are too obsessed with documentation to define the issue so simply. For them, documents and statehood form a closed circuit, with each defining the other. The flaws in the RF documents, then, must in themselves function as proof of the RF's illegitimacy and must illustrate the basic tenets of the movement.

The Citizens of the USSR are fixated on the fine points of Russian money and passports. Their argument about the codes indicated on the Russian ruble is too complex and, frankly, too boring to go into. Suffice to say that for them, this question of codes is enough to prove that the Russian ruble is worthless. The passport argument is more significant, although the reasoning is no less convoluted. Soviet passports use upper and lower case to indicate the bearer's last name, first name, and patronymic, while the Russian version uses all capitals, usage more appropriate for tombstones, a comparison that will become clear soon enough (Rodionova).

As this example shows, the Citizens of the USSR give Soviet passports the kind of close, exegetical readings usually reserved for scripture or contract law, seizing on the smallest detail to prove their point. Their primary argument about the invalidity of RF passports comes down to the use of a word and an abbreviation: "registration" and "UFMS" (the Administration of the Federal Migration Service).

Soviet internal passports were issued at the passport office of the Ministry of Internal Affairs, and among the many pieces of information it contained was the *propiska* for the domicile where the passport bearer was officially permitted (and expected) to reside. In 1992, the responsibility for issuing passports in the Russian Federation was handed to the newly formed Federal Migration Service—which, as the name implies, also processed applications for migration into the RF.[3] New legislation replaced the *propiska* with registration (*registratsiia*), which actually removed a number of obstacles to the free movement of Russian citizens and to their access to education and social services. But registration, particularly when combined with migration, has been used to argue that the RF passport system turns Russians into migrants rather than citizens.

This comes up repeatedly in interviews with the Citizens of the USSR. A sixty-one-year-old retired woman named Lidia Frolova told a journalist that a friend pointed out the terminology to her back in 2013: "Take a look at your passport. It says we're migrants and has an immigration service stamp" (Klimova).

Another followed the trail to the records office, where she asked if they had any paperwork on her renouncing her USSR citizenship and "migrating" to the RF. Naturally, they did not: "So it's like I was married when I wasn't looking!" (Charodeyy).

The Citizens of the USSR's literalism is selective. When a reporter asked how it happened that their "Soviet" passports were printed in Ukraine, they explained that these were leftover blank passports from the old days: "You see ... thirty years ago one of the passport series codes accidentally formed a bad word. So these passports were set aside ... And now we've put them to use! They are real Soviet passports!" (Charodeyy).

---

3. The UFMS was disbanded in 2016, and its functions were transferred to the Main Directorate of Migration Affairs under the Ministry of Internal Affairs. This does not seem to have figured into the arguments made by the Citizens of the USSR, probably because their passports would likely have been issued before this reorganization and would therefore still bear the abbreviation UFMS.

The fact that the letters spelled "KhAM" (rude person, boor) somehow did not bother them, despite their attribution of near-magical significance to other words on official documents. Nothing gets in the way of what for all intents and purposes looks like a classic case of projection. To the Citizens of the USSR, all of these documents prove that the Russian Federation is not really a state but rather a commercial entity. Meanwhile, the group's main source of income is selling invalid documents to its members. Clearly, the Citizens of the USSR are not lacking in sheer gall. Perhaps the label "KhAM" on their passports is more significant than they think.

The USSR as Conspiracy Theory

One of the many weaknesses of Western pundits' accusation that Putin and his supporters want to resurrect the Soviet Union is how little thought is put into exactly what the "Soviet Union" is supposed to signify. Is it a question of revived imperialism, a return to communism, pure nostalgia, or something else entirely? It would be easy to make the same mistake about the Citizens of the USSR. Without asking what the group members themselves mean when they talk about the USSR, we are left simply imposing our own preconceptions onto them. Assuming they must be Stalinists, quasi-nationalists, or old people longing for the Brezhnev days says more about the commentators than it does about the movement.

Should we really be surprised, then, to find out that even the group members themselves do not all agree on their vision of a Soviet radiant present? Part of the problem is the movement's decentralization, but the real issue is a combination of ideology and epistemology (while also begging for a bit of ethnography that I am in a poor position to provide). The Citizens of the USSR is a group that starts out with an idea that is almost too simple—the Soviet Union never collapsed—allowing its adherents to project a wide variety of fears and desires onto what is essentially a blank slate. The result is an ideological syncretism that has transformed the Citizens of the USSR into a collection of the usual preoccupations found among Russian conspiracy theorists.

In fact, if we set aside the obvious genealogical connections to the Sovereign Citizens and the Reichsbürger, the movement that the Citizens of the USSR most resembles is QAnon. Like QAnon, the organization thrives on the culture of the Internet in general and social media in particular (with YouTube hosting a number of the movement's most prominent speakers). Like QAnon, the Citizens of the USSR's demographic skews toward (but is not limited to) the middle-aged and elderly. In the Citizens' case, this would be the segment of the population with the greatest affective ties to the Soviet Union based on their own lived experience, as well as the most traumatized by the 1990s. And, like QAnon, the Citizens of the USSR rapidly accrued a set of familiar xenophobic, conspiracist tropes that were not part of the initial stages of the theory.

Just as QAnon did not initially traffic in antisemitic fear-mongering, the basic premise of the Citizens of the USSR had nothing to do with Jews. And yet it is hard to be surprised at the news that some Citizens of the USSR in the Kuban were arrested for plotting to murder a rabbi ("Grazhdane SSSR arestovany"). Or that some of them believe that Jews are poisoning children's food, eating Christian babies, and brainwashing innocent Russians (Varlamov, "'Grazhdane SSSR' protiv Rossii"). By no means am I suggesting that all the Citizens of the USSR hold such beliefs, or that *only* Citizens do; quite the opposite, the tropes and memes of antisemitism are already so prevalent in the discourse of authoritarian, conspiratorial, and hard-core nationalist groups that their migration into the worldview of some Citizens of the USSR was inevitable. My aim here is not to uncover antisemitism (especially when it barely bothers to cover itself) but to highlight the ideological work that goes into the development of the various subgroups. There is no need for a single mastermind to put all these tropes together; for one thing, the Citizens of the USSR have many candidates vying for mastermind status. For another, it is far more likely that individuals cobble together a familiar conspiratorial ideology on their own.[4]

The stories that the Citizens of the USSR tell one another are inconsistent, underdeveloped, and often quite distant from the basic idea of a Soviet Union that never fell. Taraskin claims to be the head not only of the USSR but also of the Russian Empire. Sergei Torgunkov believed he was the second coming of Christ even before copying from Taraskin's playbook; he published a tract about his divinity and suggested an alliance with Alfa Bank ("Jesus Christ is a VIP client of the new Alfa Bank!") (Merlizkin). Another group is preparing for a great battle against the Reptiloids (Polovinko).[5] And I haven't even brought up one of the most common tenets of the Citizens of the USSR: they insist that they are the only "living people" on the territory of the Russian Federation.[6]

---

4. QAnon seems to do just fine generating new content even in the absence of new "Q drops" (public posts from the anonymous person or persons behind the "Q" identity).

5. Nor is it surprising that many of the Citizens are anti-mask COVID deniers, who call the epidemic a "global conspiracy" (Kozlov).

6. The Living People of the USSR insist on making affidavits based on the 1666 British proclamation called the Cestui Qui Vie Act, which provided for the disposition of property for those who had vanished at sea or not been heard from for seven years. A number of conspiracists, particularly the Freemen on the Land (a Canadian offshoot of the Sovereign Citizens), have interpreted the act in a much more sweeping manner: anyone who does not declare themselves "alive" after seven years becomes the property of either the British Crown, the Vatican, or global Jewish capital. The only defense the Living People have against this sinister dehumanization is their own legal assertion that they are, indeed, "living."

In a 2018 interview published on Lenta.ru, Acting USSR President Sergei Taraskin seems much more committed to the Soviet Union as an entity than to the Soviet system. The "fact" that Lenin was an agent of anti-Russian Western forces does not bother him: "You're connecting large legal entities to concrete individuals. But you must understand that such a large state always had plenty of scoundrels and traitors, and heroes, and so on. An individual whom you like or don't like should not be connected to the whole entity" ("'Rossiiskaia Federatsiia—eto okkupant'").

In and of itself, this statement sounds like common sense, but when applied to the founder of the very state that Taraskin claims to represent, it should undercut the foundations of everything Taraskin is trying to (re)build. But it does not, because Taraskin's reflexive syncretism and lack of interest in ideology render the search for consistency foolish. Taraskin says that socialism will play a role, because the word's root is "society," and a person can't live without a society. There will be a planned economy ("How can you create something without planning?") but not Marxism. Socialism for him is based on "honor, conscience, [and] justice."

While there are no doubt plenty of Stalinists among the Citizens of the USSR, as well as others who are committed to their own understanding of the tenets of communism, expecting the entire movement to display such ideological dedication is to fall into the trap that so often awaits liberal observers of conspiracy theories. We search in vain for ideological consistency when what we really should be looking for is *affect*. The Citizens of the USSR's appeal is emotional, not logical, which is one of the reasons that they cannot be swayed by rational argument.

Yet there is still a very potent irony about this USSR that lacks a coherent political program. However much Soviet practice deviated from Soviet theory, the historical USSR was dependent on the *idea* of an ideology to an unprecedented extent. The Citizens of the USSR either cannot come to a consensus or cannot be bothered to dwell on social and economic theory. The contours of their USSR might resemble a utopia, in that it is both idealized and unrealized, but modern utopias, while often mirroring an imagined Golden Age, have tended to look forward to the creation of something new. Borrowing from the title of Edward Bellamy's famous utopian novel, the Citizens of the USSR are looking backward (in every sense of the phrase's meaning). They want what they have lost: decent living standards and pride in a powerful country. The rest, from grand ideological theorizing down to the minutiae of daily life, is a set of details that can be addressed later.

Cult Phenomena

I have not done any kind of ethnographic work with the Citizens of the USSR and cannot claim to have unmediated access to their story. Instead, careful attention to the ways that the group has been positioned in the media and framed by experts can tell a story of its own. As fascinating as the Citizens of the USSR are on their own terms, the reactions to them have been at least as significant.

While it is easy to follow the lead of the blogger Ilya Varlamov ("'Grazhdane SSSR' ostalis'") and dismiss most Citizens of the USSR as "freaks who are nostalgic for the Soviet Union" (*prosto friki, nostalgiruiushchie po Sovku*), their presentation in the media tends to grab the audience's attention with some of their more bizarre beliefs or activities before eventually sounding the alarm about the danger the Citizens allegedly pose.[7] The only thing that stops the media coverage from turning into a full-fledged moral panic is how limited that coverage has been so far.

There does seem to be a concerted effort to turn the Citizens of the USSR into the kind of threat that must be confronted by the power of the state that the movement itself rejects. Since Putin's return to the presidency in 2012, the state and the media have marshaled their considerable might for the purpose of suppressing what liberal politicians have long called "civil society," the non-governmental organizations (NGOs) and formations that have been the mainstays of liberal democracies. In the 1990s, when the experience of the Soviet Union and a tendency to look toward the West made the proliferation of independent institutions generally appear to be a good thing, such organizations experienced rapid growth. For example, George Soros, now uniformly depicted in the Russian media as the country's enemy, funded a variety of organizations in support of educational reform, international exchange, and the growth of democratic institutions. The current state approach to independent organizations seems predicated on defining them as competitive threats to the country's sovereignty. Volunteerism is generally viewed as suspicious, unless it is associated with state or church structures (Englund and Lally).

In 2008, President Dmitry Medvedev signed an order creating the Center for Combating Extremism (commonly known as the Center E), officially mandated to fight extremism and terrorism. Center E agents are reliable attendees of all manner of political rallies and have been at the forefront of a battle that the Russian state began in the late 1990s, the fight against so-called sects (i.e., cults), often categorized as totalitarian or destructive. The 1997 Law on Freedom of Conscience and Religious Associations defined Islam, Buddhism, Judaism, and "Christianity" (i.e., Russian Orthodoxy) as "traditional religions" in Russia and established a registration regime for all other religious groups

---

7. Even Varlamov engages in a a similar approach, if in a more casual manner. Immediately after his statement about the "freaks," he writes "But as for the organizers . . . of course, something has to be done."

effective December 31, 1999. This law, in combination with subsequent legislation aimed at NGOs and "extremism," has facilitated the criminalization and demonization of a wide range of religious organizations, most notably the Jehovah's Witnesses.

The Citizens of the USSR would find themselves demonized as both a secular extremist movement *and* a dangerous cult. In a political situation where the boundaries between church and state are being brazenly ignored, the Citizens of the USSR are a perfect folk devil.

The campaign against so-called cults began long before the establishment of Center E. In fact, it is part of the process that led to the adoption of the 1997 law. In the 1990s, both foreign protestant evangelists and new religious movements (NRMs, the neutral term scholars prefer to "cults") saw the former Soviet Union as an untapped market for the business of saving souls. During those same years, the Branch Davidians and Heaven's Gate in the United States and Aum Shinrikyo in Japan became object lessons in the dangers of "cults" (especially since Aum Shinrikyo was also active in Russia). Homegrown NRMs such as the Great White Brotherhood of Maria Devi Khristos, the Mother of God Center, and the followers of Vissarion fueled a panic about malevolent Svengalis "zombifying" the country's youth (Shterin; Borenstein, "Suspending Disbelief").

Much of the blame for the panic can be cast on the sensationalist media, but they had a great deal of help from self-proclaimed "experts" who warned of the dangers of NRMs in no uncertain terms. These experts were usually affiliated with the Russian Orthodox Church (the organization that had the most to lose), most notably Alexander Dvorkin. Dvorkin's most significant intellectual contribution to the anti-cult movement is the phrase that will (soon!) bring us back to the Citizens of the USSR: to describe organizations such as the Society for Krishna Consciousness and the Great White Brotherhood, he coined the term "totalitarian sect" (Dvorkin).

It was a brilliant, if ironic, turn of phrase. Ironic in that the American panic over NRMs "brainwashing" naive recruits was a repackaging of 1950s Cold War anxieties about communist "thought reform" (most notably dramatized in *The Manchurian Candidate*), and brilliant because it took advantage of the then-current desire for distance from the Soviet "totalitarian" past. Dvorkin creates a folk devil who is both foreign (like the Hare Krishnas) and disturbingly familiar (a variation on his country's own experience with the suppression of individual freedoms). "Totalitarian sect" reconciles two ideas that might seem mutually exclusive, in that totalitarian theory posits the attempt at a total control that admits no difference of opinion or approach, while the word "sect" denotes a group that has splintered off from the mainstream. Totalitarianism thus gets projected onto a small group that can be condemned in good conscience, a group that can be despised by cultural conservatives for its deviation from the norms and by liberals for its offenses against human agency.

Perhaps one of the inevitable ramifications of defining the state as the subject and hero of history is how easily the deviation from social norms is traduced as a crime against the state. The fight against totalitarian sects (I'm abandoning the scare quotes, but only because they are tedious) became part of the ever-expanding scope of Center E, lumping religious minorities and political protesters together with terrorists and anarchists. Recently, Dvorkin's mantle has been taken up by Roman Silantiev, a professor of the history of religion who has held a series of positions within the Russian Orthodox Church. As a specialist on Islam, Silantiev has spent most of his career offending Muslims, but he also frequently speaks out about new religious movements (Ragozina 289–92). Now Silantiev is developing a unified theory of social deviance that implicitly justifies Center E's determination to lump all perceived threats into a single category: destructology. And the Citizens of the USSR are the theory's most visible test case.

In the run-up to unveiling his new theory, Silantiev was frequently asked to comment on the Citizens, and he wasted no opportunity to paint them as a cult-like threat to the country's morals. Even without Silantiev, the media had frequently compared the group to religious "sects," even deploying a nickname sure to set off alarm bells: Witnesses of the USSR. The association in the mind of a Russian speaker is obvious: the Russian name for the Jehovah's Witnesses translates back into English as the Witnesses of Jehovah. American nonbelievers tend to dismiss the Witnesses as a minor annoyance ("How can I close the door on them without being rude?"), but in Russia, they are more likely to be perceived as sinister. The Jehovah's Witnesses have a long history of persecution dating back to the Soviet period, and they remain in the public mind as a prominent example of a totalitarian sect.[8]

Silantiev's only problem with this term for the citizens is apparently that it is not derogatory enough. Together with Olga Strelakova, he published a short book in 2020 called *Necromancers of Our Times* (Nekromanty nashikh dnei). The book is about the Citizens of the USSR, or, as he and Strelakova like to call them, the "necrocommunists." In so doing, they are focusing on the magical thinking that I have already argued is at the heart of the movement, but for them, this is no playful metaphor. While it does contain a fair amount of useful information about the ideological similarities between the Citizens and the Western groups we have already discussed, *Necromancers of Our Times* has one task: to make the

---

8. See Baran, *Dissent on the Margins*, as well as her "From Sectarians to Extremists" and "Contested Victims."

reader see the Citizens of the USSR as a totalitarian cult. The Citizens' ideology thus loses any political import, since the group is now just an extravagant variation on the familiar theme of religious sectarianism.

In particular, Silantiev and Strelakova are at great pains to connect the Citizens of the USSR with the various strains of neopaganism that have developed throughout Russia over the past three decades. These connections are real but not primary; like the group's antisemitism, neopaganism is something that part of the movement picked up through the predictable process of conspiratorial osmosis. The Foundation for Traditional Religions, a Russian neopagan website that monitors media coverage of pagan themes, responded to a positive review of the book by pointing out that Silantiev and Strelakova are continuing the process of "connecting (neo)paganism with yet another extremist marker" ("Neoiazychestvo"). In other words, the authors are using the years of negative press about neopagans to show the Citizens of the USSR in a bad light, while also using the Citizens to smear the pagans. As vilification goes, it's quite efficient.

Shrinking the Public Sphere

The conflation of fringe politics with fringe religion has obvious value for the state, promoting the narrative that deviation from the (Putinist) mainstream is a matter of fanaticism rather than legitimate political differences. Here the Citizens of the USSR make the perfect poster children, because, to anyone not already inclined to take them seriously, their claims are patently absurd. But what Silantiev and Strelakova are doing in *Necromancers of Our Time*, and what Silantiev and his other coauthor Sergei Chekmaev do in *Destructology*, goes several steps further.[9] In applying anti-cult methodology to groups that are not, at their core, religions, they willfully ignore the boundary between the spiritual and the secular. Just as anti-extremist legislation and police work shrink the available space for legitimate political dissent, Silantiev and his co-authors are trying to redefine the public sphere as a realm with no room for the secular.

---

9. Chekmaev's involvement is noteworthy. A journalist best known as a science fiction writer and editor, Chekmaev has long been a driving force behind the socially conservative science fiction coming out of the liberpunk movement (*Plots against Russia* 169–77). He has edited anthologies about the dangers of tolerance, the decline of the family, and a future USSR at war in space. Religion is not a new theme for him. In 2018 he published *Modnoverie*, an anthology devoted to satirizing neopaganism. He is closely associated with Snezhnii kom, a publishing house that, although dealing primarily with science fiction, brought out Silantiev and Strelakova's *Necromancers of Our Time*. The boundaries between sociological science fiction and science fictional sociology appear to be wearing thin.

Silantiev does not repeat the mistakes of more familiar Bible-thumpers who alienate the less committed with fire-and-brimstone rhetoric. The veneer of sociology covers up an unacknowledged debt to the theology known as presuppositionalism. Presuppositionalism rejects the very idea of rational disputation with nonbelievers, because the unerrant Bible is the only source of truth. As Chrissy Stroop writes in "Is Being Trans a Religion?," "The 'unsaved,' bringing their own presuppositions to the evidence, will come to different conclusions—about the Bible, for example, or about the formation of the Grand Canyon, which the 'evolutionist' will see in terms of geologic time, while the creationist will see the impact of Noah's flood . . . Based on human observation of the evidence alone, the reasoning goes, there is no way to adjudicate between these two incommensurate 'worldviews.' The 'saved' Christian, with his 'biblical worldview,' simply 'knows' that he . . . is right."

Stroop, a prominent "exvangelical" writer, argues that the American Christian Right characterizes all opposing views and phenomena as "religions" (including "transgenderism," the subject of this particular post) in order to ensure that "there can be no religiously neutral space, no concept of equal accommodation as a way to manage the fact of pluralism in any modern society democratically. Instead, there can be only a struggle for the domination of your religion or worldview over those held by others."

Presuppositionalism has a longer way to go in the Russian Federation. Decades of official atheism have left their mark, and even most people who identify themselves as Orthodox Christians have no particular church affiliation. But just as Putin's third and fourth terms have demonstrated the increasing entanglement between the priorities of the Russian government and those of the Russian Orthodox Church, Silantiev's destructology represents a hybrid of the presupposionalist insistence on viewing all opposing views as false religions and the Russian state's criminalization of dissent. Extremism and sectarianism are on the verge of becoming synonyms.

After Russia's invasion of Ukraine in February 2022, the Citizens of the USSR were obviously no longer a priority for either the state or the media, but that does not mean they vanished from the public consciousness. Once several of the Citizens' organizations (including the Union of Slavic Forces of Rus) were banned by the Komi Supreme Court ("Miniust vnes"), believers in the Soviet Union's continued existence were more likely to be covered as a legal problem than as a fringe sociological phenomenon. Two Citizens of the USSR were charged in the murder attempt aimed at the rabbi in Krasnodarsk; on December 25, 2021, one was found incompetent to stand trial and sent to a psychiatric hospital, while the other (a seventy-year-old woman) was sentenced to six years' hard time ("Piat' storonnikov"). With the outbreak of the war and the massive repression of even the slightest public disagreement with Russian government policies, an uptick in the Citizens of the USSR's activity was unlikely. When they did start making the news again, it was always in stories about arrests and prosecutions. First, on May 4, when Taraskin was sentenced to eight years in a prison colony on charges of extremism ("Samoprovozglashennogo 'prezidenta SSSR' posadili"), but this was merely the denouement of a story that had begun with his arrest in 2020. In June, two Citizens in Orenburg were sentenced to two years and three months of "corrective labor" for their activities in an illegal organization, with a third committed to a psychiatric hospital (Melikhov). The only story about the Citizens that might have had a connection with the war in Ukraine was the August 22 arrest of five members of the Union of Slavic Forces of Rus in Rostov oblast for, among other things, calling for violent attacks on "military, government, and law enforcement personnel" ("Piat' storonnikov"). One might have expected Russia's attempted conquest of its neighbor to be the Citizens of the USSR's moment, since annexing Ukraine could be a step toward some kind of Soviet restoration. But for the Citizens, the Soviet Union still exists; there is nothing to restore. As for the Putinist state, it has no patience for any competing political agenda, even if there might be room for making common cause. To the contrary, the Citizens of the USSR are an affront to Russian sovereignty, and an embarrassing one at that.

Styob and the Soviet Superposition

It is easy to mock the Citizens of the USSR; certainly, I've done my fair share of laughing at their expense. Experts such as Silantiev and commentators in the media try to have it both ways, highlighting the absurdity of some of their views while still insisting that they represent a clear and present danger. That the group lends itself to diametrically opposed critiques might set off alarm bells. Are we being played?

If we are, it is not by the Citizens, whose rank and file appear to be depressingly earnest, while their leaders shift back and forth on the spectrum from grifter to deranged. The Citizens are not engaged in ironic performance art. But we can learn something if we engage in a brief thought experiment, imagining an alternate history in which the Citizens engage in the kind of ironic overidentification that Russians call *styob*.

Brought into the English scholarly lexicon by Alexei Yurchak in *Everything Was Forever until It Was No More*, *styob* (commonly spelled "stiob" and occasionally "steb") superficially resembles more familiar forms of sarcasm or mockery, but with an important innovation. Styob "required such a degree of *overidentification*" with its target "that it was often impossible to tell whether it was a form of sincere support, subtle ridicule, or a peculiar mixture of the two" (250). Before 2015, the most obvious American analog was Stephen Colbert on *The Daily Show* and *The Colbert Report*: Colbert's right-wing blowhard persona (based on that of the Fox personality Bill O'Reilly) was a long-running joke always played straight. Colbert mocked O'Reilly by inhabiting him thoroughly, exaggerating the Fox host's worst tendencies while never stepping out of character.

The Citizens of the USSR are, of course, not a character; they are a social movement. But that alone would not make it impossible for them to be engaging in styob. In the United States in the 1980s, a group of activists repeatedly disrupted rallies featuring the antifeminist, homophobic Phyllis Schlafly. Calling themselves "Ladies against Women" (LAW), they donned hats, gloves, and aprons; carried picket signs with such slogans as "My home is his castle"; and chanted, "Hit us again, hit us again, harder, harder." When speaking to the press, they always stayed in character, admonishing female reporters for neglecting their domestic duties by asking, for example, "Did your husband give you permission to come to this rally?" (Winslow).[10] Ladies against Women were not merely funny; every one of their actions and utterances ridiculed the target of their overidentification. If the Citizens of the USSR were engaging in styob, what would it say about their target(s)? And what would that explain about the hostility mobilized against them?

The obvious answer is Soviet nostalgia and imperial revanchism. Nostalgia is structured around loss, absence, and distance: why be nostalgic when you've never left home? In their insistence that the USSR never fell, the Citizens are literalizing the metaphor behind the constant backward glance toward the Soviet Union, the compression of history by the New Chronology, and the trite plot device central to Time Crasher stories: they collapse the Soviet past and the post-Soviet present into one time frame. Their assertion that a defunct country supersedes the reality of currently recognized nation-states uses deliberate conflation of space (the USSR/the Russian Federation) to perform a similar feat for time.

In "Our Nuthouse Is Voting for Putin," the lead singer of Rabfak asks, "Why is today yesterday and not tomorrow?"—explicitly calling attention to Putinism's retrohistorical orientation and its inability to imagine a future that is not some kind of revival of a lost past. But that is in one of the song's verses, not the chorus. A closer examination of the song shows that its satire is based on a structural tension between the overt, oppositional critique of the lyrics (which complain about the living conditions in the "nuthouse") and the styob of the chorus, which

---

10. Ladies against Women came out of the Berkeley-based Plutonium Players, who included it on a list of fictitious groups endorsing one of their rallies in 1979, along with Reagan for Shah and Mutants for Nuclear Power (Jones).

always reaffirms the authority of those in power ("The doctor is right / I'm guilty / Our nuthouse is voting for Putin / Putin is definitely our candidate").

As performers of styob, the Citizens of the USSR occupy the subject position of the song's chorus rather than its verses. The Putinist regime views the Soviet past through rose-colored glasses, but the Citizens love it so much that they simply refuse to accept the idea that the Soviet Union is gone. The fact that so many of the Citizens are of retirement age only sharpens the joke. What better way to show a country fixated on the past than to create a social movement dominated by people whose youth is behind them?

Crazed, belligerent, or at least outraged pensioners abound in post-Soviet culture. Their plight can be poignant, as in Eldar Riazanov's 1991 film *The Promised Heavens* (Nebesa obetovannye), about displaced, homeless pensioners living on a landfill, whose self-appointed "president" convinces them that benevolent aliens are going to take them away to a better world. Or they can be murderous, as in Mikhail Elizarov's *The Librarian*, the best set piece in which is about hundreds of previously comatose grandmas fighting gang wars.[11] In the media and online, Russian viewers have long been treated to the antics of "Putin's Brigades," a network of elderly women who rant publicly about anti-Russian conspiracies and the New World Order (Olevskii and Davletgil'deev). Soviet nostalgia is not exclusive to the old, but angry pensioners are a handy tool for ridiculing the impulse to look backward.

The problem with styob is, ultimately, part of the problem that the Putinist state has with the Citizens of the USSR: the ridiculousness cannot be contained. Styob is absurdity at its stickiest. You can touch it, but it comes at a cost to your self-seriousness. For the past decade, Putinism has faced the intermittent challenge of oppositionists who refuse to grant the regime the kind of evil solemnity previously accorded to the Soviet state by late Soviet dissidents (Gabowitsch 60–62). One of the earliest moves of the new Putin administration was the February 2000 closure of the satirical television program *Puppets* after it aired an episode portraying the Russian president as an evil gnome. Yet mockery could not be silenced for long, and one of the galling things about the 2011–2012 street protests or the overall demeanor of the leading opposition figure Alexei Navalny was not a 1960s-era earnest demand to "live without lies," but the constant readiness to laugh in the face of the regime's stupidity and incompetence. When Navalny was nearly killed by an (alleged) poisoning presumed to be the work of

---

11. The elderly women are revived and given super-strength and endurance thanks to the mysterious effects of one of a set of obscure socialist realist novels, each of which briefly grants its readers a superpower. Groups of power-hungry collectors (called "libraries") fight each other for possession of the few remaining copies, hence the gang wars.

the state security forces, the regime suffered a double hit: first, the simple fact of depositing the poison in Navalny's underwear meant that the name "Putin" and the words "Navalny's underwear" often found themselves sharing a sentence; and second, that Navalny and his team were able to expose his poisoners live over the Internet by essentially prank-calling them.

By the end of post-Soviet Russia's third decade, styob had become such a reflexive framework for Putinist excess that it had become self-perpetuating. Agency was no longer required. Or perhaps it would be better to say that *intent* was no longer a prerequisite: styob could arise on its own, independent of its authors' point of view. Styob is now as much an interpretive strategy as it is an artistic device. In this, as always, it mirrors its object. Not only can we no longer tell if the propagandists on state television believe their most outlandish stories, but, as I have argued in *Plots against Russia* and elsewhere, their belief is irrelevant. They are putting propagandistic, conspiratorial utterances out in the world, to circulate as they will.

The same holds true for statements and positions that could function as styob, and this is one of the things that makes the Citizens of the USSR a problem. Their extended rants about the USSR's century-long life span may be drivel, but they also sound like an overidentified parody of Putinist nostalgia. The state and the media can either ignore them or demonize them, but they always run the risk of being tainted by the fundamental similarity between the Citizens' belief system and the discourse of the state. The Citizens of the USSR are Putinism's embarrassing, snaggle-toothed backwater cousins, the relatives one might prefer never to have to acknowledge. But they do exist, and they do share a lineage with their more powerful and respectable kin. Where the Citizens of the USSR strive to resurrect a fallen kingdom through sheer force of will, the state is not trying to create something from whole cloth. Instead, the state/media apparatus is engaging in demiurgic magic, an attempt to redefine and transform this embarrassing movement into a quasi-terrorist, quasi-sectarian threat. Inflating the danger they pose makes them a more worthy adversary or, at the very least, a serious enough opponent that engaging with them will not make the state look absurd. One does not need the dreams of a thousand cats to make this happen; all that is required is the much more realistic attempt to make a handful of kittens look like bloodthirsty lions.

4
NOT DEAD YET

While You Were Sleeping

After the leaders of the Russian, Belorussian, and Ukrainian Soviet Social Republics signed the USSR's death certificate (otherwise known as the Belovezha Accords), *Komsomol'skaia pravda*, the venerable central youth newspaper that was already well on its way to becoming a tabloid, published a cleverly titled obituary: "Ia prosnulsia—zdras'te! Net sovetskoi vlasti!"[1] In English, that would be, "I woke up and—hello! Soviet power is gone!," but the original Russian is a catchy rhyme. It dates back to a popular saying from the 1960s, referring, among other things, to crossing the border into Poland by night train. Before 1991, it was merely ironic, or perhaps wishful thinking, but now it summed up the strangeness of the USSR's death by pen stroke.[2]

The appeal of the Rip Van Winkle time travel trope after 1991 is undeniable: the entire country fell asleep, only to wake up to a different world. Where Soviet citizens once marched forward into the future, now they found themselves sleeping through history. The key question though, is not how they slept but rather how they felt, and what they did, when they woke up. Where some were ecstatic,

---

1. Despite numerous references to this headline, I have not been able to find the associated article. For a recent reference to it, see Chesnokov and Kashin.

2. Apparently, the original document has gone missing. Former Belarusian President Stanislav Shushkevich was told as much when he asked to see it in order to work on his memoirs (Parfitt). The Citizens of the USSR have not, to my knowledge, used this fact as evidence of the USSR's continued existence, which strikes me as a missed opportunity.

others hoped they were simply having a bad dream. Or wished they could go back to sleep until things changed again.

This metaphorical time travel is probably the only kind that does not defy the laws of conventional physics, since the technical passage of time is unaltered. It is a variation on future shock, except that the unease has nothing to do with developments in technology. Instead, the idea of either waking up in a new world or doggedly refusing to do so keeps the Soviet order alive through sheer force of will.

The common tropes surrounding the end of communism are primarily about motion. An obstacle to be removed, communism "fell" or "collapsed," as illustrated by two recurring images: people marching in the streets (forward motion) or statues toppled from their pedestals (downward motion). This was supposed to be the march of history, with the dismantling of the Berlin Wall as the visual representation of people's refusal to be stopped or contained. The Soviet Union's end was anticlimactic, but it was preceded by two unprecedentedly kinetic years.

To keep the Soviet Union alive, then, was anti-kinetic, a concerted effort to remain inert. One of America's most rabid anticommunists, William F. Buckley Jr., inaugurated his *National Review* in 1955 with a mission statement that the magazine would "stand athwart history, yelling Stop." Ironically, this is not a bad description of the imaginary Soviet Union in the years immediately following 1991, but with an important change of position. The people remaining in imaginary communism after its fall would be taking things lying down.

When a country confronts malaise and even, possibly, termination, metaphors of morbidity and mortality are not far behind. In the run-up to the Crimean War (the nineteenth-century one, not its twenty-first-century echo), the Ottoman Empire was diagnosed as the "sick man of Europe," supposedly by Tsar Nicholas I, although the attribution remains debatable (Livianos 299–300). In the century and a half that followed, the rest of the continent's constituent parts have unwillingly vied for that (dis)honor, with the term applied to Serbia in 1997 (O'Rourke), Germany after reunification (Dustman), Italy on more than one occasion (Mammone and Vetri), Portugal in 2007 ("New Sick Man"), Greece after the 2008 financial crisis (Carassava), Scotland (McCartney), the United Kingdom (Buttonwood), and post-Soviet Russia (Eberstadt) repeatedly over the past three decades.

Toward the end of the Cold War, the gerontocracies of the Warsaw Pact succeeded in making the metaphor of the failing country as a sick man literal, with Brezhnev's failing faculties, incomprehensible diction, and moribund bearing setting the tone. At the time, the aging of the leadership did not inspire much hope for significant change, let alone far-fetched fantasies of total regime collapse. After Brezhnev's demise, his replacement by two old men who died in rapid succession appeared to make geriatric leadership death an ongoing feature of

Soviet life. When Konstantin Chernenko became the third general secretary to die in four years, a popular joke made the rounds about someone being asked for his ticket to Chernenko's funeral and replying, "I have a subscription."

The actual death of the Soviet Union took place after six years of intense dynamism rather than quasi-vegetative stagnation. The drama and trauma of the old system's passing would sometimes find itself embodied in the figure of the dying elder who lies in bed and slowly recedes from life while the outside world moves forward at breakneck speed. That contrast has long been at the center of stories that focus on the experience of the bedridden dying, from Tolstoy's Ivan Ilich (1886), who is outraged that the world will continue without him, to the protagonist of Yuri Olesha's 1928 "Liompa," who despairs that he is slowly forgetting the names of all the objects and creatures that will remain after he is gone. One year before "Liompa," and just ten years after the October Revolution, Olesha published his short novel *Envy*, whose protagonist and initial narrator, like Olesha himself, was born in 1899. At one point, the narrator, Nikolai Kavalerov, writes:

> "My youth coincided with the youth of the era," I say . . .
> "I often think about our era. Our era is renowned. Isn't it marvelous when the youth of an era [*molodost' veka*] and the youth of a man [*molodost' cheloveka*] coincide." (26)

Technically, Kavalerov could have lived to the ripe old age of ninety-one or ninety-two and seen that same era's passing, although his drinking habits and dissolute lifestyle combined with the ravages of Soviet history make this scenario unlikely. The novel ends with its hero in bed, and it is not difficult to imagine him back there again, dying along with the Soviet Union.

Have a Nice Funeral

In any case, Olesha died in 1960, and so he never had the chance to bring his horizontal hero to a post-Soviet resting place. That task would fall to others. One of the earlier examples is Lyudmila Ulitskaya's short novel *The Funeral Party* (1997), which complicates matters by taking place in New York rather than the former Soviet Union. *The Funeral Party* is about the last days of Alik, a Soviet émigré painter dying in his tiny New York apartment. Most of the narrative attention is devoted to the women attending to him—former and current lovers, neighbors, and one quasi-stepdaughter. All of them except the neighbor are immigrants from the USSR, a country that, for them, has long been in a twilight state between life and death.

Since the early days of the USSR, emigration has been associated with notions of living death. The White émigrés of Mikhail Bulgakov's play *Flight* (1927) may as well be living in a squalid version of the Tibetan Bardo; the heroine of Olesha's *A List of Blessings* (1931) is an actress whose flirtation with emigration is redeemed in the end only by a heroic, pro-Soviet martyrdom. In 1986, Soviet television aired "The Russians Are Here," a 1983 episode of the American documentary television series *Frontline*; this was a profile of Russian émigrés in New York, which the Soviets broadcast under the title *Byvshie* (former people), continuing the tradition of portraying emigration as a hellish afterlife.

Ulitskaya's ex-Soviet heroes, by contrast, are doing rather well. Alik and his fellow émigrés have spent years in the United States; "even their bodies changed their composition: the molecules of the New World entered their blood and replaced everything old from home" (90). The land of their birth "existed for them only in their dreams" (90–91). If their sense of self depended on Russia, it was primarily through negation, as "proof of the correctness" of their decision to leave: "Consciously or not, the news from Moscow about the growing stupidity, lack of talent and criminality of life there during these years provided the proof they needed. But none could have imagined that what was happening in that far-off place which they had all but erased from their lives would be so painful for them now. It turned out that this country sat in their souls, their guts, and that whatever they thought about it—and they all thought different things—their links with it were unbreakable" (90).

All the same, Alik, at least, has kept close track of events in the Soviet Union. At the outbreak of the August Coup in 1991, he gloats, "I said something would happen before that treaty was signed," to which a new visitor from Moscow asks, "What treaty?" (86–87).[3]

The Funeral Party is decidedly not about the fate of Russia; instead, it is a showcase for Ulitskaya's ability to create groups of characters who feel individual and real rather than symbolic or abstract. Nonetheless, she structures the eleventh chapter around the coup; as soon as it is over (in chapter 13), Alik's decline accelerates. He watches the statues being torn down and the public funeral of the three men who died in the fighting, and he starts to confuse the crowds on the television with the crowd of people outside his window. He speaks briefly only five more times before lapsing into unconsciousness and, eventually, death.

Alik does not live to witness the Soviet Union's official demise, but he does keep his wits about him long enough to see the most dramatic events that led to

---

3. Alik is referring to the proposed new, more flexible Union treaty that would have converted the USSR into the Union of Sovereign States.

his homeland's end. Again, *The Funeral Party* is far more concerned with its characters as people than as allegorical figures, but the parallels between Alik's last days and the rapid decline of the USSR are easy to see. Each is shocking and (with the benefit of hindsight) inevitable, and each remains somewhat inexplicable. Alik's illness never gets a proper diagnosis, but he dies of a creeping paralysis that eventually stops his lungs and his heart. In life, Alik had been joyful, creative, and irrepressible, a man who, the narrator tells us, was capable of being at home just about anywhere. In *The Funeral Party*, Ulitskaya bids farewell not just to an individual man (who is the object of love and mourning) or even a country (which, at least here, is not) but to a relationship between the two. Despite the occasional talk of souls, this is not a metaphysical or primordial tie as much as it is about the inextricable links between personal and national history. It is the story of an ordinary man's unasked-for connection to the country of his birth. For the émigré such as Alik, it was always there, leading a parallel life. And now it was dying along with him.

Goodbye, Brezhnev!, or, The Lenin Who Couldn't Die

Ulitskaya was not alone in linking the slow death of an aging character with the decline and fall of late socialism. But Alik, despite his emotional attachment to Russian culture, had little in the way of a lingering investment in the Soviet system. Two much more famous works would find greater drama and comedy in the symbiotic connection between a bedridden elder and a vanished Second World: Wolfgang Becker's 2003 film *Goodbye, Lenin!* and Olga Slavnikova's 2001 novel *The Man Who Couldn't Die*. The shared general conceit (a family's attempt to pretend that their socialist country never collapsed out of fear that the shock would kill their ailing parent/spouse) is a sore point for Slavnikova, who has publicly insisted that Becker stole her idea ("Slavnikova v Chekhovke"). Even if her accusation is unfounded, the coincidence is unfortunate, since to the broader, non-Russophone world it puts Slavnikova in the position of the person who wrote a book "like *Goodbye, Lenin!*," although she published it two years earlier.[4]

Slavnikova's frustration is understandable. Her original idea ends up looking second-hand. Even worse, *The Man Who Couldn't Die* is unlikely ever to reach the popularity of *Goodbye, Lenin!*. Nor is it likely to be filmed, and not only because Becker's movie will always stand in the way. Slavnikova's novel is, like much of

---

4. The book would appear in English only in 2018.

her work, far more concerned with her characters' inner worlds than anything else. Even though *The Man Who Couldn't Die* does have plotlines that go beyond the characters (a local election is at the heart of the story), the book pays much more attention to what is going on in the paralyzed old Alexei Afanasievich's bed and in his wife's and stepdaughter's heads. To add insult to injury, a German work and a Russian work use the same conceit, but it is in Germany—Germany!—that the results are funny.

For what it's worth, I find Mark Lipovetsky's assessment of the situation convincing: "The metaphor juxtaposing physical immobility and being stuck in the past and/or awakening in a different country was too obvious to anybody living through the postsocialist transition not to become a common trope" ("Introduction," x). As I hope the previous chapters already show, the post-Soviet imagination has produced a plethora of stories involving sudden time jumps and, as we will soon see, thriving twenty-first-century Soviet Unions. If we add in the late- and post-Soviet preoccupation with simulation and the unavoidable figure of Lenin slumbering in his tomb, the conceit of both works does start to look inevitable.

Goodbye, Lenin!, of course, is broadly postsocialist rather than specifically post-Soviet; it is a German film whose action takes place almost entirely in (the former) East Berlin. The film has the iconographic advantage of its Cold War border setting, with the Berlin Wall having divided the socialist East from the capitalist West. The Soviet Union is decentered, if not absent: where the protagonist's father abandoned his family and married a West German years ago, young Alex is in love with Lara, a Soviet nurse in the hospital that treats his mother, Christiane. Alex's sister, meanwhile, follows in her father's footsteps by getting involved with a West German man, with the crucial difference that these footsteps are far fewer: in her case, the West has come to her. The romantic entanglements of *Goodbye, Lenin!* are one of the many things that show how crucial the setting is in each of the two stories, even if the now defunct political system was more or less the same. Germany has plenty of cities, but *Goodbye, Lenin!* is set in East Berlin, not only to exploit the drama of the Berlin Wall but to highlight the effect that proximity had always had. The West was accessible and relatively familiar in a way that could not possibly have been true for Slavnikova's characters, who make their home in the Urals. If they live in Slavnikova's native Yekaterinburg, their (internal) border is with Siberia—how much farther could they be?[5]

---

5. Yekaterinburg is often assumed to be part of Siberia by people living in the Western part of Russia. But never say that to someone from Yekaterinburg (Filippov).

The story of *Goodbye Lenin!* is straightforward: Christiane, a schoolteacher and apparent true believer in East Germany's communist path, sees her son Alex embroiled in a scuffle with police at a demonstration by the Wall. She has a heart attack and falls into a coma that lasts eight months. During that time, the Berlin Wall comes down; Alex's sister, Ariane, leaves school to work at a Burger King and invites her new, West German boyfriend to move in with them; Alex takes a job installing satellite dishes and starts a romance with Lara, his mother's nurse from the Soviet Union. When Christiane finally wakes up, the doctors warn her children that any shock to her system might be fatal. Roping in his unwilling sister, and with the help of his tech-savvy friend Denis, Alex recreates socialist East Germany within the confines of their apartment. They replace their new furniture with the older items they had put in storage, and Alex is on the constant hunt for some of his mother's favorite foods that are no longer sold. He and Denis even create fake news broadcasts that his mother watches on her TV and a hidden VCR.

When Christiane regains some of her strength, she leaves the apartment to discover foreign cars, advertising billboards, and even a statue of Lenin being towed off into the distance by a helicopter. Her children quickly concoct a new lie: West Germans, fed up with the predations of capitalism, are coming to the East in droves.

Not long before her death, Christiane reveals that she had been supposed to bring the family and rejoin their father in the West after his escape but had changed her mind out of fear that the state might seize her children. She asks to see her former husband one last time, a brief, personal reunification that Alex facilitates. In anticipation of the upcoming national reunification celebrations, Alex and Denis invent one last outrageous news story about the new East German leader's opening of the borders with the West. Unbeknownst to them, Lara has told her the truth about the collapse of the Eastern bloc. Christiane dies a few days later.

The challenges involved in recreating the socialism of a bygone era (even one that ended mere months ago) provide *Goodbye, Lenin!* with both comedy and pathos: Alex and Denis's film shoots for their fake news programs are delightfully absurd, even going as far as convincing a taxi driver who resembles East Germany's most famous cosmonaut to imitate his lookalike and pretend to be the nonexistent country's new head of state. All their efforts are ultimately doomed because this quixotic rescue mission is not merely out of step with the surroundings: it is anti-entropic. It requires the enforced, falsified order of a closed system (the apartment) that is nonetheless fatally vulnerable to the chaotic outside world. Even Lara's revelation of the truth to Christiane is not just a matter of ethics—it is the final proof that one cannot stop information from leaking or control all variables. Out of love for his mother, Alex is trying to create a self-contained world that cannot allow any contradictory information to seep in from the outside world. In doing so, he is not just re-creating the material trappings of East Germany but also mimicking its oppressive and restrictive structure. Their apartment is made of four Berlin Walls.

In physics, the idea of a struggle against entropy is senseless, since it would involve the movement of energy, which, by definition, increases entropy. But entropy is also a question of time: each moves in only one direction. Warm-hearted as the film is, *Goodbye, Lenin!* reminds its viewers that nostalgia's fatal flaw is its unwillingness to reconcile with the passage of time. This is all the more poignant because the nostalgia in this case is secondhand; Christiane does not know that she is living in a simulation, and Alex is interested in preserving the illusion of a persistent East Germany only to hang onto his childhood and, more important, his mother. Once again, the attachment to the lost world is melancholic, although in Alex's case, it is more a matter of anticipatory mourning for his mother's impending death. It is only through his mother's eyes that Alex can vicariously feel any sense of loss at East Germany's passing.

Yet, as I indicated at the beginning of this chapter, Christiane's static journey to the grave is counterbalanced by other instances of symbolic motion. First, there is her collapse at the protest that marks the beginning of her illness (she falls not long before both the Wall and her beloved regime do). Second is the movement back and forth across the no longer meaningful border between East and West Germany. In the fantasy world constructed by her son, the mad rush of East Germans into the West becomes its mirror opposite, a communist fairy tale of West German refugees from capitalism. This not only allows for the admission that the barrier between the two Germanies has fallen, but once again resembles watching a film as it rewinds. With the fall of the Wall, East Germany was like a water balloon that had sprung a leak, but Alex's fake broadcast would have Christiane believe that the water is flowing into the balloon rather than out.

Christiane's illness also ties into the film's most persistent vertical motif: the space program. As a boy, Alex is obsessed with Sigmund Jahn, the first German cosmonaut to fly into space as part of the Soviet Union's cooperative program with fellow socialist states. In his mind, Jahn's launch into space becomes mixed up with Alex's father's defection to the West, and it is Jahn's lookalike that Alex and Denis dress up for their final fake news broadcast. Christiane herself went nowhere when she was alive, declining to join her husband abroad, but after her death, Alex and his family launch her ashes on a toy rocket that he had built with his father long ago.

But the most obviously significant contrast to the mostly bedridden Christiane is the bizarre spectacle to which she is exposed during her brief, unsupervised excursion from her apartment: the huge statue of Vladimir Lenin, carried aloft and away by a helicopter. Lenin's outstretched arm, a common feature of communist iconography, is no longer the commanding gesture of a leader addressing a crowd, but the odd farewell salute that gives the film its title. If we ignore the helicopter (as the camera does at key moments), the ascent of this ponderously heavy monument appears to defy gravity, in keeping with the Stalinist utopian emphasis on flight as a symbol of the communist trajectory. It is also a striking contrast with what we know about the fate of such statues in the wake of the Warsaw Pact, that they are torn down rather than elevated. Moreover, there is the matter of Lenin himself, whose body—like that of the sick and dying elders in *Goodbye, Lenin!*, *The Funeral Party*, and *The Man Who Couldn't Die*—lies still in the mausoleum that had long been the symbolic center of Soviet power. What could be a more ironic end for one of the twentieth century's most famous materialists than his ascension into heaven?

Socialism in One Bedroom

Next to *Goodbye, Lenin!*, *The Man Who Couldn't Die* looks like a much grimmer affair, despite their shared premise. The World War II veteran Alexei Afanasievich Kharitonov has spent the past fifteen years confined to his bed after a stroke. His wife and stepdaughter are taking care of him, but not just out of a sense of filial obligation: they need his pension to get by. True, the children in *Goodbye, Lenin!* at one point are also in a budgetary bind thanks to their sick mother (she can't remember where she has hidden a substantial amount of cash that is about to become worthless once the country switches to the Deutschmark), but their devotion to her survives the financial disaster Christiane inadvertently causes.

But it is the time frame that makes the most significant difference. *Goodbye, Lenin!* takes place in the months between the fall of the Wall and German reunification, when young people like Alex could still be excited about their future. *The Man Who Couldn't Die* unfolds years after the collapse of the USSR, and optimism is in short supply. Alexei Afanasievich's bedroom is dismal and oppressive, but the world outside his window is hardly joyous. Alexei Afanasievich's stepdaughter, Marina, gets wrapped up in a corrupt election campaign for a candidate who has decided that bribing voters is simply paying for services rendered, and crass, rich New Russians show off their dubiously accumulated wealth.

Marina's mother (and Alexei Afanasievich's wife) Nina Alexandrovna is completely at a loss to understand the new society that has supplanted Soviet everyday life. For her and, to a lesser extent, for Marina, the timelessness of the old man's bedroom has become something of a refuge. Indeed, everything they do for Alexei Afanasievich can be viewed as a kind of displaced self-interest: are they keeping him alive because they love him or because they need his money? Their years-long maintenance of the illusion of a perpetual Brezhnev era starts out as a way to avoid a fatal shock to the old man's system, but it is the women who start to find comfort in their simulation. Alexei Afanasievich spends most of the novel trying to figure out how to kill himself with the little voluntary muscle control he has left.

The Man Who Couldn't Die takes place mostly during the aforementioned election campaign, but its temporal scope is much broader. At Marina's instigation, the two women began to curate Alexei Afanasievich's reality years before the Soviet collapse:

> At the first historic tremor, [Marina] had divined in the decrepit general secretary's replacement by a younger, more energetic one not a pledge of Soviet life's continuity but the beginning of the end. She immediately began preserving the substance of the era for future use and purging it of any new admixtures, no matter how harmless they seemed at first. So it came to pass that their good old Horizon television—on which only impressionistic bursts of static were still in color—showed the farewell to that great figure. (18–19)

Compared to the machinations of Alex and his friend in *Goodbye, Lenin!*, their scheme starts out low-tech: "Nina Alexandrovna was charged with reading the paralyzed man specific articles, which Marina made fat deletions in and supplied with handwritten insertions. Nina Alexandrovna carried out these instructions, although she was embarrassed by both the articles and her own voice" (19). Their task becomes more complicated when the gap between their simulation and the reality of perestroika grows too wide: "Very quickly, outside time became so altered that there wasn't even anything in *Pravda* for Marina's pen to rework" (19). Eventually, with the help of "computer whiz Kostik" (28) they begin to make their own fake news broadcasts: "they got so good at it that they were able to create the Twenty-Eighth and Twenty-Ninth Congresses of the Soviet Communist Party for the paralyzed man" (28).

Alex and his friend in *Goodbye, Lenin!* may occasionally enjoy themselves while maintaining an illusory East Germany, but their sense of purpose does not waver: their job is to keep Christiane alive. On at least two occasions, the film hints that their efforts might not be as necessary as they think (first, when we learn that Christiane had been willing to consider defecting to the West, and second, when Lara's revelation of the truth does not cause her to immediately drop dead), but Christiane is always at the center of the simulation, as both inspiration and audience. *The Man Who Couldn't Die* complicates the relationship between the deceivers and the deceived almost from the very beginning. Alexei Afanasievich is mute, so his family members can only guess about the effectiveness of their work, and even its necessity:

> No one could say for certain whether their playacting was fooling the sick man, of course. Nina Alexandrovna, at least, thought she picked up a certain agreement, a semblance of approval in the signals emitted by his asymmetrical brain. Of course, Alexei Afanasievich had always not so much liked as considered it proper that his innumerable family wait on him hand and foot, so he may simply have been pleased with their efforts and the theatricalized fuss occasioned by his illness. (29)

In the absence of the kind of feedback that Christiane provides her children, the simulation in Slavnikova's novel seems to exist for its own sake or, more properly, for the sake of the very people who have engineered it. Alexei Afanasievich's bedroom, nicknamed the "Red Corner" after the Soviet propaganda displays that were encouraged in the country's early decades, becomes a shrine to the undead Soviet past as embodied by Leonid Ilich Brezhnev, the long-dead Soviet leader who, in the book, is as functionally immortal as Alexei Afanasievich himself:

> These properties had something to do with immortality. The general secretary's rejuvenated photo—half documentary print and half retouched and clearly made during his lifetime—was striking for that very quasi-drawnness you see only in a dead person's features . . . But what was amazing was this: the general secretary, whose death had here been reversed and whose longevity had become a natural feature that only kept increasing, had somehow borrowed an authenticity from Alexei Afanasievich that Brezhnev himself had never possessed. (21–22)

Of all the Soviet leaders who could have been chosen for the role of immortal icon, Brezhnev is the most appropriate for Slavnikova's purposes. Once glasnost took hold under Gorbachev, one word that would doggedly attach itself to Brezhnev and his era: stagnation (*zastoi*). The word is equally applicable to the stifling bedroom that houses Alexei Afanasievich's body, which, like Brezhnev in his last years, seems stuck in a liminal state between life and death. Marina's Soviet charade is so good that "her stagnation had achieved perfection":

> Apparently, the period of stagnation preserved in the Red Corner would not allow for forward movement, so everything had fallen back in place; now that was even more true. At night, the window sealed shut for the winter would crackle and tinkle as if holding back the press of some

growing mass, as if the paralyzed immortality were flexing an invisible muscle. (94)

After years of pretending to live in a never-ending Brezhnev era, both Marina and Nina Alexandrovna occasionally find themselves confused about basic questions of reality. Marina starts to see her political candidate, Apofeozov, as a threat, "the embodiment of the realest reality, . . . the opposite of the immortal little world she was defending" (49–50). Nina Alexandrovna sometime has the feeling that "Brezhnev's funeral had indeed been a deception, a film someone had spliced together, that the years were still divided into five-year plans and the country, with all its heavy industry, was continuing to build communism in the heavens above" (29). The contrast between the imaginary USSR that they have so painstakingly maintained in Alexei Afanasievich's bedroom and the world outside its walls produces an uncanny effect for the characters, if not the readers: both worlds are equally familiar, and yet both are always a bit "off."

Their confusion is thematically appropriate. In keeping the Brezhnev era alive, they are inadvertently recapitulating that era's salient feature: simulation itself. Countless jokes from the last years of Brezhnev's life play on the idea that the general secretary is little more than a vegetable. But even more jokes highlight the gap in the Brezhnev era's reality and its contemporary representation. One classic story about Soviet leaders on a broken-down train (updated each time a new leader came to power) contrasted each leader's absurd approach to problem solving. When the train stops moving, Lenin calls for a voluntary work day to get it fixed, Stalin demands that all the train workers be executed, and Nikita Khrushchev posthumously rehabilitates them. And Brezhnev? He proposes pulling down the shades on all the windows, rocking back and forth, and pretending that the train is still moving.

Later versions of the joke are extended to include Gorbachev and Yeltsin, but the whole point of the family's deception is to act as if the joke could not possibly be updated. No one else is ever going to get on that train. Alexei Afanasievich's bedroom is more than simply a sanctuary for a nearly extinct Soviet habitat; it is a simulacrum of a simulation. The stagnation in this apartment is more perfect than the Brezhnev era could ever be, because it has divorced itself from time (the past several decades) and even biology (Alexei Afanasievich cannot [be allowed to] die). The novel's indictment of Soviet nostalgia (realized here as an apartment-sized Brezhnev theme park) could not be more cutting, for the entire project represents the ever-shrinking horizons of a dying man in a simulated world that, whatever appeal it might have, can only be stifling. Small wonder that Alexei Afanasievich is suicidal; he is the last vestige of a world that self-destructed long ago.

Both *The Man Who Couldn't Die* and *Goodbye, Lenin!* are thought experiments: how could we pretend that what Ken Jowitt called the "Leninist Extinction" never happened? To the extent that they inspire sympathy in their audience, their stories, like Ulitskaya's *The Funeral Party*, rely on the very familiar human impulse to resist the death of a loved one. Both Slavnikova and Becker give us characters whose ongoing attempts to reconstruct the dead socialist system are motivated at least in part by love and are made possible by their particular time frame. The reconstruction projects begin either in the final days of the USSR (Slavnikova) or within a few months after the end of state socialism (Becker). Both the socialist systems and the moribund parents are steps away from death; they just happen to be on opposite sides of the dividing line between existence and oblivion. *Goodbye, Lenin!* and *The Man Who Couldn't Die* derive their pathos from the fact that they are, in every way, near-death experiences.

Earlier I described *Goodbye, Lenin!* as melancholic, even if the objects of their melancholy are different. The juxtaposition of (anticipatory) mourning for a lost parent and retrospective mourning for a lost world has the advantage of drawing the focus to affect; while the stories are by no means apolitical, they remind audiences across the political spectrum that grief over a loss does not require that the lost object be unequivocally good or admirable. This even holds true for *The Funeral Party*. Ulitskaya's characters have no love for the Soviet system, but the dying man at the center of the novel cannot escape his affective connection to his former homeland that is falling apart just slightly faster than he is. We grieve because we lost something that was ours.

Alik does not experience melancholia over the demise of the Soviet Union (to be fair, even if he were so inclined, this would require time that he no longer has). Alex, in contrast, rediscovers an attachment to East Germany's space program that would not have been at the forefront of his mind; rather than bury his mother, he shoots her ashes into the atmosphere on a homemade rocket, a simultaneous farewell to mother and motherland. The end of the film points to successful mourning rather than endless melancholia: Alex has held a funeral for his mother, started a life with a young woman, and is poised to look toward the future. Situating the story of the attempted reconstruction of the socialist past so closely to the time of the system's collapse creates the hope that this obsessive attachment will prove to be just a phase. *The Man Who Couldn't Die* leaves much less room for such a hope, because even though the reconstruction begins at the moment of the system's death, the story (and Alexei Afanasievich's dying) extends for years. Slavnikova makes melancholia an ongoing feature of post-Soviet life.

Building Communism through Time Travel

Maintaining the illusion that the Soviet Union continues to exist is a grueling effort requiring unrelenting vigilance. Over time, it is doomed to fail. There are simply too many variables to account for, too many opportunities for the truth to seep into a carefully constructed bubble of alternative Soviet reality. The limits of realism, however, are no match for the tropes of science fiction. A present-day Soviet Union is as credible an alternate history scenario as Hitler winning World War II, but the most prominent examples are from a genre we have already examined at great length. This is a job for Time Crashers.

Preventing the downfall of the USSR is the main goal of the time-traveling Natasha in Arsenyev's *Student, Komsomol Girl, Athlete*, but Natasha has to die to make it happen. Only in the novel's brief epilogue do we get a glimpse of twenty-first-century Soviet life, while the other stories in the collection propose a joint Soviet/Nazi empire to ensure a radiant future. We get a fuller vision of today's Soviet Union on the two television series that brought the Time Crasher genre to the small screen: *The Dark Side of the Moon* and *Chernobyl: Exclusion Zone* (Chernobyl': Zona otchuzhdeniia).

In chapter 2, I analyze the first season of *The Dark Side of the Moon* as an example of a Time Crasher ending up in the Soviet past; the second and final season returns its hero to a 2011 that, thanks to Solovyov's actions in 1979, is dominated by a technologically advanced and largely benevolent USSR. The second season aired in 2016, four years after the first. With sixteen hour-length episodes, Season 2 is one of the most extensive presentations of a persistent Soviet Union ever produced.

Chernobyl: Exclusion Zone, though populated by very different characters from those of *The Dark Side of the Moon* and revolving around the Chernobyl disaster, oddly mirrors its predecessor. The show began broadcasting its first season in October 2014. It was such a hit that a second season appeared three years later, and the story concluded in 2019 in a series of three television films that told a single story from different angles, with different endings in each film.

Chernobyl: Exclusion Zone centers around a group of teenage characters who seem designed to remind older viewers why they hate teenagers. The plot is set in motion by Igor Matveev, a particularly unsavory young man who, pretending to be emergency tech support, steals the cash that the parents of Pasha, the de facto leader of his friend group, had set aside for purchasing a new apartment. Igor is on his way to Chernobyl, and the friends follow him by subscribing to his video podcast, in which he describes his travels at the same time as he demonstrates the rapid decline of his mental equilibrium. One of Pasha's friends, Anna, lost her older sister in Pripyat right before the disaster, so the trip takes on a personal significance for her. The upshot is that the group travels back in time to the day before the disaster and avert it. Then, in Season 2, the teens find themselves back in the present but in an alternate future in which a nuclear disaster in Maryland has led to the collapse of the United States, while the USSR has managed to live long and prosper. In the final three movies, they fight and defeat the malign mystical forces that had been toying with them from the start.

Each of these series features an involuntary trip to the past: 1979 for *Dark Side* and 1986 for *Chernobyl*. In the latter series, the trip takes place only toward the end of the first season, but the stakes are obviously higher: the teenagers are traveling to one of the most significant, and deadly, moments of late Soviet history. Where *Chernobyl*'s focus on crisis is obvious in its very name, *Dark Side* invites its viewers to join Solovyov on a journey to a time defined by crisis's opposite: stability, stagnation, and order. The historical change wrought by Solovyov is easily explained by the Butterfly Effect, helpfully and clumsily introduced in the second season's first episode by the hero's random encounter with a little boy reading Ray Bradbury's 1952 short story "A Sound of Thunder."[6]

Nevertheless, each series incorporates a state-destroying crisis into its alternate present—one explicitly, the other more vaguely. In both *Chernobyl* and *Dark Side*, the USSR is flourishing, but the United States has collapsed. *Chernobyl* appears to be governed by a law of conservation of disaster. Thanks to the teens' intervention at the end of Season 1, the Chernobyl reactor does not melt down, but, for reasons that are never made clear, on August 7, 1986, the Calvert Cliffs Nuclear Power Plant near Lusby, Maryland, melts down instead.[7] Since the entire plot of the series revolves around the mystical consequences of nuclear disaster, the US nuclear accident serves as the impetus for moving most of the series' action from the USSR to the Divided States of America (Raz"edenennnye shtaty Ameriki). As a result, the viewers' exposure to the twenty-first-century Soviet Union is rather brief.

In *Dark Side*, the United States is also in chaos, with would-be refugees desperate to immigrate to the USSR. Unfortunately, any North American visitors who might think of staying in the Soviet Union have been chipped by the US Embassy, and unless they can get access to a technology called a "Russifier" (*russifikator*), they will die. As for the USSR, it has expanded from fifteen to more

---

6. In this story, a time traveler to the prehistoric past accidentally steps on a butterfly, and when he returns home, his world has become a fascist dictatorship.

7. Calvert Cliffs is an actual nuclear power plant in our reality. It is possible that the brief shutdown of the plant on September 10, 2013, after a malfunction brought the plant to the producers' attention ahead of the second season's 2017 premiere.

than two dozen constituent Soviet Socialist Republics and is a global economic and technological leader.

One might ask: why does the fantasy of a persistent Soviet Union seem to necessitate the collapse of the United States? But an even better question might be: what does it mean to ask this question, and what does it mean not to? *Chernobyl*, at least, implicitly acknowledges the role of the USSR's internal problems; in both the USSR and the alternate United States, nuclear meltdowns kickstart the state's disintegration. But framing the collapse of a global superpower as a zero-sum game in these two works implies a theory behind the downfall of the USSR. If the Soviet Union truly fell apart on its own, then there is no need to imagine its survival would have such an effect on the United States. The complementary distribution of civilizational collapse means something quite different: the end of the USSR is understood as a defeat in its conflict with its US rival. Two things are at work here: first, the persistence not only of the USSR but of the Cold War framework that died with it; and second, the transformation of what was once a fringe conspiracy theory into something close to common knowledge. The USSR did not fall; it was pushed, by a vast network of US espionage and subversive influence, possibly even including Gorbachev as an American agent of influence.

Even without this conspiratorial framework, imagining the destruction of the United States has its own appeal. After years of humiliation, not to mention highhanded treatment on the part of the United States and its allies, watching the United States suffer the Soviet Union's fate has to be intensely gratifying.

Both *Chernobyl: Exclusion Zone* and *Dark Side of the Moon* temper Soviet nostalgia with a post-Soviet desire for the good life. The Soviet Union endures not by reverting to Stalinist repression or even by maintaining Brezhnevian stagnation on never-ending life support. The fantasy sold by each is that the Soviet Union remains a great power, preserves the most salient (and fondly remembered) aspects of Soviet mass culture and daily life, and keeps immorality in check, all while ushering in an age of economic prosperity that the USSR never lived to see.

While each alternate present gestures toward a power structure that is familiarly Soviet (a general secretary, a Communist Party, and all its associated organizations), the economic miracle that provides Soviet citizens with a high standard of living in *Chernobyl* looks suspiciously un-Soviet. *Dark Side* still has variations on familiar consumer restrictions (batteries can be purchased only two at a time); its economic growth appears to be the result of the general secretary's knowledge of the other timeline (Solovyov revealed it to him in Season 1) and the fulfilled potential of Soviet science. *Chernobyl* has both a ruling Communist Party and private corporations, with little sign that anything remotely resembling communism is actually being built.

Chernobyl's Soviet present is a relatively brief stopover for our time-traveling teens. They stay in this timeline for all of Season 2 but spend most of it in the United States—and even there, they also jump farther into the past for a couple of episodes. The show's producers seem more interested in the changes this timeline has wrought on our heroes: the nerd (Gosha) and the bully (Lyosha) switch roles, and the tough redhead Nastya switches romantic ties from one to the other at the same time. The four main characters, led by the heroic Pasha, are no longer a group, and some of them do not even know each other. Anya, who joins the gang by chance in Season 1, rejoins them in Season 2 because she happens to be a flight attendant on the plane taking them to America. Though all of them have their circumstances changed, Pasha is initially the only one who remembers the original timeline, and, in any case, the course of these characters' lives is determined less by sociopolitical circumstance than by the mystical forces behind both the Chernobyl and Calvert Cliff accidents (or, less charitably, the ham-handed plotting of the show's producers).

Aside from the characters themselves, what is most striking about the twenty-first-century USSR is how much it has in common with the original timeline. Both versions have overprivileged gilded youth (in Season 2, they are the offspring of party bigwigs); both have powerful security ministries to contend with, and, curiously, both have large corporations that are presumably private. The second season's villain, Dmitry Kinyaev, is an American refugee child who grows up to run GlobalKintek, a sinister atomic energy company.[8] If we set aside the mysticism, time travel, and alternate dimensions, *Chernobyl*'s twenty-first-century Soviet Union looks a lot like . . . China.

China, we should recall, has long represented the late Soviet Union's road not taken. Where the USSR liberalized the political and public spheres while having a chaotic approach to economics, China did the opposite. Its leaders liberalized the economy while keeping a tight rein on politics and speech. This alternative started to look appealing to the large swaths of the impoverished and humiliated in the Russian Federation, especially during the 1990s. *Chernobyl: Exclusion Zone* offers its viewers a Chinese model of avoiding the Soviet collapse: state capitalism with a communist face.

The twenty-first-century USSR of *The Dark Side of the Moon* is more complicated, which is fitting; where *Chernobyl* uses an alternate Soviet present primarily to complicate an already elaborate plot, *The Dark Side of the Moon*'s second season is devoted entirely to the ramifications of its Soviet premise. This was not

---

8. Kinyaev is also a telekinetic who in his childhood was believed to be possessed by an evil spirit, though in fact he is possessed by the spirit of the Zone. Like all good executives, he multitasks.

a foregone conclusion; even by the end of the first season, there was no reason to expect the series to bring its hero to a present-day Soviet Union. When Mikhail Mikhailovich Solovyov awakens in the first episode of *Dark Side of the Moon*'s second season, his 1979 odyssey is finally over. But the story is only beginning or, really, beginning again. In real time, three years have passed since the first season's premiere, while on the show, Solovyov has jumped thirty-two years into the future/his original present. The show has been rebooted, not once but twice. The first season ended with a cliffhanger. Solovyov, who had spent the first season in the body of his father, tells the doctor who addresses him that he is not Mikhail Mikhailovich (the Solovyov of 2011), but Mikhail Ivanovich (Solovyov's father, who died in the very first episode of the series). The scene is set for a new round of disorientation, this time a form of future shock: how will Solovyov *père* react to the twenty-first-century world of Solovyov *fils*?

Unfortunately for any viewers who might have spent almost three years waiting on the edge of their seats to find out, this question is left unanswered. During the series hiatus, the producers must have rejected this conceit for their sequel season. In Episode 1 of Season 1, Solovyov repeats the claim that he is Mikhail Ivanovich but immediately retracts it. Mikhail Ivanovich remains stubbornly dead. Instead of enacting a mere inversion of the first season, now Solovyov slowly comes to realize that the 2011 to which he has returned is not the same as the 2011 he left after his initial car accident. He is still in the militia, but he is a beat cop instead of an officer. Unmarried in the original timeline, now he is separated from his wife, who is raising his daughter with her new lover. His daughter's schoolteacher is Katya (his love interest from Season 1), and the redheaded murderer he chased into the past now teaches at the same school. But the biggest difference, of course, is that the Soviet Union never collapsed.[9]

---

9. In the interval between the first and second seasons, Vladimir Yankovsky directed a twenty-episode Ukrainian television series called *Citizen Nobody* (Grazhdanin Nikto), released in 2016. Set in Kyiv and filmed in Russian, *Citizen Nobody* tells the story of Maksim Orlov, a detective who wakes up after twenty-two years in a coma to find the USSR dismantled and Ukraine an independent country. Though every episode features at least one moment when Orlov is nonplussed by current mores and corruption, most of the series is simply a set of "cases of the week." Like Solovyov in *Dark Side of the Moon*, Orlov faces complex challenges in his personal life. While he was comatose, his wife gave birth to their daughter and married his best friend. The resulting love triangle could have been the basis for a nuanced exploration of divided loyalties in an impossible situation, but instead it quickly descends into high melodrama: Masha, Orlov's (ex-)wife had a nervous breakdown after his accident, and her current husband—who now turns out to be an evil, cynical mastermind—threatens to return her to the psych ward if she tries to run off with Orlov. Meanwhile, their somewhat wayward daughter Nastya is being courted by Orlov's new young partner on the police force. The exploration of post-Soviet displacement is limited to Orlov's laments about the downfall of the "honest" militia system from his Soviet days, along with a possible allegorical reading of the love triangle, in which the noble, Soviet Orlov fights his corrupt post-Soviet rival over Masha (the motherland) and Nastya (the future).

One might expect that, after the first season, Solovyov would adjust to his new world like an experienced Time Crasher, but instead, he makes the same rookie mistakes, repeatedly exposing his ignorance to his colleagues and family and letting them chalk it up to a post-accident concussion. As in the previous season, the producers treat the viewers to numerous in-jokes and easter eggs. In Season 1, when Solovyov insists on finding his mobile phone, a doctor offers him a toy telephone on wheels and a string. Now, everyone has a phone, but the Soviet-made phones are oversized and made of wood. Muscovites still watch the TV show *Dom-2* (literally, *House 2*), but instead of the familiar "Big Brother" reality show clone, the Soviet version is a documentary about groups of young people building actual houses without competing to live in them. And when a case brings Solovyov in contact with an eccentric beekeeper, the man turns out to be named Sergei Sobyanin (in our world, the mayor of Moscow since 2010).

These trivial examples are dwarfed by the scope of the USSR's transformation since 1979 (when Solovyov was in the past) or since the late 1980s (when perestroika apparently never materialized). From news reports and throwaway lines, we learn that there is a bridge to Alaska under construction in the Aleutian Soviet Socialist Republic (SSR), that Finland is the twenty-third SSR, and that, thanks to a deal signed by the "Baron of the Gypsies" making him a "Baron of the USSR" (!), the Gypsy Soviet Socialist Republic brings the overall count up to twenty-six (as opposed to the historical fifteen).[10] It is not enough for the USSR to fail to collapse; it has expanded both in territory and hegemonic influence.

As in the first season, Solovyov has to relearn a great deal about the profession to which he has devoted his entire adult life. The crime rate is apparently even lower than it was in the 1970s, but with little evidence of a significantly repressive state security apparatus ferreting out freethinkers and suppressing dissent. True, some of the system's success has dystopian overtones. The militia is completely unprepared to hunt a serial killer such as the redhead because it solved its "maniac" problem years ago. Children with mental problems are detected early and "fixed." Overall, the militia seems to have degraded in the absence of any real challenge. Solovyov meets with indignation when he casually reminds his superior that, in an investigation, you always toss out your first theory; any good militiaman knows that the first theory is always right.

For Solovyov, at least, the flaws in the Soviet 2011 are hardly deal breakers. This revitalized Soviet Union is closer to a utopia than the country ever came, even if

---

10. The Russian equivalent of "Gypsy" is what is used on the show. No effort is made in Russian to replace a term that is at best Orientalist and at worst a slur. Television shows such as *The Dark Side of the Moon* make no efforts to move away from anti-Roma stereotypes, so I have reluctantly come to the conclusion that "Gypsy" is a more appropriate translation.

minor imperfections help make it seem more grounded. By creating a brave new world that feels somehow lived in (lived, in fact, in Minsk, since Belarus does a good job standing in for a twenty-first-century USSR without any special effects at all), *Dark Side of the Moon*, Season 2, offers an extended twist on some of the phenomena we've already seen in this book. The series projects the past onto the present without ignoring the passage of time. *Dark Side of the Moon* presents its alternate Soviet Union as a kind of conditional-subjunctive nostalgia.

The Rise and Fall of Great Powers

For reasons never made clear, the prosperity of the alternate Soviet Union in *Dark Side of the Moon* entails a total realignment of the rest of the world. Desperate would-be immigrants from the "United French Emirates" line up in front of the Soviet Embassy, while Soviet-born Israeli refugees are welcomed back with open arms, as Premier Savrasov declares that there is "no such thing as an-ex citizen of the USSR."[11] At one point, faced with an overly controlling father, a grown daughter, fumes: "What kind of *domostroi* is this? As if we lived in Holland, and not the Soviet Union!" A little girl in one episode was adopted from England right before pogroms broke out and cured of a disease thanks to superior Soviet medicine. Technically, these are all throwaway lines, the geopolitical equivalent of the references to Sobyanin and Russian reality TV. But they are significant to the show's world building, in part because they betray the origins of this particular alternate scenario. Europe and the Western world in Season 2 suffer the fate that conspiracy theorists and state propaganda have been predicting for years: France is overrun by Muslims, and the most liberal of Western countries (the Netherlands) is now in the grips of a fundamentalist revanche.

Unsurprisingly, it is the United States that has it worst. Or rather, the former United States. Now that the country has broken apart, the Southern states have recreated the Confederacy under the presidency of Chuck Norris. The previously mentioned North American refugees in the USSR (nicknamed *sevushki* from the word for "north") are fleeing a country torn not just by political strife but by chronic insomnia, the breakdown of interpersonal communication (too much texting), and the dictatorship of the dollar. The miseries of capitalism become soapy entertainment in a TV drama called *The Fall of the Oligarch*, with plot

---

11. Curiously, these refugees are fleeing from damage brought on by a tornado, which is not high on the list of natural disasters to which the region is prone.

twists including a woman who says "I love you" only after being given a check and a terrible boss who encourages a subordinate to jump out the office window to his death.[12] Moscow audiences flock to a musical called *My Fair American*, about an ignorant girl from the former United States trying to learn how to act and speak Soviet.

And, really, who wouldn't want a Soviet life in the world of Season 2? Toys for children are free. The state has a reality television-style social program to try to rescue failing marriages. If you're caught speeding, you simply apologize and promise to try to do better. True, tobacco, junk food, and alcohol have been banned, and people in key professions have to watch their weight in order to keep their jobs. Batteries can be bought only two at a time, and woe betide the scofflaw who tries to get immediately back in line. But Solovyov finds this a small price to pay. As he tells his friends in one of the last episodes, he comes from a world with no USSR. There's more crime, the telephones are better, but the people are pettier.

If anything, Solovyov undersells the contemporary Soviet Union's appeal, because he neglects to mention the key difference that accounts for the country's prosperity: the triumph of Soviet science. Sick people from around the world flock to the USSR for treatment; even cancer is no match for the power of Soviet medicine. Soviet scientists have also invented a special device to treat sleeplessness, with bootleg versions sought out by desperate American insomniacs. But the most emblematic accomplishment is revealed in the second season's premiere: the Soviet Union has sent cosmonauts to Mars.

In practical terms, the success of the Soviet space program means little, but symbolically, it signals that the country has fulfilled its postwar promise. The national pride in sending Yuri Gagarin into space in 1961 cannot be overstated. For Soviets in the 1960s, space was a site of scientific romance. As we see in the next chapter, a revitalized space program is the key to numerous twenty-first-century fantasies of a Soviet future. A triumphant Soviet Union is almost impossible to imagine without somehow winning the space race. As if to signal the centrality of space exploration, the second season returns to the series' primal scene: the site of Solovyov's accident. In the first season, Solovyov just happens to be injured right in front of the Cathedral of Christ the Savior (torn down in the early Soviet years and rebuilt in the 1990s); he knows he is in 1979 when the cathedral is replaced by the large public swimming pool located on that site for most of the Soviet era. In Soviet 2011, the same spot is now occupied by a Museum of Space Construction.

---

12. One of Solovyov's colleagues doesn't watch that show, because he hates "science fiction."

An Officer of the Law

Science and geopolitics create the setting for Season 2, but they rarely rank among its hero's top concerns. At heart, the show is still a police procedural. As in the first season, many of the legal violations that Solovyov encounters are difficult for the contemporary viewer to call "crimes." Take, for example, the store managers who manipulate the algorithm that determines eligibility for purchasing new furniture; because of them, some select customers can buy a couch in two months rather than eight. Certainly, there is an element of corruption involved (the managers are probably accepting bribes), but the algorithm itself is hard to take seriously. As always, Solovyov might have an opinion, but it does not affect the performance of his duties. His willingness to enforce the law—any law—makes him a good cop. But why are his actions so acceptable within the framework of the series?

Solovyov's refusal to engage with the ideology behind his country's laws—whether in the 1979 Soviet Union, the 2011 Russian Federation, or the 2011 USSR—makes him the perfect hero for the twenty-first century's second decade. One of the great successes of Putinism has been its ability to push back any cognitive dissonance one might have about unconditional love for the motherland in any of its historical iterations. The Russian Empire, the Soviet Union, and the Russian Federation are all instances of the hero of the country's history: the state. Its laws and actions may be just or unjust, but that is not up to the individual to decide.

Here the imperatives of the genre come close to clashing with the overriding logic of the state. As an action hero, Solovyov must make decisions that will almost always be correct, and as a police officer, he must uphold the law, but as an accidental time traveler who inadvertently disrupts history, he exemplifies the dangers of individual improvisation. Upon his return to the proper timeline in the last few minutes of the series, Solovyov asks a passerby, "Who's the president? Putin?" and gets the response, "No, Medvedev!" The answer is correct, and it does not matter that, after thirty-two episodes of time travel, Solovyov forgot that Medvedev was (technically) running the country. The Russian Federation's leadership matters to him only to the extent that the leader is whoever the leader is supposed to be.

Fables of Reconstruction

The lessons of Solovyov's travel to an alternative Soviet present and his return to a briefly estranged Medvedev era are about the irrelevance of politics and ideology to the life of the post-Soviet individual. Wherever he goes, his concerns are basically the same: saving the people he loves and finding personal happiness. The subtext of *The Dark Side of the Moon* is not only that the personal is not political in contemporary Russia, but that we can even imagine the personal as apolitical during Soviet times. Solovyov's experience suggests the possibility that the Soviet past can be mined for its cultural and historical treasures without yielding the ideological equivalent of blood diamonds.

When recreating the Soviet era moves from the global scope of alternative history to the controlled experiments of local "real life," the ability to separate ideology from the everyday becomes a contested question. Reconstructing the past is a different project from maintaining that a pivotal historical event (the collapse of the USSR) never happened. Moreover, these reconstruction projects are comfortably distant from the traumatic event, set at more than a generation's remove, making room for theme park kitsch and the formulas of the reality show. Out of a diverse set of aesthetic and political motivations, the 2006 film *Park of the Soviet Period*, a subsequent real-life event by the same name in Moscow, a three-volume novel by Alexandra Marinina, and the notorious art project *DAU* all create Soviet simulacra within the tightly controlled geographical and ideological boundaries of a localized social experiment. What most of these works fail to engage with, however, is the gap between the Soviet Union as lived experience and the USSR as ideological simulacrum. When the Soviet Union still existed, that gap required little explanation. Indeed, it was arguably a part of that very lived experience that the post-Soviet simulations attempt to reconstruct.

With 1991 well in the rearview mirror, what purpose could a small-scale reconstruction of the Soviet Union serve? On the most superficial level, it is a profit-seeking (i.e., capitalist) attempt to capitalize on nostalgia for the days of Soviet state socialism. It is also a matter of working with what one has. Russia may not be the home of Disney, but as one entrepreneur brags in the *Park of the Soviet Period* film, "We'll prove that our horrors are the most horrible in all the world!"

Actual attempts at Soviet reconstructions as an entertainment event have been few and far between. In 2008, the small Volga city of Tutaev opened a Park of the Soviet Period (presumably taking the name from the movie) as both a tourist attraction and a local recreation site constructed on an existing town square. More humble than the other examples considered in this chapter, the Tutaev park was never meant to be a miniature model of the Soviet Union in its entirety. Instead, it is designed to look like a typical "park of culture and rest" *from* the late Soviet period. As one reviewer on autotravel.ru put in in 2011: "O, Park of the Soviet Period is an exaggeration. It's just a local park. Tiny. The most noteworthy part of the park is the sign at the entrance. There are thematic sculptures along the pathways. That's it" ("Park sovetsokogo perioda").

The Tutaev park inverts the logic of Soviet simulation. As Mikhail Epstein writes:

> Signs of a new reality, of which Soviet citizens were so proud in the thirties and fifties, from Stalin's massive hydroelectric plant on the Dnieper River to Khrushchev's decision to raise corn and Brezhnev's numerous autobiographies, were actually pure ideological simulations of reality. This artificial reality was intended to demonstrate the superiority of ideas over simple facts . . . The presence of the idea of a sausage confronts the absence of real meat therein. The presence of a plan for manufacturing confronts the absence of actual production. (194)

The city officials promoting Tutaev's park are making the opposite sort of promise: in their Park of the Soviet Period, visitors will encounter a satisfying simulation of a significant aspect of the Soviet experience, but the result was a shoddy, underwhelming product that could not live up to its hype. They promised a facsimile of Soviet ideology but delivered a worthy successor to actual Soviet workmanship.

The Park of the Soviet Period advertised in Moscow in 2019 had more resources available to it and had the advantage of being more an event than a place. Located in the area surrounding the Ostankino television station, this park opened on July 20 and closed on August 2, a two-week period that the organizers were determined to pack with fun for the whole family: "Tabletop games—a feature of Soviet parks, racing with retro-bicycles, a model club, an air rifle range, young pioneer groups, volleyball and foosball, and guitar poetry will transport the guests to the atmosphere of the Sixties and Seventies" ("'Park sovetskogo perioda' poiavitsia"). In addition, from July 20 to 27, visitors could also attend Soviet fashion shows and dance parties, where they could learn to dance the Boogie-Woogie.

The video advertisement circulating on VKontakte ("Iunost'") underscores how the event underplayed ideological symbols in favor of sheer entertainment. Yes, we see people dressed in Pioneer costumes and military garb, but the emphasis is on the games and the dancing. What is on offer here is not so much a trip back to the Soviet Union per se as a nostalgic revisiting of the songs, dances, and games that were popular in late Soviet times. For decades after the Soviet collapse, critics have debated the significance of Soviet symbols deployed in post-Soviet entertainment: was there such a thing as innocent nostalgia, or were the films and television shows that used Soviet music and imagery to touch viewers' heartstrings a Trojan horse for more pernicious content?[13] At the very least, events such as the Ostankino Soviet park helped normalize the Soviet past as something to either be proud of or simply not be ashamed of, enabling the general tendency to downplay the regime's crimes in favor of "the positive."

But even if this project were intended to be ideologically neutral, the spectacle of Russian citizens partying in Soviet drag becomes more difficult to watch in the aftermath of the 2022 Ukrainian invasion. As scholars have argued since the days of Louis Marin's 1977 semiotic analysis of Disneyland, theme parks are efficient vehicles for repackaging and transmitting ideology in the most anodyne of forms. The commercial for the Ostankino park project puts dancing, gaming, and donning Soviet garb on the same level by cutting from one to the other quickly; no matter what they are doing, everyone is smiling. At least as presented in the commercial (unfortunately, I missed the two-week window for visiting by about three years), the ideology Ostankino is selling is not exactly Soviet. Rather, it is a fantasy *about* the Soviet, and the way that the Soviet can be seamlessly integrated into a post-Soviet life. The only visible slogan is Stalin's "Life has become better, life has become happier!," which takes on new meaning in this twenty-first-century context. Stalinism also prominently featured smiling people in its propaganda, but the Stalinist smile is fixed and determined, making it all the more noteworthy given the fact that, generally, public smiling was not a feature of Soviet life. The smiles in the commercial are completely different: they look like the smiles of people who are actually enjoying themselves. Their smiles look spontaneous (which could just be good acting), directing the focus to the subjective pleasurable experience of the park visitors (never a prominent feature in Stalinist propaganda). Life has truly become better, but not in the way that Stalin's slogan implied. Instead, the visitors are prosperous bourgeois subjects of Putinist capitalism, and the Soviet past is both their inheritance and their playground.

As discussed in the introduction, the Jurassic-Park influenced phrase "Park of the Soviet Period" is an almost inevitable Russian locution; it is as catchy in Russian as it is clunky in English. Nevertheless, both instantiations of the post-Soviet Soviet Park clearly owe their name to the 2006 film. Directed by Yuli Guzman from a screenplay by Guzman and Eduard Akopov, *Park of the Soviet Period* was a commercial flop ($130,000 in ticket sales versus a $5.2 million budget) (Lavrov) that nevertheless sparked heated critical discussion and even a novelization by the screenwriters in conjunction with Aleksei Kozuliaev. Jam-packed

---

13. A key concept in this debate is Lipovetsky's "post-sots," which shares certain formal traits with postmodernism (particularly the recycling of socialist realist tropes) without the irony or self-consciousness that fuels most postmodern art (*Postmodern Crises* 169–94).

with celebrity cameos (the Soviet crooner-turned-Putinist legislator Iosif Kobzon; Vladimir Etush, reprising his role from the beloved 1967 film *Kidnapping, Caucasian Style*; the journalist Elena Khanga; and even the journalist and future master propagandist Vladimir Solovyov), *Park of the Soviet Period* is overstuffed on every level: the plot is a strange mishmash of genres and pastiches, the characters' motivations conflict in a manner less suggestive of depth than of shoddy writing. Most important, the film's point of view on the Soviet legacy is, by the end, almost incomprehensible. If the film's representation of the Soviet past is muddled, it inadvertently succeeds as the incarnation of early Putinism: when it comes to history, the film is trying to have it all ways at once.

The hero of the film is Oleg Zimin, a television journalist who is assigned to visit the new Park of the Soviet Period as an honored guest, in order to eventually produce a flattering review. The park, which is meant to provide an "exclusive experience of the USSR," is supposedly divided up into all fifteen Soviet republics, but most of what we see and hear about is thematic rather than national: there are plans for a "Gulag experience," complete with interrogations for guests who meet the minimum health requirements; there's a Civil War parade, a rocket launch meant to replicate Gagarin's famous flight, and a reenactment of the Virgin Lands campaign (an agricultural mobilization movement that ran from 1954 to 1963 and was romanticized in Soviet film and fiction). One reviewer on kinopoisk.ru ("Retsenzii") compared the premise to *Westworld* (the 1973 Michael Crichton film—this was before the HBO television series came out), but *Park of the Soviet Period* is both more complex and less consistent in its treatment of simulated history as fantasy. The Park of the Soviet Period is not just a resort where people can experience the Soviet past; it is also a twenty-first-century resort designed to mimic a Soviet-era resort. The facility Zimin stays in accepts Soviet rubles, has "Soviet" staff, and even serves "Soviet" beer. ("There's no better beer than our Zhigulevskoe," a staff member tells Zimin, before admitting that it's actually German.) As the last example demonstrates, the staff are in character by default but willing to break the frame every now and then. Dinner is served in a luxurious dining hall, with Soviet-style food and Soviet-style entertainment and speeches, but also the possibility of sitting at a table with three different men dressed as the legendary World War II secret agent Stirlitz. The announcements maintain the overall pretense of living in the Soviet Union while still reminding guests of entertainment options that involve visiting various non-overlapping historical eras.

Since the park is a resort, it offers all the comforts of a high-end Soviet spa, and Zimin discovers he is partial to Charcot showers, a common Soviet-era hydrotherapy treatment which involves spraying the patient with a hose-like device that issues high-pressure streams of water. He is even more partial to Alyona, the staff member who administers the showers, and he spends the first part of the film crudely courting her. The resort administration warns him off, explaining that there is a nonfraternization rule, but he persists and eventually wins her over. Soon their forbidden love turns the resort experience into a dystopian nightmare: Zimin is falsely accused of rape, drugged, and tortured (with the very same Charcot shower he liked so much). He escapes captivity, gets into physical fights with the staff, and even (portentously) knocks over one of the Lenin statues that decorates the park. Just when he and Alyona are about to be released, his captors are attacked by... Soviet Cossacks and soldiers, apparently led by the famous Red Army Commander Vasily Ivanovich Chapaev.

Zimin is introduced at the beginning of the film as a cynical, burnt-out media figure fighting a hangover and waking up next to a woman who surprises him with a request for money. After just a few blasts from Alyona's Charcot shower, he is head over heels in love with a woman he has just met. Alyona, it turns out, is a true believer. When they argue on the set of the Virgin Lands reenactment, she rebukes him for treating the park as just a source of entertainment: "For me, this is something holy. My grandfather told me about the Virgin Lands, how they worked for the state for free. And you act like it's a zoo, Oleg, and we're in a cage, and the whole world is outside. It was more pure. And you ruined it! I hate you!"

Of course, in keeping with the hackneyed plotting and muddled ideology, this exchange is followed by a passionate kiss. But when contrasted with Zimin's behavior in the film's opening scene, it does give the impression that *Park of the Soviet Period* will show us how immersion in the Soviet past makes Oleg a better man. And, indeed, Oleg does become a better man, but it is as much from having Soviet institutions to resist as it is from any moral superiority monopolized by the previous regime. His fight against the senseless and hypocritical rules of the park gives him what the Soviet Union gave its believers: purpose. If that purpose is in itself anti-Soviet, so be it; he needs the oppressive regime as an enemy in order to free himself from the mere hedonism of his post-Soviet existence.

In fact, this is what truly makes *Park of the Soviet Period* an effective theme park and historical reenactment. Zimin is now the hero in an unimaginative story of an individualist's rebellion against a dystopian state. He gets to rail against tyranny, topple statues, and (in a visual echo of the classic British dystopian television series *The Prisoner*) engage in fist fights with reactionaries on a giant chess board. Zimin himself has mixed feelings about nostalgia, but once the plot gets moving, he is trapped in a secondhand *1984*, with forbidden romance as a gateway to subversion. But once again, the film's approach to ideology blurs the picture. Alyona, after all, is a true believer. It is as if Winston Smith fell in love with a Julia who, rather than pretending to be overzealous in order to avoid scrutiny, was absolutely committed to her work in the Anti-Sex League.

Even his opponents are poor stand-ins for totalitarian despots. Their cause is not Stalinism per se, or even communism; it is simply the Soviet past itself. As one of them tells Zimin: "We have ideals. You gave up all the good things, the social services, the equality." He then dismisses Zimin's critique of the park's severity: "As soon as a liberal screws a girl, he remembers 1937." Later, one of Zimin's torturers tells him, "You took everything from us! You were raised by us, got so much, and threw it all away! . . . Our ancestors knew what they were living for!" It may look as though Zimin is reviving the fight against Stalinist repression, but his fight, which is with living people who refused to acknowledge that the regime's crimes outweighed its benefits, is actually once removed. At moments like these, the film seems to have a clear target: pernicious nostalgia for an overidealized past that was abusive and cruel.

For most of the film, it is possible to believe that the director is luring his viewers in with the charms of the Soviet past, only to remind them how terrible things actually were. Zimin's arrival at the park is accompanied by Timur Shaov's "Soviet Tango," which enacts this very process:

Ah, time, the Soviet time!
The memory warms the heart,
And you scratch the back of your head—
Where did that time go? . . .

You could drink your fill for a ruble,
Ride the metro for five kopecks,
And the summer lighting shone in the sky,
Flashing the beacon of communism!

And we were all humanists,
And we never knew spit,
Even our filmmakers
Loved each other back then . . .

And women gave birth to citizens,
And Lenin lit their path,
Then those citizens were jailed,
And then the jailers themselves were jailed.

This all works, more or less, until that final scene with the Soviet Cossacks saving the day, as Alyona cries out with joy, "It's our guys!" (*Nashi!*). If these men are "ours," then what does that make the quasi-Soviet tin tyrants who run the park? Or, for that matter, Zimin, whose nostalgia for the past has never included the communists?

After the credits start to roll, Guzman and Akopov leave the viewers with one last moment of ideological portent: Zimin and Alyona are driving a flatbed truck laden with cargo that is mostly covered by tarps, with the exception of statues of two Soviet Young Pioneers gazing off into the distance. They meet a smaller truck heading the opposite direction, whose driver asks them, "Does this road lead to the Park of the Soviet Period?" Zimin replies, "No, this is Shosse Svobody [Freedom Highway]." The driver, who turns out to be transporting Lenin's Mausoleum, says, "What good is a road if it doesn't lead to the Park of the Soviet Period?" The line is an almost word-for-word restatement of the famous phrase from Tengiz Abuladze's groundbreaking perestroika film, *Repentance* (1984), the story of a local tyrant with clear parallels to the Stalin years. At the end of that film, an old woman asks one of the protagonists if the road leads to the church, only to hear the reply, "No, this is Valam Street" (named after the tyrant). The old woman responds, "What good is a road if it doesn't lead to a church?" In the Abuladze film, this is a spiritual rebuke to the tyrant's cult of personality, which makes the paraphrase in *Park of the Soviet Period* all the more puzzling. Zimin offers freedom, but the driver sees value only in the Soviet past. Yet Zimin himself is transporting a statue of Young Pioneers. As the credits continue, a warning appears at the top of the frame: "The autopilot has been turned off! All responsibility lies with you!"

The message in those words, at least, is clear: think for yourself. *Park of the Soviet Period* is using roads and routes as a metaphor for political choices, but the conflicting maps and signs are more suggestive of a ten-car pileup. Perhaps this is a comment on the very syncretism that characterizes so much Soviet and imperial nostalgia. The problem is that the affective relationship with the past entails an almost total suspension of judgment: Lenin is "ours," the Cossacks are "ours," and in the imperial nostalgic culture of late Putinism, the tsars are also "ours." More to the point, so is Zimin.

Products of Their Times

Implicit in the stories of Soviet reenactments is an unquestioned axiom about the relationship between people, their times, and their environment. The Park of the Soviet Period was ostensibly built for the twin purposes of recreation and profit, but the unfolding of the plot demonstrates the power that even a simulated environment has on its participants. The park cannot automatically transform every participant into a Soviet true believer; on Zimin, it has precisely the opposite effect. But this is still an effect, and, more important, a *Soviet* effect. Zimin has gone from a jaded, post-Soviet libertine to a cross between a dissident and a (counter)revolutionary, but both the pro-Soviet and anti-Soviet stances are evidence of a Soviet subject position. Anti-Soviet subjectivity is just Soviet subjectivity with the polarity reversed.

As a representation of a sociological experiment in reconstructing the past, *Park of the Soviet Period* is hopelessly scattershot: the park, with its multiple attractions and themes, refuses to commit to a specific time period. Its value is as a perhaps inadvertent representation of the syncretic, inconsistent "Soviet past" that has been the object of popular nostalgia: the nostalgia isn't for a particular period that existed but for an imaginary Sovietness that can exist only as a fiction. In her 2018 novel, *Gorky Quest*, Alexandra Marinina goes in a different direction: she chronicles the attempt to reconstruct the Soviet 1970s in one building, populating it with young people who were born long after the USSR collapsed. Now we are dealing with the recreation of a period that many of her readers, like the author herself, remember personally.

Much of the novel is devoted to the design of the experiment, reflecting both the fictional masterminds' and the author's dedication to their idea of accuracy. Though the novel represents a departure from Marinina's best-known books (which usually feature an investigator trying to solve a murder), it shares the philosophy that underlies all her work: with the proper application of professional, systematic thinking, anything is possible. In *Gorky Quest*, as in most of her novels, characters indulge in pages-long monologues in which they demonstrate just how thoroughly they have thought about a particular question. For the reader, the mileage on such speeches may vary, but the characters who deliver the monologues derive immense satisfaction from elaborating just how right they are.

Underneath its convoluted plotting, *Gorky Quest* is a drama about the problem of nature vs. nurture. They key word, however, is "about." The books do not actually engage with this problem on the level of action and character. Instead, the premise is that, in order to conclude a 150-year-long crackpot experiment in eugenics, a group of young twenty-first-century Russians must pretend to live in the 1970s so as to replicate the thinking habits of a young man of that time. Richard Wiley, an aging Russian-to-English translator from the United States, has come to Moscow in the hopes of gaining information that will allow him to claim a prize set up as part of his family's trust. The Wiley-Cooper clan traces its roots back to the mid-nineteenth century, when its patriarch became convinced that he could turn his offspring into super--geniuses and learn the secrets of heredity if they would only live properly and keep a journal detailing every significant aspect of their lives. One branch of the family ended up in the Soviet Union, and at least a few of them continued to keep their journals and mail them off to the Wiley-Cooper family foundation in the United States. They emigrate to the United States in 1992, and the youngest member of the family (Anton, now Anthony) starts conducting research to cure migraines, to which many of his relatives, including Richard, are prone. Richard Wiley realizes that if Anthony wins the family prize, he will use his money to produce a medicine that provides temporary relief at the cost of the migraine patient's future mental health. Richard wants to win the money to keep it out of Anthony's hands.

The key to winning the prize somehow lies in the journals kept by Vladimir, a young schoolteacher (and member of the Wiley-Cooper clan) who died under mysterious circumstances. If Richard can just understand how Vladimir thought, the prize will be his. But as an old American man, he cannot be sure that he is reading Vladimir's diaries correctly, and even Russians of Vladimir's generation would fail, because they are now so much older than Vladimir was when he taught Russian literature to Soviet schoolchildren. Current twenty-something Russians would have a completely different frame of reference.

The solution? Pay a group of young Russians to live in a hotel under conditions that maximally reproduce the USSR of the 1970s, then have them read the same literary works Vladimir discussed in his journal. As a result, parts of *Gorky Quest* are the prose equivalent of a Seventies-themed Russian reality show, with much of the entertainment stemming from the young people's shock at their strange living conditions.

After reading this novel twice, I am forced to admit that I still find the premise baffling, if not incomprehensible, at least on the level of plot. When Marinina talks about this book, she is most excited about discussing the differences between her generation (which came of age in the 1970s) and the young people of 2018. As research, she conducted focus groups with young Russians to get a sense of their perceptions of the world around them and claims that she came to truly value the younger generation. Young people today are different, she says, but still wonderful. This conclusion does not conflict with her characterization of her protagonists, who, like any group, consist of both charming and unlikable people. What, then, is the point of her exercise, and how does it differ from other fictional reconstructions of the Soviet past?

First and foremost, the young people's reactions and the older characters' reminiscences are meant to be entertaining. Many of them are the equivalent of US viral videos of Gen Z children baffled when they try to use a rotary phone, while others (such as the Komsomol meetings in which the young characters are forced to participate) are reminders of the hypocrisy and unpleasantness of late Soviet life. But *Gorky Quest* also expresses a naïve faith in the logic of generations and in the direct, simplistic relationship between a time period and the people who live in it. There is something inherently anti-novelistic about this belief, at least in Marinina's case: why populate a fictional world with a variety of characters, all of whom have unique personalities, only to argue that environment shapes everyone in ultimately predictable ways?

Readers looking for a rosy-tinted view of the Soviet Seventies will be disappointed by the older characters' repeated emphasis on the hypocrisy, senselessness, and inconvenience of the system in which they grew up (even if those same characters also can wax wistful when they recall those years). Marinina's reconstructed 1970s are neither heaven nor hell, but merely different from the 2010s. Unlike *Park of the Soviet Period*, *Gorky Quest*'s reconstruction has little inherent drama to it; instead, the author's emphasis on the everyday, prosaic aspects of her characters' lives (one of the strengths of most of her writing) demystifies the return to the past. Where *Park of the Soviet Period* reproduces a past that seems to seep beyond its borders, and that at least some of its visitors and staff wish were actually real, *Gorky Quest* is more content to function like a theme park ought to: it's a nice place to visit, but eventually, it is time to go home.

Camp Concentration

The most famous (or perhaps infamous) Soviet reconstruction is a project whose scope and scale are so vast that few of the scholars who write about it (myself included) have been able to view the entire thing. In 2005, the Russian film director Ilya Khrzhanovsky began planning a film biography of the legendary Soviet physicist and Nobel laureate Lev Landau. Over the next several years, this project (called DAU after Landau's nickname) grew into an unprecedented immersive, multimedia video and research project funded by the oligarch Sergei Adonyev. Khrzhanovsky built an entire institute, which operated between 2008 and 2011 at the site of a stadium in the Ukrainian city of Kharkiv. The largest film set in Europe, the DAU Institute was populated by hundreds of people from all walks of life, who committed to a total historical simulation twenty-four hours a day. As the project's website describes it:

> Scientists could live and work in the Institute and it was also populated by hundreds of carefully selected willing participants—artists, waiters, secret police, ordinary families—all cut off from time and space.
>
> Several hundred people left their everyday lives to go back in time to the Soviet Union, taking up residence at the Institute in a spatially and temporally parallel universe. It was a meticulous historical simulation where everything, from uniforms to kitchen appliances, food, money, and vocabulary, matched the objects and habits of the time. The Institute had its own newspaper (with daily bulletins informing the participants of historical events from the time) and the currency used was the ruble. ("About DAU")

Real-life physicists, mathematicians, and scientists of various profiles moved to the DAU Institute and even continued their research on the premises. Religious leaders and artists visited, including the renowned performance artist Marina Abramovic, the theater director Peter Sellars, and the composer and performer Brian Eno. Only four participants in the project were professional actors (playing Dau, his wife, their son, and Institute Director Krupitsa). Nearly everyone else acted under their own names, improvising their lines and subject to filming at any moment during the day or night.

By the time filming was over, the director had over seven hundred hours of footage as the source material for what had become much more than a single feature. As of July 2022, *DAU* consists of fifteen films and six series, with one of the films (*Degeneration*) clocking in at six hours and nine minutes. *DAU* debuted in Paris on January 25, 2019, as a series of screenings at two city theaters and an immersive experience at the Pompidou Center. Visitors to the Pompidou, who purchased "DAU visas" rather than ordinary tickets, could encounter members of the cast who were living at the center and remaining in character, much as they had on the Kharkiv set. Parts of the Pompidou were transformed into a "Soviet" space, including an apartment for the scientists who took part in the project.

Where *Park of the Soviet Period* turned the blurred boundaries between life and historical reenactment into the subject of fiction, and *Gorky Quest* portrayed a similar phenomenon as a quasi-sociological experiment, Khrzhanovsky's totalizing ambitions disrupted the categories of "real" and "reenactment" for both its participants and its viewers (in the case of the latter, this worked primarily at the Paris installation, which obliged the visitors to become participants themselves).[14] Unsurprisingly, *DAU* has also sparked serious ethical concerns that continue to be debated, mostly involving the people (and animals) who appear on screen. The numerous sex scenes were not simulated, and some of them depicted rape.[15] To what extent was *DAU* enacting a complex sexual assault on some of the actresses? What about the involvement of children with Down Syndrome from a nearby orphanage—can they really be said to have consented to take part in this

---

14. The experience of viewing *DAU*, at least in Paris, is ultimately as physical as it is aesthetic. As Tatyana Efremova writes: "*DAU* offered the viewers intense bodily immersion into the world of the past through activating their sensorium (smell and touch, as well as sound and vision) and radically blurring the boundary between the fantasy and the real. It also encouraged the spectators to build their own narrative of the event—to revisit their own memories and personal histories, to enjoy suggested encounters, or to choose one's own experiences" (149). Or, as Il'ia Kukui puts it, "there was the sense that everything, literally everything in this project was created in order to subject the viewer to torture."

15. The "real" sex performed by people playing fictional characters nonetheless manages to break the frame. As Iampol'skii notes, it's a shock when Dau's wife Nora has sex with her son Denis as the cleaning woman watches, and yet that shock leads to cognitive dissonance: "The sex on the screen is real, but the whole incest situation is simulated, and that's quite clear."

film, and was their treatment appropriate?[16] *Degeneration* is a powerful statement about the triumph of fascists over intellectuals, but was it really necessary to invite Tesak, an actual neo-Nazi, to play one of the film's murderous thugs?[17] Or to have Tesak slaughter a pig in front of the *DAU* participants, on camera, leaving both the actors and the audience to watch it bleed out on a carpet?

DAU is a phenomenon that cannot escape discussions of the moral dimensions of art, and even its defenders (who dispute the allegations about the disabled children and the harmfulness of the simulated rapes) cannot reasonably assert that *DAU* is just "art for art's sake." A project that demands so much of its participants over so many years, requiring them to live in a compound and pretend to be in the Soviet Union, cannot be just a work of aesthetics. Going back at least as far as Plato's *Republic*, philosophers and critics have debated the effects of artistic representation on readers and audiences (with *The Republic*, for example, assuming that the reader is a passive recipient easily led astray by a text's bad example). One of the controversial aspects of Soviet nostalgia in general and Soviet reenactments in particular concerns the social role of representation: does nostalgic content produce politically nostalgic (if not reactionary) audiences? *DAU* turns representation into just one of at least three dimensions to consider, along with the function of the performers and of the active viewer/participant (at the Pompidou Center). What does it mean to be playing the role of a scientist if one is already a scientist, or a fascist if one is already a fascist? When the actors live versions of their own lives in the Soviet DAU research institute, what does this metaphorical time travel do to their own subjectivity?

DAU prompts these questions, but as one would expect from any complex work of art, particularly one as postmodern and slippery as this one, it does not provide definitive answers. Khrzhanovsky is a provocateur, and as a provocation, *DAU* is a huge success. As a meditation on historical reconstruction, *DAU* is effective less as a set of films than as the collection of controversies that the filming sparked. If one knew nothing of the project before viewing any of the *DAU* videos, the historical or sociological questions raised would be about the era represented and about the films' fidelity to historical fact. But our knowledge of the three-year lifespan of the DAU Institute inevitably informs the viewing experience. Reception of the films is also reception of the making of the films,

---

16. For a (mostly) English-language debate over these very issues, see the collection of seventeen scholarly reactions to *DAU* edited by Natascha Drubek et al. in the October 2020 issue of *Apparatus*.

17. Maxim Martinskevich, better known by the nickname Tesak (Hatchet), was a skinhead with several convictions for extremism. In addition to calling for all democrats to be put to death, he founded a vigilante organization that lured gay men to trysts, only to kidnap them and post videos of their torture online. He died in pretrial detention in 2020.

often boiling down to an ethical question: under the conditions that prevailed in Kharkiv, should these films even have been made at all? This is not a job for formalism or New Criticism but an invitation to explore context.[18]

The context of *DAU* is an object lesson about (restored) historical forms and their creation of a period-appropriate subjectivity. Part of this is clearly intentional. Why else would the participants have to forswear the Internet and wear Soviet underwear, if it were not to put them in the proper historical mindset? This not only prefigures Marinina's faith in the power of historical forms to form predictable, period-specific consciousness in *Gorky Quest*, it practically weaponizes it. *DAU* is not just an exercise in implicit time travel; generically, the scene of *DAU* suggests a different fantastic genre: horror, or more specifically, the tale of the haunted house. Like a decaying manse whose ghosts possess visitors and make them act out dramas of long-ago suffering, the *DAU* set encouraged an identification with the spirits of the past. Accusations that Khrzhanovsky ran the set like a megalomaniacal tyrant are believable precisely because they so perfectly fit the historical/fictional framework. Of course, the director would be "possessed" by the spirit of a minor Stalin: the whole point of the project was to recreate these horrible times in miniature; not "socialism in one country" but "Stalinism on one film set." This is method acting as horror story.

DAU was always vulnerable to the accusation that, in reconstructing the Soviet Union covering the period from 1938 to 1968, it was also replicating its flaws and excesses.[19] It is an unrealizable monument to something that could not be realized, a perhaps unintentional echo of one of the most powerful critiques of the Stalinist project written when Stalinism was still in its early stages, Andrei Platonov's *The Foundation Pit* (1930). Ostensibly the story of exhausted but mostly committed communist workers digging the foundation for a future "Proletarian Home" (a huge workers' housing complex), by the end it becomes clear that all they have been doing is digging their own mass grave. The Proletarian Home is never built, while *DAU* mutated into a sprawling monster that virtually no one will see in its totality.

Does this make *DAU* a failure? Perhaps, but it is a failure that also constitutes an unprecedented success. The other restorationist projects discussed in this chapter are not just smaller in scale or ambition; they somehow manage to

---

18. Here I agree with Lipovetsky, who writes, "Sadly, it is more interesting to talk about these films than to watch them: for me, this is proof of the experiment's failure" ("Introduction," 391).

19. See, for example, Robert Bird: "Though it purports to replicate Soviet experience, DAU really enacts the revenge of what Soviet discourse sublimated, at least in its public manifestations. As an aesthetic strategy, this eruption of what was previously suppressed is familiar from bleak late- and post-Soviet cinema (known in Russian as chernukha)."

minimize and tame their subject matter. This is built into the premise of both *Goodbye, Lenin!* and *The Man Who Couldn't Die*, which create the tiniest possible pseudosocialist habitats within the confines of two different bedrooms. Compared to the symphonic majesty of *DAU*, Becker's and Slavnikova's tales are chamber music. Marinina's novel, while sprawling and interminable, also limits its faux Soviet Seventies to one house. Hardly a supporter of the Soviet system, Marinina still subjects her protagonists only to the mildest of indignities, while she is unable to resist the decade's nostalgic charms. The various Parks of the Socialist Period defang and dehistoricize the Soviet Union in order to recreate it; granted, Zimin quickly finds the dark side of the theme park/resort where he is a guest, but only because he puts in the effort. The twentieth-century USSR in both *Dark Side of the Moon* and *Chernobyl: Exclusion Zone* are also reassuringly bland; ideology comes up in *Dark Side*, and the season-long exploration of this brave new world reveals a number of unappealing features, but ideology has been put on the back burner.

Like a Borgesian map that expands to the size of the territory it represents, *DAU* comes far closer to recreating a vanished USSR on former Soviet territory, while also, intentionally or not, enabling a critique of this very process of re-creation. The more Khrzhanovsky's project focuses on minutiae (Soviet money, Soviet clothing, Soviet food, Soviet vocabulary), the more it manages to resemble both the USSR and a theme park simultaneously. An overly precious preoccupation with reproducing Soviet material culture coexists with both a system of institutionalized violence and all the petty ways people transgressed and found joy, or at least the illusion of agency. Finally, *DAU*, by virtue of its location, includes an element that rarely finds its way into other reenactments, reconstructions, and imaginary contemporary Soviet Unions: *DAU* is a colonial/imperialist project. While it is true that Landau taught in Kharkiv between 1932 and 1937, his Institute for Physical Problems was located in Moscow. The multiyear film set, however, was located in Kharkiv. Philip Cavendish points to Khrzhanovsky's "weak cultural connections to Ukraine" and the fact that *DAU* is an example of what Yuri Shevchuk has called "cinematic depopulation as a variety of cultural imperialism." Ivan Kozlenko goes further: "DAU is a fundamentally Russian project. It is a project on which is branded the entire history of Russia's re-embrace of aggressive imperialistic instincts, one in which the function of the individual is purely instrumental." For him, the positive reception of *DAU* in the Russian Federation is "a symptom of the complete ethical perversion of Russia's cultural elite, which has become resistant to, and developed a tolerance for, extreme violence and the oppression of human rights."

Constructing a Soviet film site in Kharkiv is not the cinematic equivalent of the Russian bombing and seizure of the same city eleven years later. To argue otherwise would downplay the massive suffering and loss of life that the 2022 invasion has caused. But the two events are on a continuum, even if they occupy very distant points from each other. Each was made possible by the cultural and imaginary persistence of an empire that officially ended in 1991. Russia's war on Ukraine denies both Ukraine's very existence and the imperialist nature of the invasion—how can it be imperialist to take back what was already "ours"?—while the film shoot in Kharkiv was made possible by the two countries' proximity, similarity, and shared past that Russians tend to treat as either a positive or neutral fact, rather than the vexed legacy it brings to modern Ukraine. Nor should we forget that *The Dark Side of the Moon*'s contemporary Soviet Moscow was filmed in the other neighboring Slavic country, Belarus. Most of the Russian fantasies of a revived or persistent USSR we have examined are set on (and produced in) the territory of the Russian Federation. The imperialist implications of this fantasy are already evident in the implicit claim on post-Soviet territory, but they are even harder to ignore when the fantasy is produced in another sovereign country. The twentieth-century Soviet fantasy is more than just a set of variations on time travel and theme parks: it is the insistence on viewing Russian and former Soviet territory as a geographical palimpsest. Every stratum of history is still reachable; it is merely buried under other strata. The former Soviet Union as palimpsest is a revanchist political nightmare, as well as an affirmation that Philip K. Dick was right: the empire never really ended.

5

THE RETURN OF THE RADIANT FUTURE

Tomorrow Never Comes

The end of the Cold War wreaked havoc with cartography, erasing three existing countries from the map (East Germany, Czechoslovakia, and the USSR) while adding seventeen (and this is not even counting the disintegration of Yugoslavia). This geographical upheaval was accompanied by a redistribution of conceptual territory whose consequences would take years to play out. The former Soviet bloc lost more than nuclear weaponry and economic and political stability. In the division of spoils, the West got custody of the future.[1]

Who, after all, was writing the epitaph for the Cold War era? I hesitate to invoke Francis Fukuyama's *The End of History and the Last Man*, both because of how wrong its predictions now seem and because the "end of history" has become such a post-Cold War cliché, but Fukuyama is an illustrative symptom. Fukuyama was nothing if not timely; his book came out in 1992 (that is, just after the Soviet collapse), and was based on an essay published in *The National Interest* in 1989 (when Eastern European communist regimes were in a race to see who could self-destruct first). Fukuyama's triumphalism is difficult to bear, but what should be even more galling to both leftists and the disgruntled denizens of the postsocialist world is his appropriation of a Marxist framework to declare the

---

1. Kirill Kobrin argues that Russians' "social atomization" and indifference to politics means that "Russian society has a weak sense of the reality of any other order besides their own personal worries." As a result, they have nothing from which they could construct an image of the future (15).

permanent dominance of the capitalist liberal democratic paradigm. Fukuyama had the vision to realize that the spoils of the Cold War were not merely economic and ideological; the winners retained the right to frame the future.

Granted, a defunct political system would appear to have no future by definition, but for Soviet discourse, the future was about more than simply continuity beyond the present day, or even the central planning five and seven years ahead for which the USSR was so famous. One would expect a Marxist regime to be teleological, but the centrality of the future in Soviet culture goes far beyond the system's Marxist foundations. The future was more than a goal off in the temporal distance: it was the thing that gave the present its meaning. The Soviet Union, particularly but not exclusively in the Stalin era, drained the present in favor of the future. Any and all suffering and sacrifice endured by the population "now" would be redeemed by what was yet to come.

Replacing the Soviet Union with the Russian Federation and the other fourteen successor states involved not just the passage of calendar time, but the inversion of the temporal hierarchy. The Soviet devaluation of the present in favor of the future suggests another interpretation of Rabfak's now familiar complaint in "Our Nuthouse Is Voting for Putin": "Why is today yesterday and not tomorrow?" A better future that is somehow qualitatively different from the present and the past is virtually inconceivable. The post-Soviet era hobbled the national imagination, reducing the future to endless variations on the historically familiar.

With, perhaps, one exception: the end of the world.

After a brief survey of post-Soviet Russia's post-apocalyptic fantasies, this chapter examines the varieties of Russian futures that could, by some stretch of the imagination, be considered positive: the neomedievalism of Mikhail Yuriev's *Third Empire* along with its implicit rejoinder, Vladimir Sorokin's *The Day of the Oprichnik*; the online communities creating Soviet futuristic video projects; the nostalgia-infused retrofuturism known in some circles as SovPunk (in video games, Internet memes, and online art exhibits); and the *USSR-2061* series of literary and artistic contest challenging amateur creators to come up with their own vision of a twenty-first-century Soviet Union that is in the process of conquering space while solving a whole host of perceived problems at home. Examining all these works together will show what kind of imagined future can reasonably be called "optimistic."

Only the End of the World Again

The post-Soviet Russian imaginary has had plenty of room for the apocalypse; the end of the world as we know it is always around the corner. There is something dreary about invoking it, on a number of levels. First, there is the prevalence of apocalyptic and postapocalyptic storytelling throughout the entire world at roughly the same time. Second, there are the potentially diminishing returns of destroying civilization on a regular basis. And third, there is the fact that I have personally written on this topic on several occasions. It is telling that the best example I can give of the iterative nature of the apocalypse is one that I have already given in *Plots against Russia*: Marina and Sergei Dyachenko's 1999 novel *Armaged-dom*, which I suggested would be best translated as "Sweet Home Armageddon" (55). In this novel, everyone has come to expect the intermittent apocalypse known as the *mryga*, which is usually scientifically predicted and announced in advance on television. Many will die, but a few will always survive to face the next *mryga* to come their way.

When post-Soviet Russia imagines the world's end, it is partaking in a long-standing cultural tradition of apocalypticism while also engaging in a conversation with popular exemplars from around the world. Perhaps as a result, Russian apocalyptic and post-apocalyptic storytelling is one of the country's more successful exports; it may not be quite as popular as the family-friendly cartoon sensation *Masha and the Bear*, but it does have the virtue of a much higher body count. Apocalypticism comes naturally to post-Soviet culture, perhaps because, like the Dyachenkos' iterative catastrophes in *Sweet Home Armageddon*, the end of the world is arguably a familiar experience. The Soviet collapse is the obvious example, to be sure, but it is not the only one.

For writers of Russian fiction, the post-Soviet apocalypse is heralded by an event that turned the key elements of Soviet science worship into the stuff of nuclear nightmare: the 1986 disaster at the Chernobyl atomic power station. Chernobyl establishes a compelling pattern for late and post-Soviet catastrophe tales. Modernity itself fails ordinary people, destroying institutions, compelling mass evacuation, and threatening public health in mysterious and unpredictable ways. Most important, catastrophe is largely invisible: we see its results (death, societal breakdown), but the event itself is always offstage. World War II may have been the formative trauma for generations of Soviet citizens, but it was a different type of horror: ubiquitous, unrelenting, and impossible not to see. It is the intangibility of Chernobyl that introduced Russia and the Soviet Union to postmodern catastrophe.

Even a cursory look at some of the most notable examples of Russian (post) apocalypticism reveals several important patterns. First, we see the reinforcement of the Chernobyl model in the writers most directly concerned with catastrophe. Second is the reassertion of a cyclical model of history, in which the often-dystopian future is established as a repetition of a familiar past. Third, we find an insistence on the inexplicable, often metaphysical nature of catastrophe, divorced from easily identifiable politics or recent history. Finally, there is a self-referential or metafictional element to catastrophe, either using an apocalyptic scenario to comment on the fate of Russian literature or showing literature's vulnerability to the collapse of supporting institutions. All of these patterns are in the service of a darkly pessimistic view not just of the future but of the eventual human condition: the inhabitants of the postapocalypse are often barely literate and superstitious, the combination of both nineteenth-century anxieties about degeneration and twentieth-century fantasies of mutation and degradation.

Our main examples will consist of two well-known works: Tatyana Tolstaya's *The Slynx* (Kys'), and Dmitry Glukhovsky's transmedia juggernaut, the *Metro 2033* franchise. *The Slynx* was the long-awaited first novel by an acclaimed highbrow short-story writer, while *Metro 2033* spawned a hit video game before launching a multimedia empire. Yet they share a set of presumptions and preoccupations that defy any critical desire to keep them hygienically separate.

The Idiocy of Postapocalyptic Village Life

The Slynx takes place in a town built on the ruins of Moscow, now called Fyodor-Kuzmichsk after its paramount leader. As a result of the Blast (*Vzryv*), most of the population is plagued by Consequences, mutations presumably caused by radiation. The few survivors of the pre-Blast world (known as the Oldeners [*Prezhnie*]) are virtually immortal—they can be killed by accident or violence, but otherwise they neither age nor die. The protagonist is Benedikt, who has the prestigious job of transcribing the few old books to survive the destruction of the old world. He would rather have been a more literal keeper of the flame—no one knows how to make a fire, so the person responsible for keeping a fire going is particularly respected. That the two choices are complementary is in itself significant.

The world of *The Slynx* is a post-apocalyptic variation on the feudal system in general, and the Russian feudal past in particular. The lowest order in Fyodor-Kuzmichsk (a name that is almost as ungainly in Russian as it is in English) are serfs, literally lorded over by the town's masters. Kudeyar Kudeyarovich Kudeyarov, the Head Saniturion (*Glavnyi sanitar'*), leads a law-enforcement organization redolent of both Stalin's terror and Ivan the Terrible's oprichnina. Everyone in town is terrified of the legendary slynx, an animal whose Russian name is a combination of "lynx" and the equivalent of "Here kitty-kitty." The lynx supposedly stalks the northern woods, but danger lurks much closer to home. Benedikt marries into Kudeyarov's family and reluctantly helps him stage a coup, realizing too late that the Head Saniturion represents the greatest danger to his world.

Russian critics are divided as to whether or not *The Slynx* constitutes an "anti-utopia" (a term that, in Russian, is even broader than the much-misused "dystopia" in English), and with good reason. As Natalia Ivanova ("I ptitsu") and Mark Lipovetsky ("Sled Kysi") argue, *The Slynx* is much more concerned with commenting on the Russian intelligentsia and traditional Russian logocentrism than it is in serving as a political cautionary tale. The temporal gap between *The Slynx* and the novel's initial readers is the same as that posited by Zamyatin in *We*, but the functions of these two novels could not be more different (Clowes 37). Even an allegorical reading of *The Slynx* fails to point to any reasonably probable alarming future. Instead, *The Slynx* fits more comfortably within the broader genre that spawned both utopia and dystopia: satire.

Yet the impulse to distance *The Slynx* from dystopia (or anti-utopia) is worthy of examination in and of itself. Reading *The Slynx* as a dystopia threatens the novel with its own distinct belatedness. Ironically for a book that posits a backward-looking future, *The Slynx* as dystopia could easily be dismissed as a dissident relic of the Cold War and Soviet times: such classic dystopias as *We* and *1984* were nourished on the fear of a totalitarian threat, while Russian literature in the Yeltsin years had been taking a much-deserved rest from decades of ideological burdens. If we also recall that Tolstaya's original inspiration for the novel was the Chernobyl disaster, then *The Slynx* is not just untimely; the book is quite simply overdue. Nor does appealing to the broader realm of science fiction help Tolstaya's case. The semiliterate narration was prefigured by Russell Hoban's *Ridley Walker* (1980), while neither radiation-induced mutation nor an ignorant reverence for the printed page is remotely novel (see Miller's *A Canticle for Leibowitz*). The mutations themselves cannot hold up to the slightest scrutiny, and the Oldeners' immortality is utterly nonsensical, at least within a science fictional framework.

Such niggling complaints do Tolstaya an injustice, and that is precisely the point. Tolstaya teases her readers with familiar dystopian tropes but refuses to make them add up to anything so simple. Both utopias and dystopias have a long-established epistemological master plot that combines Plato's Allegory of the Cave with the myth of Prometheus (Morson 88–90). Traveling to utopia is a journey to wisdom, and returning from utopia necessitates the often vain attempt to keep the flame of wisdom alive, bringing it back in the hopes of sharing it with others. Dystopia is also the story of the acquisition of wisdom, but with conspiratorial overtones: it is wisdom that is being deliberately hidden by a regime built on lies (or hoarded, like the stoker's flames in *The Slynx*). Within the fictional framework, the wisdom acquired in utopia is usually experiential or discursive; that is, it can be transmitted dynamically, through demonstration or oral speech. Dystopian wisdom tends to require access to static media that are better suited to preservation—in particular, books. This focus on preservation is something dystopias share with post-apocalyptic fiction more broadly (since catastrophe all but obliterates history). Hence the reverence for the printed word, raised almost to the level of fetish: the illuminated manuscripts of *A Canticle for Leibowitz*; the lost book containing the word "I" in Ayn Rand's *Anthem;* the complete works of Shakespeare in Aldous Huxley's *Brave New World*; Goldstein's admittedly falsified counterrevolutionary tract in *1984*; and virtually every book ever printed in Ray Bradbury's *Fahrenheit 451*. Dystopias are an extended plea on behalf of the printed word, while utopias are books to end all books.

The Slynx revisits the book-as-fetish only to interrogate it. Previous dystopias essentially treat old books as taboo: the fact that they are forbidden elevates them to virtually totemic power. Books also leave room for optimism, raising the possibility that postapocalyptic survivors might learn from them and rebuild the best of the past. In other words, postapocalyptic dystopias can recapitulate the power and danger that books usually get only through the apparatus of censorship. In *The Slynx*, all books are banned, but in both senses of this polysemous word; they are too dangerous to be entrusted to ordinary people in their homes but too precious to be damaged, destroyed, or entirely forgotten (Agamben 28). When the inhabitants of Fyodor-Kuzmichsk fear the presumably radioactive danger of "Oldenprint" books, Tolstaya is subverting the traditional prometheanism that the book embodies for the dystopian tradition: the light these books bring may well be deadly.

Like Zamyatin's *We* (*My*, 1921), *The Slynx* repeatedly refers to its own status as text, but in a much less direct fashion than D-504's journal. The book's chapter titles come from old-fashioned pronunciations of all the letters in the Russian alphabet (including those removed by the Soviet orthography reform of 1917–1918). In form, *The Slynx* is a *bukvar'*, a book used to teach children the alphabet and, by extension, literacy. Benedikt himself is repeatedly accused of illiteracy by the Dissident Lev Lvovich, in terms that recall the novel's form: "You don't know your ABCs"; "You haven't learned the alphabet of life. Of life, do you hear me?" Benedikt is appalled: "Do you know how many books I've read? How many I've copied?" But Lev Lvovich is unrelenting and hurls an accusation that crystallizes the role books have acquired in post-Blast Moscow: "You don't really know how to read, books are of no use to you. They're just empty page-turning, a collection of letters" (Tolstaya 227).

Books can be preserved for future generations, but the preservation pays off only if one assumes that they will reach an audience who can understand them. One of the most familiar clichés of Russian book reviews asks whether a book "will find its reader." Transposed into the terms of *The Slynx*, that question becomes: Can the book be truly understood as something other than mere words? Will the future reader have the intellect, spirit, and context to do something with it, other than protect or destroy it? These are not abstract questions for Tolstaya, or for her own post-Soviet milieu. The Soviet Union, which prided itself on reading more than any other country, yielded to a Russian Federation that changed the status of reading forever. On one hand, more books were in circulation, but most of them were the sort that intellectuals could not take seriously. On the other, "serious" books were published in ever smaller print runs, with competition from mass-market books (not to mention film, television, the Internet, and gaming), diminishing the chances that such a book could make a difference.

The Slynx reproduces the idolatry of a logocentric, book-worshipping culture; even Pushkin is reduced to a literal wooden idol. The surviving Oldeners speak the language of the Soviet intelligentsia, and their endless preoccupation with completely irrelevant concerns (party cards, dissidence, whether or not "the West will come to our aid") renders them laughable. Lev Lvovich's accusations against Benedikt are completely on target: after gaining unfettered access to Oldenprint books, all Benedikt wants to do is alphabetize them, resulting in a pages-long list of titles and authors whose humor and pathos come from their senseless juxtaposition. Like post-Soviet Russia, Fyodor-Kuzmichsk turns out to be awash with books, but these books can do no good for anyone. Scriptures here are not sacred; instead, they are the textual equivalent of the golden calf. The books are taboo, in Freud's sense of the term: objects of both worship and terror, they are the final form taken by the unexamined elitism of the intelligentsia: the repression of all culture.

Sheltering in Place

What more appropriate antagonists could there be for a transmedia project that includes novels, interactive websites, and video games than mutated, bloodthirsty librarians? Dmitry Glukhovsky's *Metro 2033* shares Tolstaya's vague postnuclear scenario, her preoccupation with human degeneration, and her transposition of old or current cultural trends into an imaginary future. Its connection to books and literacy, however, is more ambiguous. *Metro 2033* in all its myriad formats is a thoroughly digital phenomenon, ranging from first-person narrator to first-person shooter. Initiated on the author's blog before its expansion and publication as a book, *Metro 2033* has migrated from platform to platform: audiobooks, e-books, paper books, comics, and, most famously, video games (now on PC, Xbox, and Steam). It has spawned sequels (*Metro 2034* and *Metro 2035*, of course), made its way through film development hell, and served as the basis for an expanded set of fictional publications: the multi-authored novels and short stories published as *The Universe of Metro 2033* (fifty-nine volumes and counting).

Though the franchise began in prose, its continual transmedia metamorphoses undermine both traditional logocentrism and Romantic notions of the autonomous author. The online versions of the books appear long before their print publication, giving the chance for readers to comment, make suggestions, and contribute to the franchise's world-building project (through art and music). By contrast, Tolstaya's novel has won a great deal of acclaim, but one would be hard pressed to find *Slynx* fan fiction.

Set only twenty years after a nuclear holocaust (as opposed to *The Slynx*'s two hundred), *Metro 2033* offers more possibilities for the survivors to encounter the remains of the past. The premise is appealingly simple: the survivors of the war have taken refuge in Moscow's vast Metro system, devolving into clans centered around the various stations. Under constant threat from mutated rats and the mysterious Dark Ones (*Chernye*), about whom little is known, they live in a state of continuous military readiness. The novel's hero, Artyom, was rescued from a rat attack as a small child and raised by a man at the Exhibition of the Achievements of the National Economy (VDNKh) station. Now an adult, Artyom meets a mysterious man named Hunter (Khanter), who sends him on a quest to stop the Dark Ones. After a series of adventures and misadventures, Artyom finds his way to Ostankino Tower; from there, he can fire missiles at the Botanical Gardens and destroy the Dark Ones forever. In a twist straight out of Orson Scott Card's *Ender's Game*, Artyom learns that the Dark Ones meant no harm, but his discovery comes too late.

On the whole, *Metro 2033* is much less book-haunted than *The Slynx*—among the many aspects of the novel that could be considered a critique of contemporary Russia is the portrayal of the surviving humans as a largely postliterate society. When the possibility of a powerful, virtually magic book is raised two-thirds of the way through the novel, one could easily dismiss it as just another talisman to be collected in a tale whose structure owed much to video games long before it was adapted into one. The hunt for a particular book (or "Book") owes as much to the novel's concern for Moscow architecture as to anything else: the Book can only be found in the Russian State Library. Whether the library itself has become a source of magic, or whether its mystique is a function of the survivors' ignorance remains unclear. Most of the information about the library is provided by Artyom's traveling companion, Daniel, who approaches his topic with all the reverence of a cargo cultist:

> "The card catalogue," said Daniel quietly, looking around with reverence. "The future can be foretold using these drawers. The initiated

know how. After a ritual, you blindly pick one of the cabinets, then randomly pull on a drawer and take any card. If the ritual is properly performed, then the name of the book will foretell your future, provide a warning, or predict success."

But Daniel's attitude toward the library proves justified, at least as far as the feral librarians are concerned:

> Two grey humped figures emerged from behind the corner of the building he and Daniel were in. They made their way slowly across the courtyard, as if they were searching for something. Suddenly, one of the creatures stopped and raised its head, and Artyom felt as if it was looking directly at the window at which he was standing....
>
> "Librarians?" he whispered with alarm, also squatting so as not to be visible from the street.

They clearly have paranormal abilities, and when they gut Daniel with their bare claws, they somehow read his mind and ventriloquize his words. Typically, Glukhovsky seems to want to have it both ways: to affirm the magic while also indulging in bathos. As Daniel dies, he gives Artyom a "bloodstained pasteboard rectangle ... the card Daniel had taken out of the card catalogue drawer in the vestibule. The card read: 'Shnurkov, N. E., Irrigation and the prospects for agriculture in the Tadzhik SSR. Dushanbe, 1965.' They come to the library in search of a book that tells the future, but only find a bibliographic reference to a maximally irrelevant relic of the past."

Like Tolstaya, Glukhovsky uses his end-times scenario for satirical purposes, transforming the Moscow Metro system into a microcosm of Russian historical, political, and intellectual trends. Here, too, the search for verisimilitude pays few dividends; the bands of survivors at the various stations display an unlikely sense of history and irony. The Ring Line (the Metro's outer belt, which connects with all the other lines) is managed by a coalition of trading partners who call themselves the "Hanseatic League." The Red Line is controlled by unreconstructed communists (naturally); the remaining scientists and intellectuals are called Brahmins; a religious retreat run by fanatics is called the Watchtower; and the majority of Metro society is in conflict with fascists who actually call themselves the Fourth Reich. The agenda behind Metro 2033's taxonomy is not a realist one, nor is it, strictly speaking, science fictional; realism would put a premium on the post-catastrophic order's psychological and political plausibility, while science fiction would apply similar principles in the name of world building. This is not to say that *Metro 2033* does not "work," but it works according to the principles of its author's satirical worldview and agenda, as well as the canons of computer games.

As with *The Slynx*, Glukhovsky's debt to Chernobyl is obvious, but there is a crucial difference. *Metro 2033* situates itself within a particular Russian science fiction tradition, first borrowing from it but then pushing it forward. The world of *Metro 2033* includes the now-ubiquitous "stalkers," men who venture out of the subway system for valuable goods and intelligence. The inspiration is, of course, the Strugatsky brothers' *Roadside Picnic* (Piknik na obochine, 1971) and its adaptation by Andrei Tarkovsky, *Stalker* (1979). Though "stalker" is originally an English word, its use in Russian is quite specific, and it lacks, for example, the connection with sexual predation. When adopted by Glukhovsky for what turned out to be the first international transmedia hit to come out of the former Soviet Union, the stalker becomes a fixture of post-Soviet science fictional adventure, as ubiquitous as the robot was to American Golden Age science fiction. The example of *Metro 2033* inspired another transmedia project that has grown even bigger than Glukhovsky, a work of stalker-like salvage and bricolage that combines all the primary tropes of post-Soviet, post-apocalyptic entertainment: *S.T.A.L.K.E.R.* is a set of Ukrainian-made, Russian-language first-person shooters that have also become a successful series of novels and comics.

Returning to the primal scene of Soviet catastrophe, *S.T.A.L.K.E.R.* unapologetically "borrows" the basic scenario outlined by the Strugatsky brothers and Tarkovsky, but with a crucial difference: now the "zone of exclusion" into which the stalkers venture is not the byproduct of an alien incursion but the aftermath of the Chernobyl disaster. The post-apocalyptic future looks more and more like a nightmare reconstituted out of the Soviet past.

Empire State

The Russian post-apocalypse takes place in the future while subverting any conventional expectation of the future as "progress." The post-apocalyptic future negates forward movement in both time and space. In all of the examples we have looked at, Russia is moving backward and shrinking at the same time. Catastrophes on the scale depicted in these stories are lethal to large-scale state structures, obliging all the survivors to live in a world that is hyperlocal. To the extent that Russia endures, it exists only as far as the eye can see or the legs can walk. From a Putinist point of view, these are tragic visions. It is the state that is the subject and hero of history, particularly of Russian history. At best, the future death of Russian statehood is a Putinist cautionary tale; at worst, it is simply inimical to the values of a system that puts sovereignty above all else.

It should be no surprise that nationalist imaginings of Russia's future are completely different. A positive vision of tomorrow's Russia usually has the trappings of empire. Again and again, Russia's future depends on political hegemony and geographic expansionism. Fortunately, empire (in both its Russian and Eurasianist forms) is one of the most commonly studied themes in post-Soviet F&SF, probably because it is both prevalent and timely. Eurasianism is a particularly productive framework for alternate Russias rooted in significantly different histories. Holm van Zaichik's multivolume *Eurasian Symphony*, for example, is a series of mysteries set in the conjoined "OrdRuss" Empire (a merger of Russia and China), while Pavel Krusanov's *The Angel's Kiss* charts a similarly Eastern path for Russia's imperial development.

Curiously, there are two important overlapping but ideologically contradictory visions of a Russian imperial future that are not based on a particularly Eurasian vision. They turn, instead, to the Russian Middle Ages: Mikhail Yuriev's *The Third Empire* and Vladimir Sorokin's *Day of the Oprichnik*. Less SovPunk than Medieval Punk, these books are an exercise in double extrapolation: they obviously use a medieval framework, but that is in the service of building on then-contemporary political and ideological trends. These two authors' goals are, of course, in complete contradiction with each other. Yuriev imagines a repressive hegemonic medieval Russia as a utopia, part of a grand vision for the world in which there is no room for anything that is not grand. Sorokin, by contrast, has created a dystopia that is as compelling in its own way as *1984*. Yet each is using the same historical and fantastic source material.

There is nothing novel about writing about these two authors together; the commonalities are too obvious to ignore. In the wake of the Russian invasion of Ukraine in 2022, it is *The Third Empire* that has gotten more renewed attention, for, as several critics have noted, the book looks like a pretty precise blueprint for Putin's bloody war and its 2014 antecedent (Ball; Bershidsky; Khapaeva). I would not deny the accuracy of this comparison, but I am always concerned when criticism lapses into the familiar and problematic pattern of analyzing science fiction in terms of how well it predicts the future. The important thing about *The Third Empire* is not that the author somehow got it right, but that he and his ideological opponents correctly laid bare the ideological forces animating Putinism.

As Maria Snegovaya notes, *The Third Empire* is not just medieval futurism; it reflects a set of ideas that have currency in both Russia and the West ("Ukrainskie sobytiia"). *The Third Empire* is a utopia that is medieval in form but Huntingtonian in content. In *The Clash of Civilizations,* Samuel Huntington insisted that, in the wake of the Cold War, history would be driven by the conflicts among civilizations rather than ideologies or nations, primarily the "West" (basically NATO and its partners), Latin America, the Muslim world, the "East" (Asia minus Australia and New Zealand), sub-Saharan Africa, and the Orthodox world. Huntington's thesis is important not for the soundness of his ideas (whose oversimplification, arbitrariness, and underlying racism have been repeatedly demonstrated) but for their appeal and influence.[2] The allure of Huntington is emotional, political, and aesthetic; it is as much a politicized fandom as the Russian Internet denizens who insist that Tolkien's Orcs can be turned into a positive image of Russian power (Borenstein, *Soviet Self-Hatred*). In each case, the best question to be asked is: what is it about that person's worldview that makes these ideas so attractive?

Huntington has proven so popular in Putin's Russia as to suggest a useful adaptation for Huntington's thesis: Putinism is a Huntingtonian civilization. As a work of speculation, *The Clash of Civilizations* is somewhere between geopolitical cosplay and an extended tournament of *Risk*; as a framework influencing leaders of actual countries (let alone nuclear powers), it becomes even more disturbing when the war toys deployed in the game are not, in fact, toys. But for the narrative to truly take hold, it must repeat itself in endless iterations, preferably localized ones. Yuriev's *Third Empire* does the important ideological labor of moving Huntington from political theory (i.e, "science") to the realm of national myth, which is encoded so well in Russian fantasy and science fiction.[3] Once Huntingtonism is Russified by means of the fantasy genre, it can re-enter Russian discourse as an explicitly Russian phenomenon, presenting Huntington's clash of civilizations as an ideological structure that was always already essential to Russian statehood (the medieval past) and crucial to Russia's future (in the Third Empire).

Imperial Bedtime Stories

Is it fair to call Sorokin's *Day of the Oprichnik* a dystopia and *The Third Empire* a utopia, simply based on what is widely known about each author's politics? Perhaps it is fair, but it is not particularly sophisticated. Yuriev, however, includes a number of textual clues for even the not-so-careful reader.

The most obvious clue is that the author does not seem to bother making the book interesting. That is, it has no real characters or plot. Instead, like such classics of the genre as Thomas More's *Utopia*, *The Third Empire* is part travelogue, part history lesson, with the only continuity of character provided by the underdeveloped figure of the narrator. Nineteenth-century utopias would try (often in vain) to improve on this form, grafting on a love plot (*Looking Backward*) or a quasi-legal drama (Charlotte Gilman Perkins's *Herland*), but, if anything, these

---

2. See the contributions to Orsi's volume for some of the most salient critiques of Huntington.

3. Suslov notes that some Russian science fiction writers "inspired by the ideology of Eurasianism and Samuel Huntington's theorization . . . reduce their plotlines to clashes of civilizations" (575).

innovations just showed exactly how poorly the utopian text tends to function as a novel.

Wisely, Yuriev dispenses with the fiction that he is writing, well, fiction (in the sense of having an actual story). Instead, the entire book is a report by a Brazilian who has studied and traveled in the Third Empire, an attempt to explain this fascinating structure to outsiders. This external framework (common to many fantasy novels as well) provides an excuse for the narrative's main task: dumping huge amounts of information on the reader.

This is not to say that the book is without its pleasures; if that were the case, it is unlikely anyone would read it. *The Third Empire* may fall flat when considered as a novel, but it has a great deal going for it when understood as a political tract. Like the utopias of old, Yuriev's book does not have to develop a dry, grounded, theoretical argument while trying to convince his readers to embrace his vision of a better future. Instead, he can describe this future as if it already exists, relieving him of some of the burden of plausibility by letting him simply declare that possibly unlikely events have already happened.

After a brief retelling of the history of the Soviet Union (the Second Empire) and the 1990s that consists of referring to historical figures by monarchical names (Joseph the First; Boris the Cursed) and placing a decidedly pro-totalitarian, antiliberal spin on events, the narrator's tale begins in the time of Vladimir II, the man who will reconstitute the Third Empire. Though he is not actually named, there is no pretense that we are talking about anyone other than Vladimir Putin. The story begins at roughly the same time as the book's publication but extends much further in time. This is a future history of Putin's Russia extrapolating from what was then current events, imagining an apocalyptic scenario, and indulging in a great deal of national imperialist wish-fulfillment fantasy.

During the period of "reforms" and "recovery" (*vosstanovlenie*) that begins in the year of the book's publication, Vladimir II abolishes the oligarchs and begins the process of territorial expansion, eventually including Turkmenistan, Kazakhstan, Belarus, Transnistria, and parts of Abkhazia in a new Russian Union. Everyone is perfectly happy to join the new Union, as they all understand that the collapse of the USSR was not a natural process but the result of US machinations (as were nearly all the terrorist incidents that took place in the post-Soviet space). When his second and constitutionally mandated final term as presidency comes to an end in 2008, Vladimir II remains in power in this successor to the Russian Federation.

He reminds his subjects that Russia has always been "a separate, ancient, and self-sufficient civilization," one where status is more important than money and where "personal success" cannot give life meaning (61). The renewed pride in all things Russian extends to the pettiest of details, from the calendar (back to the

Julian system!) to motor vehicles (no longer will the automobile-driving population face the indignity of license plates using Latin rather than Cyrillic letters!).

Still, Vladimir merely lays the groundwork for his successor, Gavril the Great. Gavril wins the presidency in 2012 and holds a successful referendum transforming the Russian Union into the Third Russian Empire, under a system of governance to which we will return shortly. As a result of the West's overreactions to Gavril's foreign policy (and his decision to stop selling gas to Europe), Russia and NATO go to war. Thanks to the superiority of the Russian military and the convenient discovery of new types of weaponry with no basis in scientific fact, the war lasts twelve days, ending in the total capitulation of the United States.

And this is where the wish-fulfillment fantasy truly comes to the fore, as Gavril arranges a parade in honor of Russia's great victory:

> [A] plane carried America's elites arrested especially for this occasion (and sent back home and released the very next day) to be displayed on Red Square: President Bush III [Jeb] and former Presidents Bill Clinton, Bush Jr. [W] and Hillary Clinton, the current and former members of the cabinet, congress, and senate, along with bankers and industrialists, newspaper columnists and television anchors, famous lawyers and top models, pop singers and Hollywood actresses. They all paraded across Red Square in handcuffs with nametags around their necks—everyone except the military prisoners, who walked with full honors. The Russian authorities let their citizens and the whole world understand that Russia fought and defeated not the American army, but American civilization. (106)

Russia's 2014 and 2022 invasions of Ukraine, which the leadership has insisted on casting as a proxy between Russian and the West, make it difficult to read *The Third Empire* as mere fiction. But Yuriev's novel was by no means the only one to imagine an East/West final battle taking place on Russia's western border. What really stands out is, instead, the text's sheer joy in every instance of advancing even the smallest element of what might be called "Russianness," while imagining a humiliating conquest of the West that is so spectacular as to be virtually pornographic. This, perhaps, is the aspect of *The Third Empire* that truly warrants praise for its prophecy: the atmosphere of intense *ressentiment* and xenophobic fury that it shares with Russia during the "special military operation."

Yuriev's vision of the Third Empire requires a complete reorganization of the planet along two guiding principles: gigantism and medievalism. Medievalism characterizes the empire itself, while gigantism encompasses both the empire and the rest of the world. Both principles reflect an imagination that is as limited as it is imperialist. The Third Empire's medieval structure is the source of the book's fame (or notoriety, depending on one's political affiliations). The book takes place in the future, but this is a future based on a scientific and social speculation that can only be called impoverished. Scientific progress certainly exists, but it consists of futuristic technology whose sole purpose is to dispel the obvious concerns about the empire's feasibility. How does the empire defeat the West? It creates a superweapon. How does the state ensure that those responsible for maintaining order are trustworthy rather than corrupt? Russian scientists invent a process called a "tech interrogation" (*tekhnodpros*) that uses an infallible truth serum. These inventions are brought into the narrative not as a result of extrapolation from scientific trends but as convenient ways to dispense with two of the most common utopian conundrums: how we get from here to there (answer: miraculous scientific weapons!); and, to paraphrase Juvenal and Alan Moore, "Who watches the watchmen?" (answer: drugs!).

All technological innovations in the novel are in the service of making the Third Empire's New Medievalism possible. Yuriev's future entails rejecting virtually every feature developed by liberal democracy since the Enlightenment; indeed, it rejects the Enlightenment itself. There can be no state institutions that are in any way based on regularly assessing the will of the people as a whole because the polity itself is redefined. First, Gavril convinces a willing Russian populace to abolish the presidency in favor of an imperial autocracy, somehow using this one last popular vote to set up an institution whose authority would no longer be beholden to the will of the people. This is not without precedent. The Romanov dynasty began with the election of the new tsar by a national assembly of nobles in 1613. Yuriev, however, creates a polity that is not rooted in nobility. Instead, the Third Empire is based on a very narrow slice of medieval Russian history: the oprichnina.

The oprichnina, which lasted for only seven years in the mid-sixteenth century, looms large over Russian history. Instituted by Ivan the Terrible at the height of his paranoia, the oprichnina was a response to his conviction that the aristocracy was plotting to overthrow him. The oprichnina was both a territory administered under different rules from the rest of Russia and the system that made this territory possible. Ivan wanted to be free of what he felt were the onerous restrictions that prevented him from prosecuting the traitors he was sure surrounded him. The result was a reign of terror against nobles he accused of treason, conducted by a special guard unit (the oprichniks) that reported directly to him. Where liberals see the oprichnina as the earliest instantiation of the repressive forces that periodically dominate throughout Russian history, conservatives and traditionalists view the oprichnina as the kind of extralegal force for truth and justice that can prosper only in a harmonious, undemocratic system unconstrained by petty procedure. In the face of widespread corruption and self-interest, the oprichnina is a model for dispensing with the complexities of liberal institutions that promise fairness but cannot deliver.

This is one of the main aspects of the oprichnina that Yuriev develops in *The Third Empire*: the new oprichnina is a set of anti-institutional institutions. Nothing about the system Yuriev describes would reassure the individual looking for procedural guarantees of justice and fairness. Instead, the reintroduction of what is essentially an estate system treats people in their aggregates, according to the category in which they are classified. This is certainly the case with the nations the Third Empire eventually conquers. Everyone's status after incorporation within the empire depends on their national/ethnic classification, with little room for exceptions on an individual basis. *The Third Empire* even returns to Stalinist notions of collective justice, with entire peoples being exiled and resettled according to imperial policy. In the case of the oprichniks, this is the class of people who are allowed to vote and take part in political life but accept other restrictions to their personal liberty for the sake of the imperial good. The lack of consideration for the individual is precisely the sort of thing that one would expect from *The Third Empire* if it were a dystopia, but the book's nature as an antiliberal, antidemocratic utopia renders individualism alien and undesirable.

This emphasis on the group over the individual is not simply a rejection of liberalism; it is something that replicates itself throughout *The Third Empire* on every scale. In Yuriev's utopia, size is everything. The empire has no patience for dealing with small political or national units. This is where Yuriev's Huntingtonism comes in. The entire world ends up divided into megastates, empires whose internal composition and political structure may differ vastly from those of the Third Empire but share with it the aesthetic and ideology of gigantism that animates the book. The Americas are reconstituted as a supra-national state united by cultural and religious ties, while most of Europe becomes part of the Third Empire. The Vatican moves to North America, which is now primarily Catholic thanks to the subsuming of Protestantism back into the Catholic Church. Protestantism, with its proliferation of squabbling churches and doctrinal differences, has no place in this new world order. The Islamic Khalifate, the Indian Confederation, and the Celestial Republic (i.e., China) round out the rest of the globe.

Yuriev's neomedieval vision is civilizational, categorical, and antithetical to the varieties of pluralism that have no place in his vision of empire. What *The Third Empire* offers is a simple world, where deviation from the principle that guides a given civilization is at best superfluous and at worst pernicious. This is not a Soviet future; even if we consider the Soviet Union to be an empire, it was built on the careful curation of accepted categories of difference, such as nationality and language. But it is consistent with the kind of nostalgia that sees the

Soviet past as proof against corruption, and as a time when people were united by a common ideal. As Marielle Wijermars explains, "The oprichnina [according to its adherents], able to cleanse the political system in a way that the system itself cannot, can move the state from its current state of degradation and stagnation towards innovation" (176).

New Medievalism, like Soviet nostalgia, is a rejection of politics as such, imagining a harmonious world governed by a shared understanding of the social good. It is a huge gamble, sacrificing any possibility for individual recourse or institutional checks and balances in favor of a system that will somehow inherently foster justice. Who needs politics when you can make a blind leap of faith?

The Executioner's Song

In *Day of the Oprichnik*, Vladimir Sorokin builds a world on roughly the same premise as *The Third Empire*, with a critical difference: *Day of the Oprichnik* would be hard to mistake for a utopia.[4] Sorokin could not have been responding to Yuriev; if anything, he is indebted to *Beyond the Thistle* (Za chertopolokhom), a 1927 novel by the former White General Pyotr Krasnov that describes an isolated, monarchic, quasi-medieval post-Soviet future.[5] Yet whatever their authors' intentions or awareness of each other might have been, Sorokin and Yuriev's books are now forever in dialogue with each other.

Yuriev's Brazilian narrator provides a bird's-eye view of the customs of *The Third Empire*, a book that, besides him, has no characters at all (unless one counts the various emperors). He covers decades of history and replicates the empire's own sensibility by focusing on groups rather than individuals. *The Day of the Oprichnik* takes the opposite approach: not only is the eponymous oprichnik, Andrei Komiaga, the first-person narrator, but, in a nod to Alexander Solzhenitsyn's Gulag classic, *One Day in the Life of Ivan Denisovich*, the action unfolds over a single twenty-four-hour period. Where *The Third Empire* is essentially a six-hundred-page info dump, *Day of the Oprichnik* parcels out information about its world at a slow pace, interspersed with both the action of the novel and the thoughts of its protagonist. The result is that, in addition to being the ideological antipode of *The Third Empire*, *Day of the Oprichnik* is aesthetically and

---

4. Hard, but not impossible. Marina Aptekman finds in Boris Sokolov a quotation by "the leader of the Union of Orthodox Oprichniks, Iosif Volotskii . . . : Finally Vladimir Sorokin has written a very good book. It will show everyone how we should treat the enemies of Russia" ("Old New Russian," 283).

5. On the connection between the two books, see Aptekman, "Forward to the Past."

generically as far from Yuriev's work as possible. *Day of the Oprichnik* immerses its readers in Komiaga's consciousness and lived experience, resulting in something novel in every sense of the word.

Perhaps the most novel aspect of *Day of the Oprichnik* is its refusal to follow either the utopian or the dystopian master plot. As Gary Saul Morson argues in *The Boundaries of Genre,* both narrative types replicate the structure of the Allegory of the Cave from Plato's *Republic* (88–92). These stories are typically epistemological quests, with the protagonist of the dystopia usually starting out as a true believer who, over the course of the novel, comes to realize the flaws of his (and it is usually his) world before joining the resistance.

This is precisely what Komiaga does *not* do. It would have been an easy task to tell the story of the victims of oprichnik terror and gain the reader's sympathy. Nor would it have been that difficult to imagine an oprichnik who grows to doubt the rules of the empire. Instead, Sorokin invites (or perhaps forces) identification with a very happy and successful torturer who is as loyal to the regime on the last page as he is on the first. *Day of the Oprichnik* is where dystopia collides with styob. Styob, as we recall from chapter 3, is the deliberate overidentification with the object of satire. The novel seduces and repulses at the same time, trapping us in the consciousness of a narrator whom most of us would find morally repugnant, but who here becomes something more complicated.

The key to that complication is violence, which is the cornerstone of both Sorokin's imaginary Russian future and Yuriev's medieval utopia. Yuriev does not shy away from violence, but he does not dwell on it. It is simply a necessity for the just operations of the Third Empire, and any qualms about its victims are simply the expression of a sentimentality that is detrimental to the administration of justice. Violence has always been at the heart of Sorokin's work, so its centrality to *Day of the Oprichnik* is no surprise. Just as his pre-1991 writings focus on physical aggression, rape, murder, and cannibalism to expose the true moral underpinnings of the Soviet system, *Day of the Oprichnik* forces the reader to understand that this kind of medieval/Eurasianist fantasy is inevitably founded on the callous destruction of human bodies. In one of the novel's best offhand jokes, Komiaga's ring tone is the sound of a man being tortured (a detail exploited to great effect in the Russian audiobook version).

Komiaga's day starts with the actual inflicting of physical violence. First, he and his men fight the servants of a disgraced nobleman ("Crack! Crack! The ribs fracture" [17]), hang the nobleman, and then brutally rape his widow ("Important work. Necessary work. Good work" [24]). As a reward, the leader of the oprichniks gives them a drug that lets them fantasize intensely about the kind of violence they have just committed:

> I stare and find the first foul creature a forty-two-year-old man wedged in a wardrobe I set the wardrobe on fire; . . .
>
> I find two children two little girls six and seven hiding under the bed under the wide bed I drench the bed in a wide stream the bed burns the pillows flame the blanket they can't stand it they scramble out from under the bed run to the door I send a fan of fire after them they run . . .
>
> my faithful flaming skewer into her narrow womb I send it and its might fills her trembling womb, my flaming skewer fills it she howls inhuman cries and slowly my fiery flaming skewer begins to fuck her to fuck her to fuck fuckfuckfuckfuckfuckfuckfuckfuckfuck. (83)

Granted, few would look at this scene and imagine it as the basis for a positive political program, but the implications are ideological through and through. In a feudalist future inspired by both the medieval past and the increasingly authoritarian present, brutality is the essence of the state's work. Neomedievalists, Eurasianists, and monarchists all share the fantasy of a state where bureaucracy and proceduralism are replaced by a mythic harmony between the ruler and the ruled. Sorokin's novel is a savage response to this romantic reactionary idyll. The oprichniks are the violent state's version of the bureaucrat. Instead of pushing paper, they push people.

But they also push each other. The brotherhood of the oprichikniks is cemented by a ritual that Batya (the leader) arranges for them at midnight. After the men all strip naked and enter the banya, they each take a drug that gives them erections and makes their genitals glow. In a logistically dubious but decidedly evocative arrangement, the men all engage in group anal sex in a single line, each entering the man in front of him while being entered by the man behind him. This "caterpillar," as they call it, ends with the serial climax of every man involved. When it is over, Komiaga thinks:

> Wisely, oh so wisely, Batya arranged everything with the caterpillar. Before it, everyone broke off in pairs, and the shadow of dangerous disorder lay across the oprichnina. Now there's a limit to the pleasures of the steam. We work together, and take our pleasure together. And the tablets help. And wisest of all is that the young oprichniks are always stuck at the tail of the caterpillar. This is wise for two reasons: first of all, the young ones know their place in the oprichnik hierarchy; second, the seed moves from the tail of the caterpillar to the head, which symbolizes

the eternal cycle of life and the renewal of our brotherhood. On the one hand, the young respect the old; on the other, they replenish them. That's our foundation. And thank God. (173)

In addition to exposing the obvious homoeroticism in a violent, all-male militaristic organization that routinely rapes women to punish men, this scene reinforces the novel's presentation of an isolated, self-absorbed Russia whose future is always about its past. Where the traditional symbol of a recursive Russia is the matryoshka doll (a smaller version of the doll within each larger version) this feminine, fertility-based image is replaced by aggressive, recursive homosexual bonding. This is not Russia as a circle but, consistent with the architecture of the novel's empire (walled off from Europe), Russia as a linear barrier. It is a perfectly self-enclosed, hierarchical system based on penetration and submission. Where Yuriev answers the classic anti-utopian question of responsible self-governance by appealing to innate harmony (plus infallible truth drugs), Sorokin implicitly rephrases the question to be about power and dominance rather than responsibility. Not "Who's watching the watchmen?" but "Who's fucking the watchmen?" This is the fundamental problem of autarky: inevitably, the country is fucking itself.

It Gets Better

Sorokin's future is a deliberately uninviting one; Yuriev's might resonate with more people, but it requires readers to wade through hundreds of pages of plotless pseudo-history. *The Third Empire*, however, is not the only "positive" view of a future Russia circulating in the literary world on the Internet. Given the prevalence of post-apocalyptic entertainment throughout the world in general and Russia in particular, a backlash against this grim pessimism was only to be expected. But the campaign for positivity was not without controversy. On June 9, 2021, Konstantin Syomin (Semin) posted a brief video to his AgitProp YouTube channel. Five months later, it had been viewed 47,807 times (as of December 11, 2021) and received 877 comments (nearly all made within a few days of its posting). The volume of response is actually on the lower side for Syomin. A popular journalist who initially made his reputation on the liberal-leaning *Vesti* news program, he has since become a Marxist with strong nationalist leanings. AgitProp, which started as a broadcast on Russia-24 in 2014, moved entirely to YouTube in 2019 after a falling out with the station's management.[6] The channel, which has

---

6. Short for "agitation and propaganda," agitprop is a term that dates back to the early Soviet days, referring to the use of popular media to make the case for communism.

136,000 subscribers, touches hot-button issues such as Belarusian protests, the opposition figure Alexei Navalny, and the rapper Oxxxymiron.

This particular video was devoted to a niche issue, directed explicitly at fellow leftists, but with the F&SF community implicated as well: "Why Is the Image of the Radiant Future Useless for AgitProp?" Syomin situates himself within what he calls an "ongoing argument" among "YouTubers, bloggers, and propagandists," with his comments occasioned by the recent release of an animated video imagining a prosperous USSR in the year 2040 (more on that in a bit). Syomin sees little point in such exercises:

> The very idea of competing with liberals or fascists on this level by trying to paint a picture of paradise strikes me as incorrect, because [to get there] there will be a revolution . . . which means that prior to [the revolution] there will be a period of terrible, awful upheaval, with struggle, loss . . . This heavenly image that we are collectively trying to convey is . . . a deception . . . People will be pushed toward socialism not by the dream of a wonderful, happy, and prosperous life but by the realization that the disgusting, horrifying, intolerable reality can't go on. Because the natural world has been ruined, because of poverty, hunger, illness, war, and unemployment. These are the horses of the apocalypse to come, when it becomes clear that the fork in the road between socialism and barbarism is unavoidable. There will be a choice between barbarism or socialism, and we must agitate for nonbarbarism.

In rejecting the very idea of optimistic futurism, Syomin manages to be both in and out of step with his time. An aesthetic preference for a dismal future would situate him within the mainstream of public taste in both Russia and the West. In the battle between what young adult authors Holly Black and Justine Larbaleister called "Zombies vs. Unicorns" (the title of their tongue-in-cheek anthology), horror and destruction beat rainbows and puppy dogs nine times out of ten.[7] But when we shift to politics, the ground beneath us shifts as well. How many fans of *The Walking Dead* view the television show or comic as a compelling roadmap for a future they wish to build? The (post)apocalypse is a nice place to (vicariously) visit, but few people really want to live there.

The occasion for Syomin's brief tirade was a curious target. Produced by the popular collective *Dumai sam, dumai seichas* (Think for Yourself, Think Now, henceforth abbreviated as DSDS), "2045: Episode 1: The Revelations of a Former Millionaire" was released on YouTube on May 1, 2021 (International Workers'

---

7. So much so that ironic positivity becomes the stuff of subcultures, like the "Brony" phenomenon, in which adult men profess to be avid fans of *My Little Pony*.

Day), and viewed over 189,000 times as of December 15, 2021 (with 17,000 likes and zero dislikes). DSDS's most popular videos make the studio's political orientation clear: "Bound to Wake Up: Class Dream of Humanity" (1 million views) and "The Real Stalin" (972,000 views; spoiler alert: the Real Stalin was a hero, slandered by Khrushchev and counterrevolutionaries). A typical DSDS video combines midlevel video-game style animation with a polemical voiceover to bring simple, communist truths to the viewer. "2045," however, is a bit different.

"2045" features retrofuturist bombast (enormous statues of cosmonauts, etc.) and a touching, if nonsensical, combination of Soviet realia with fantastic high-tech (walking, talking vending machines offering passersby Soviet-style soft drinks by the glass). Syomin is certainly correct in identifying "2045" as anodyne, if not kitschy, although there is an implication of unrest, if not bloodshed, in the past: the second socialist revolution took place in 2029. But somehow, in just sixteen years, the new Eurasian Alliance has achieved miracles. A news broadcaster tells his viewers (who would, presumably, already know these facts) that rates of tuberculosis and sexually transmitted diseases have plummeted, and that life expectancies are skyrocketing thanks to the revival of two staples of early Soviet health propaganda: a "sober lifestyle" and "physical culture" (cue a brief animation of happy, healthy citizens doing group calisthenics). Even (physical) disabilities are being "solved": soon any citizen who needs a bionic limb will receive a fully functional one at no cost.

The video's paper-thin plot tracks the postrevolutionary life of a former oligarch. In 2029, he fully capitulated to the new regime, gave over all his assets, and rehabilitated himself as an ordinary worker in an auto factory. Even in his retirement, he still insists on working. In addition, he has a popular video blog called "Planting with the Oligarch" (the title is a pun referring to both planting seeds and sending someone to prison). The bulk of this thirty-minute video is devoted to an interview with the protagonist, Upyrev (a name that comes from the Russian word for vampire, as if to suggest that he was born to be a capitalist bloodsucker). He readily admits that his old life as a capitalist, while glamorous, was founded on exploitation and misery, and he has nothing but praise for the new world.

Any viewer looking for signs of brainwashing or duress is bound to be disappointed. Voiced by an actor with the velvet tones of a kindly grandfather from central casting, Upyrev is the picture of contentment. In this regard, he fits in perfectly with his surroundings: soporific background music and long, wordless shots of the new Soviet Union's majestic architecture. "2045: Episode 1," with its beatifically smiling old man and montages of happy people somehow manages to combine retrocommunist imagery with the kitschy stylings of a late-night commercial for adult diapers.

If the comments are any indication, however, DSDS knows exactly how to inspire its target audience. "Ellen Ripley" writes, "Thank you, it brought me to tears, this is what we've been missing for so long: an image of the future, the radiant future!" Bomberfoxx comments: "Now this is something that's worth dying in battle for. Thank you, authors!" Zarina Dzotsieva agrees: "Finally, positive video material from communists! Thanks, it's great!" These commenters, along with the thousands of other viewers who upvoted the video, are evaluating it according to criteria that have little in common with those of its critic, Syomin, even though they are all presumably on the same side.

Syomin frames agitational art in general, and "2045" in particular, in terms of its effectiveness as a tool of persuasion, where the viewers are reacting in their capacity as an audience that needs no persuasion. One might then conclude that DSDS is preaching to the choir, but the viewers' enthusiasm shows the limits of Syomin's critique. In terms of the revolution that both Syomin and the viewers seem to revere, Syomin's view of art is more Menshevik: agitational art must enlighten the ignorant and convert the skeptical. Meanwhile, the commenters implicitly understand the value of inspiring the smaller vanguard of conscious revolutionary supporters. Like a fight song, videos such as "2045" rev up the enthusiasm of the people already on your side.

Syomin's normally loyal audience flooded the comments section with objections. One commenter using the name "Andrei Kapitan" succinctly expressed the view shared by most of his YouTube comrades: "We need an image of the future! Otherwise, it's not clear where to go and what to strive for!" The debate quickly spilled over from Syomin's YouTube page and onto various VKontakte and LiveJournal pages.

2061: A Frederic Jameson Odyssey

Syomin's audience, while clearly literate in science fiction, overlaps with fandom only partly. In rejecting a radiant future, however, he drew the ire of a set of ideological comrades for whom the literary and artistic representation of a twenty-first-century Soviet utopia is of crucial importance: the editorial team behind the *USSR-2061* project. I'll be going into much more detail about their work in a bit; for now, though, it is their polemic with Syomin that is important.

In a LiveJournal post titled "An Image of the Future Is Unnecessary?" by kpt_flint on June 12 (three days after Syomin's video), one of the founders of *USSR-2061* takes apart Syomin's argument step by step. Why, he asks, should the steady immiseration of everyday life be the only argument? The standard of living in the USSR rose steadily before perestroika, but people still turned away from socialism toward capitalism. And if we don't paint a picture of the future, our enemies will.

Ultimately, kpt_flint argues for the power of the imagination: "In order to build [a better] world, we must first understand what exactly we want to build... For that, we need red science fiction and red futurology. Honest, thoughtful, and scientific."

kpt_flint casts the political argument as a struggle between genres. Dystopian fiction has tended to be more entertaining, but he is unwilling to write off utopianism as both political program and fictional genre. Yes, the radiant future easily descends into a set of familiar clichés (which is why kpt_flint and his partner in the *USSR-2061* project are at such pains to steer participants clear of a whole host of aesthetic and political sins), but that only means that imagining a convincing utopia takes much more work than churning out the latest variation on *1984* or *Brave New World*. Pessimism is easy; optimism is not for the lazy or the faint of heart.

At the beginning of this chapter, I claimed that after the Cold War, the West inherited the discursive tools for imagining the future. The polemics occasioned by "2045: Episode 1" remind us that this custody battle is as much about Left and Right as it is about East and West. After 1989/1991, what avenues remained for imagining an alternative to an increasingly hegemonic neoliberal capitalism? In a much more reader-friendly fashion, the Marxist kpt_flint is making largely the same argument as the critic Frederic Jameson, particularly in his *Archaeologies of the Future*.

Best known as one of North America's foremost Marxist literary theorists, Jameson is also an accomplished scholar of science fiction. *Archaeologies of the Future*, in addition to being a comprehensive typology of American postwar science fiction, takes as its project the aesthetic and political rehabilitation of utopia and utopianism. As both genre and political theory, utopia has long been the whipping boy of sophisticated critics. Marxism, with its explicit refutation of utopianism (despite its obvious utopian elements), rendered utopian socialism passé, while the excess of communist regimes in the twentieth century have fueled the long-standing conservative critique of leftism as naïvely utopian in its understanding of 'human nature." If anything, the fate of utopia in literature has been even more dismal. As Gary Saul Morson (no friend to utopians or leftists) puts it, utopia and the novel are opposites. Utopias are tendentious, plotless, and boring almost by definition. Utopias are analogous to the "all happy families" Tolstoy invokes in the first line of *Anna Karenina*; we may want our family to be happy, but it is the unhappy family that will keep us reading over the course of several hundreds of pages.

Jameson does not try to pretend that the utopian classics are more interesting than they seem, though he does champion modern novels whose utopian aspirations are not an obstacle to reading pleasure. Utopianism is particularly redeemed in his reading of Kim Stanley Robinson's *Red Mars* trilogy, about the settling and transformation of our neighboring planet. Robinson populates Mars with complex, flawed, and believable characters who often violently disagree about the proper course of action but still manage to create a society that is, if not perfect, far closer to perfection than anything the Earth has ever seen. Utopia for Robinson is a process, not a place, as Jameson explains: "What is Utopian becomes, then, not the commitment to a specific machinery or blueprint, but rather the commitment to imagining possible Utopias as such, in their greatest variety of forms. Utopia is no longer the invention and defense of a specific floorplan, but rather the story of all the arguments about how Utopia should be constructed in the first place. It is no longer the exhibit of an achieved Utopian construct, but rather the story of its production and of the very process of construction as such" (217).

With its focus on utopia-in-the-making, Robinson's trilogy is an unusually successful example of a compelling engagement with utopian thought. Even in works that do not share Robinson's focus on process, however, Jameson sees utopia as a crucial exercise in political imagination: "The Utopian form itself is the answer to the universal ideological conviction that no alternative is possible, that there is no alternative to the system. But it asserts this by forcing us to think the break itself, and not by offering a more traditional picture of what things would be like after the break" (232). Or, in the words of Ursula K. Le Guin in her speech at the 2014 National Book Awards, "We live in capitalism. Its power seems inescapable. So did the divine right of kings. Any human power can be resisted and changed by human beings. Resistance and change often begin in art, and very often in our art, the art of words."

Though Jameson is writing specifically about science fiction, his defense of utopia, particularly in light of the online arguments about Russia's radiant future, should push the reader in the direction of SF's most famous allied genre (despite Jameson's own apparent lack of interest in it): fantasy. Or rather, the multiple meanings carried by the genre's name. Perhaps the argument over utopia is a proxy for a larger debate about fantasy itself? "Fantasy" also connotes "imagination" (in Russian, the two meanings are divided between two very similar words, *fantastika* and *fantaziia*, along with the more recently imported term for epic fantasy, *fentezi*), while for Freud, fantasy can refer to either something desired or something dreaded. Jameson subtitles his book "The Desire Called Utopia, and Other Science Fictions"; might utopia and dystopia map onto Freud's positive and negative fantasies?

What is at stake in the post-Soviet Russian fantasies of a Soviet future (and perhaps in their shadow, the coming apocalyptic hellscape), is the function and value of this kind of imaginative play. What does the Soviet future fantasy actually *do*? Is it a form of banal entertainment, an opiate for the nostalgic post-Soviet masses? A call to action? A productive exercise of the political imagination? A return of repressed anxiety and desire?

For that, we must look at both the *USSR-2061* project and the broader aesthetic phenomenon sometimes called SovPunk.

SovPunk, Indirectly

Depending on just how online one is, SovPunk is either a marginal phenomenon that sounds vaguely familiar or a useful term for a style that is all over the Internet but is only just taking shape as a primarily visual trend. Also called "Sovietpunk," the word usually refers to the deployment of Soviet aesthetic signifiers in futuristic or apocalyptic settings.

The term jumped the species barrier from online chatter to highbrow fiction with the publication of Aleksei Salnikov's book *Indirectly* (Oposredovanno [2018/2019]).[8] *Indirectly* is the third novel by this Yekaterinburg-based author, whose star has been steadily rising. His second novel, *The Petrovs in and around the Flu*, was awarded two of Russia's most prestigious literary prizes in 2018 (NOS and the National Bestseller), adapted for the stage twice, and made into a film by the leading director Kirill Serebrennikov in 2021. While I have no statistics on readership, it is safe to say that a new release by Salnikov is guaranteed attention from Russian intellectuals.

Indirectly gets to the idea of SovPunk . . . indirectly. The novel is set in an alternate world that is fundamentally the same as ours but with one major distinction: poems are considered a narcotic. The book's last chapter features a conversation with one of the supporting characters, Dmitry, a writer who another character claims has recently given up the fantasy (*fentezi*) genre to which he had dedicated his career. But Dmitry explains that he has not given up on fantasy at all:

> It's just that one day I was reading one of our contemporary classics and suddenly realized that they're writing fantasy, just like me. It's just the genre hasn't been named yet; to myself, I've been calling it "sovpunk";

---

8. Here I am following Lisa Hayden's lead ("Big Wheel Effect") in my translation of this title. *Oposredovanno* first appeared in the journal *Volga* in 2018, before being published by the prestigious Redaktsiia Elena Shubinoi as a separate book the following year.

that is, there's cyberpunk, steampunk, and in Russia we now have the sovpunk genre, and not only in Russia. There's light sovpunk, which borrows the Odessa film studio aesthetic whole cloth; there's dark sovpunk, which is dominant, and it's the basis for a whole host of things, like a gross political officer harassing a lady, bullying her family one after another, and then it's payback time, or he bullies an engineer out of envy, does something awful, then there's the barking of the Gulag German shepherds... People just put their heroes in this prefab scenery and use these plots, moving between the camps, the factory... the communal apartment and the party meeting, an endless board game, where you already know what the book is, because it's like the Conan series, which has had shitloads of sequels slapped onto it... There are lots of subgenres, like soft sovpunk without camps, but with some intellectual's travails, and he's surrounded by such thugs, such thugs!

Presumably Salnikov got the word "sovpunk" from the Internet, in which case his distortion of the term is probably willful. Salnikov's comparison of SovPunk to steampunk and cyberpunk makes sense, but it is clear that he is interpreting them all primarily as historically inflected styles: if it looks Victorian, it's steampunk; if it looks futuristic, it's cyberpunk; and if it looks Soviet, it's SovPunk. Salnikov's SovPunk is the opposite of the phenomenon as it's generally understood. Rather than taking place in the present or future, his SovPunk is closer to historical fiction, and its preoccupation with misery resembles that of 1990s' *chernukha*. In *Indirectly,* SovPunk is the antithesis of the rosy Soviet nostalgia that has taken hold in the twenty-first century. If it describes a literary trend, it is the liberal intellectual response to two decades of soft-peddling Stalinism. His SovPunk would fit Guzel Yakhina's dekulakization novel, *Zuleikha*, and its 2020 television adaptation, even as the actual SovPunk on the Internet would be much more acceptable to *Zuleikha*'s many detractors (who condemned the novel and the series as exaggerations of Stalin's crimes).

Salnikov's displacement of SovPunk to the past highlights what is actually at stake: the extent to which Soviet history says something about Russia today and can serve as a model for Russia tomorrow. Like it or not, the Soviet Union now *matters*. Though the fantasy writer in *Indirectly* dwells much more on the negative, he does mention SovPunk's "light" variety, which means that really any story that seems to go out of its way to immerse the reader in Soviet realia is SovPunk, regardless of any given ideological spin. This is Salnikov's own "fantasy" of SovPunk; to borrow a phrase from the Brezhnev era, "actually existing SovPunk" tends to be both "light" *and* aggressively pro-Soviet. Salnikov's apparently deliberate misprision of SovPunk in *Indirectly* nevertheless does valuable work, however indirectly. Salnikov's version of SovPunk renders it a form of wish fulfillment or sympathetic magic. The important thing is not the ideological content but the simple fact of the reconstruction of the Soviet Union in the realm of the imagination. This version of SovPunk, then, is an aesthetic variation on the work of the Citizens of the USSR from chapter 3: a recreation of a lost world through the assertion of sheer will.

The Red Cape Diaries

It took over a decade of evolution and mutation in the memetic stew of the Internet before SovPunk made its way to old media, through Salnikov's novel. Perhaps this is how it earns its "punk" label: dredging up the analog visual culture of a world marked by a notoriously restrictive information regime, only to let it prosper on what used to be the free-for-all of post-Soviet cyberspace. Sovietpunk (as it was more commonly called) first appeared on an obscure forum before finding new homes on VKontakte, YouTube, and Reddit. In all these spaces, SovPunk is marginal, but its proponents often use it to lay claim to more mainstream post-Soviet pleasures, from well-known video games and transmedia franchises (such as *S.T.A.L.K.E.R.*) to hit TV series (*Chernobyl: Exclusion Zone*, of course) and even, stretching the aesthetic ties to their breaking point, the blockbuster cartoon *Masha and the Bear*. In other words, SovPunk is actually popular, but the people who like it don't know that this is what they're seeing.

In October 2015, a LiveJournal user going by the handle "siesit siesit" posted a brief history of Sovietpunk ("Chto takoe Sovetpank"), which was then rewritten and republished a few months later (without attribution) on the Russian Orthodox website eparkhia.ru ("Sovetpank kak forma"). (The eparkhia.ru version has the advantage of being more compact, but the LiveJournal post has more illustrations.) siesit siesit traces Sovietpunk back to the now-moribund forum lomasm.ru, which hosted a discussion in 2007 about creating a thread for fans of the USSR. Their initial name for this community, "Union Maniac" (Soiuz man'iak), was perhaps too ambiguous (and too aggressive); siesit siesit claims that the "Union Maniac" aesthetic was obviously a real phenomenon, but the term describes a person rather than a set of tastes. "Sovietpunk" and "SovPunk" would prove more useful and appropriate.

siesit siesit divided Sovietpunk into three categories: style, genre, and history. "Style" concerns mostly illustrations and video games; anything that reproduces Soviet realia in its background ends up counting as Sovietpunk. Most of the examples he cites could simply be chalked up to Soviet nostalgia (which, indeed, he sees as the foundation of all varieties of Sovietpunk), with one intriguing exception: the now-defunct Internet meme featuring a superhero called "The Red Cape" (Krasnyi plashch').[9] A character implies something more than a mere style; a character might have a story. Granted, the Red Cape memes do not pretend to form anything like a coherent narrative, but at the very least, the Red Cape functions as a folk hero with a set of traits making him recognizable from one meme to the next.

For a character who emerged from a Soviet nostalgia forum, the Red Cape has a surprising tendency toward political ambiguity. To begin with, his appearance is less heroic than it is off-putting. We only see him from the waist up, a Soviet flag draped across his shoulders and a green gas mask covering his head. He is as far from the smiling, spandex-clad classic superheroes of North American comics as could be. In real life, his presence would likely cause panic ("Why is he wearing a gas mask, and how can I get one?").[10] Surrounded by the trappings of Soviet life, he is both a throwback to another time and a visitor from a post-apocalyptic future.

No matter the subject, all the Red Cape memes are too ironic to be taken entirely at face value. In one of the rare memes based on a drawing rather than a photo, a young Red Cape is walking with his mother and father, all three wearing the familiar gas mask, accompanied by a text that rhymes in Russian ("His parents raised / The Red Cape, / Following the precepts of Ilich" [Lenin]) (lomasm, "Sleduia zavetam"). In another, the Red Cape examines a map of the United States placed on top of a drawing of a mushroom cloud: "Ah, Comrade Kurchatov, where are you when we need you?—the Red Cape" (Kurchatov was the father of the Soviet atomic bomb) (siesit siesit, "Gde zhe ty"). In a third, he looks out over a bleak urban landscape and thinks, "Every day, life is getting more joyous!" (lomasm, "Vse radostnee zhit'). Even the Red Cape's alleged heroism is more humorous than serious. One meme has the Red Cape sitting alone at his kitchen table, resting his head against one hand while staring down at an empty plate and a bottle of vodka: "The Red Cape spent the whole day saving the Soviet Union. And now he's a little depressed" (siesit siesit, "Chet priunyl").

If this is nostalgia for the good old days of the Soviet Union, it is a nostalgia that must always take a back seat to irony. Much of the pleasure to be found in

---

9. Or maybe not so heroic. I have been unable to access the complete gallery of Red Cape memes included on siesit siesit's page; my Internet provider classifies the website as malware. Fortunately, the Red Cape has a VKontakte page (with only four members, including siesit siesit). It seems likely that whoever siesit siesit is, he is also the author of the Red Cape, talking about his creation as if he were merely a critic (as Nadya Tolokonnikova and Ekaterina Samutsevitch did when they first gave a public lecture about Pussy Riot before the group ever appeared in public).

10. DC Comics did publish the adventures of the gas-mask wearing Sandman in the 1940s, but he was meant to look intimidating.

a Red Cape meme comes from the contrast between the Red Cape's function as an (at times, literal) icon and his visual appearance, which is always somewhere between the ominous and the ridiculous. In one meme, a young boy waving a Soviet flag stares at the icon of the Red Cape on the wall: "Happy New Year, Beloved Red Cape" (lomasm, "S novym godom"). In another, the Red Cape points to an instructional display about proper gas mask use, but his finger's position is reminiscent of Russian Orthodox saints. The tag line under the picture combines the diction of Leninism and the New Testament: "And let he who has no gas mask sell his clothing to buy a gas mask. The Red Testament of the Red Cape" (the word for "testament" here, of course, refers to the Bible, but it is also the same one used for Lenin's "precept" in one of the memes discussed above) (lomasm, "Krasnyi zavet"). Yet the Red Cape is no friend of the Church: "They say you said something negative about the ROC [Russian Orthodox Church]?—Me? Like I could give a shit?" (lomasm, "Da na kher"). If the Red Cape is leading his viewers on a path to Soviet nostalgia as a political program, it is the same path originally taken by the alt-right appropriation of Pepe the Frog: with irony paving the way for something deadly earnest. In any case, the Red Cape is out of Pepe's league: he survives as a historical curiosity in the development of SovPunk rather than as an effective tool for post-Soviet red-pilling.

The Couch Potatoes of Developed Socialism

Despite the origins of SovPunk in the "Union Maniac" community, some of its theorists and interpreters insisted on the movement's nonaggressive character. Their ideal SovPunk seemed to be the unlikely offspring of the highly militarized late Soviet culture and the milder aesthetic subculture it spawned in the 1980s, the Mitki (whose slogan was "The Mitki don't want to defeat anyone"). As siesit siesit puts it: "this 'movement' is not destructive; the subculture's goal is not overthrowing the current order and the violent return to socialism. Everyone must understand the USSR is no more and will never be again, and if something like it is ever formed in the future, it will be something new, a new era."

siesit siesit is making a crucial distinction here between fantasy and a political program, since he also specifically includes an alternate history in which the USSR never collapsed, but instead became a superpower greater than all others, "taking only the best from the old USSR we knew, that is, an extended and improved USSR 2.0," while still allowing for the possibility of a more negative alternate USSR. Particularly noteworthy is his description of the SovPunk's typical hero. Like so many of the Time Crashers we examined earlier, this hero is an only slightly idealized version of the story's imaginary reader, with a touch of socialist realism: "A dreamer, a student, a scientist, or simply a worker; humble, a bit naive, but still dashing, but still, as a rule, without any particularly supernatural superpowers; everything he achieves is thanks to work, persistence, and knowledge."

Perhaps this hero should have been siesit siesit's starting point. This hero is a Mary Sue, but only barely, capable of more than the genre's readers might be yet with skills that are not quite unattainable. For him to be effective, the SovPunk world in which he operates must be, as the Russians like to put it, "vegetarian," with no room for bloodthirsty tyrants or fanatical revolutionaries. It is a Soviet Union made to order for its hero, rather than the expression of political yearnings or the result of copious historical research. It is a USSR as *Star Trek* holodeck program, with all the safety protocols dutifully enabled.

Like so many nostalgic productions, SovPunk is anti-entropic: the past cannot be allowed simply to be gone. The sheer evocation of the vanished era is both a balm for melancholia and the insistence on melancholia's permanence, externalizing the feeling of endless loss as something that can be seen, enjoyed, mourned, and visited. SovPunk is fundamentally a refusal to let go and move on. But it is also playful and creative. If we look at the USSR as the equivalent of a dead loved one, SovPunk does not insist on preserving its beloved in amber. By the same token, SovPunk is melancholic but not psychotic, with no need to mummify the mother(land) like Norman Bates does his mother in Hitchcock's classic film. To continue the comparison with *Psycho* a bit longer, the SovPunk community is not dressing in drag and pretending to be its dead mother but indulging in cosplay and having a good time.

In many cases, SovPunk is literally a game. The list of SovPunk exemplars inevitably includes a set of video games with an aesthetic derived from the Soviet past. Besides *Metro 2033*, some of the most famous games to earn the SovPunk classification are American or European rather than purely post-Soviet. From 1996 to 2009, the popular Westwood Studios franchise Command & Conquer produced games in its Red Alert subseries (along with several expansion packs and an iOS version). Set in an alternate timeline that managed to avoid World War II only to see Stalin invade Europe in 1946, it develops both a counterfactual Soviet past and an equally fanciful Soviet "present" in the 1990s (in *Counterstrike*, one of the expansion packs).[11] Though both the Allied and the Soviet factions are playable, the game designers cannot be bothered to hide their Western bias. The results are entertaining (particularly Tim Curry's meme-worthy performance as

---

11. "Alternate timeline" is an inadequate designation, since the *Red Alert* series, with its multiple endings, changing geographic and temporal settings, and convoluted connections to the larger Command & Conquer franchise, has become a multiverse of its own.

a Soviet premier declaring his intention to escape into the "one place that hasn't been corrupted by capitalism—space!") But Russian enthusiasm for the Soviet particularities of the games leaves plenty of space for irony,

By contrast, Russian-produced SovPunk video games have the home field advantage. Not only are their creators better acquainted with Soviet regalia, but they presumably have a stronger sense of what might appeal to gamers in the post-Soviet space. On the Russian-language Internet, every announcement of a new SovPunk-inflected game inevitably draws comparison to *Endless Summer* (Beskonechnoe leto), a game whose informal development began in 2008 before its commercial release in December 2013 on PCs (made available on Steam the following year). *Endless Summer* is not the first visual novel (a term for games combining animation, video clips, and text) to be created in Russia, but its iconic status in Russian gaming is so undisputed that the opening paragraph to an article on the history of Russian visual novels posted to stopgrame.ru in 2019 reminds the reader that the genre did not begin with this famous game (Stillbro).

Endless Summer appears to be a deliberately derivative story, built as much on allusion as on innovation. The plot, at least initially, is typical Time Crasher material: the hero falls asleep on a bus in 2009 and wakes up as a seventeen-year-old on his way to a Soviet summer camp in 1987. Soon, however, *Endless Summer* turns into a variation on *Groundhog Day*: the summer camp is a time loop, and the player's job is to find a way out. As for the characters, their names are Runet in-jokes. The protagonist is Semyon Persunov, a Russification of the English "same person" used as an anonymous handle on early twenty-first-century Russian image boards, while the heroine, Alisa Dvachevskaya, is named after "Dvach," or "2chan," a Russian equivalent to the notorious 4chan.[12]

More striking are the game's visuals, even though here, too, the aesthetic is more familiar than innovative. The visual novel is originally a Japanese form, with anime character designs. *Endless Summer* produces a delightful cognitive dissonance with Soviet realia surrounding Soviet characters drawn like the heroes of Japanese animation (the Pioneer scarf and uniform serving as an appropriate analog for anime's ubiquitous Japanese school garb).[13] *Endless Summer* handily encapsulates the appeal and the peril of the nostalgia that drives so much SovPunk: the summer camp is a nice place to spend some time, but it takes on a sinister overtone when the hero (and the player) realizes they're stuck in a time loop. Granted, nearly all video games resemble a time loop for the player, since

---

12. She is modeled on the anime-inspired mascot for 2chan, Dvach-chan. The mascot was conceived on the same image board that gave birth to *Endless Summer*, Ychan.

13. The original release also included erotic content in the manner of the *eroge* (Japanese erotic video games), but the game was cleaned up for its release on Steam.

players keep coming back to play the same game again and again, at least until they manage to win. The time loop of *Endless Summer* is both a proxy for game play and a cautionary tale about nostalgia itself. We may want to (imaginatively, or even politically) visit the past, but to stay there is to admit defeat.

Stories of time loops have an intrinsic, puzzle-box appeal: what do I have to do differently in order to get out? But they are also an adventure-themed equivalent to the successful work of mourning: the mourner must grieve, even wallow, but only for a culturally specified duration (or, here, a given set of iterations of the loop). The longer one is trapped in the loop, the closer the player's predicament resembles melancholia. The player is fixated on the past (here, literally fixated *in* it), incapable of moving forward. Even summers should not be endless.

Equally appropriate is the development of the two most anticipated SovPunk games to cash in on *Endless Summer*'s appeal: Mundfish Studio's *Atomic Heart* and GM Reds' visual novel *SovietPunk: Nostalgia for the Present*. *SovietPunk* takes place in a twenty-first-century USSR, populated by anime Komsomol girls who could have stepped right out of *Endless Summer*. GM Reds launched a very small but successful Kickstarter campaign in February 2021 to raise money for a demo, which, as of the summer of 2022, is available on Steam as the first part of the game, but there is no information available about the time frame for its full release. *Atomic Heart*, set in an alternate Soviet 1950s, made a splash when it dropped an action-packed, visually sophisticated trailer in May 2018, but anonymous reports of layoffs and strife may explain why, by 2022, even a demo version has yet to be seen. The endless anticipation for both games inadvertently recapitulates the temporality of the lost USSR itself, which continually deferred communism to a later date. Even in the world of video games, the radiant future rarely manifests as the radiant present.

When *Atomic Heart* did finally appear, the five years between the trailer and release did not do Mundfish Studios any favors. It came out on February 21, 2023, just three days short of the first anniversary of Russia's invasion of Ukraine and two days before Russia's Defenders of the Fatherland military holiday. While this could easily be an accident, the atmosphere in both countries does not exactly lend itself to the calm acceptance of coincidence. The developers have been excused of creating a love letter to the Soviet past, while the game's defenders point out that the picture it portrays of an alternate 1950s is far from rosy. Had the game come out just two years earlier, it would have been simply one of many cultural productions that toy with Soviet nostalgia without completely committing to it. Instead, this game became something of a Time Crasher itself, launched into an era that no longer provided it with a reasonable pretense to neutrality. Is there anything more pathetic than a tale of an alternate timeline faltering because it is either untimely or too timely to be accepted at face value?

Welcome to *Carbongrad*

In its least ideological form, SovPunk comes to (still) life in Evgeny Zubkov's series of online artwork known collectively as *Carbongrad 1999* (rebranded as *Russia 2077*). Steeped in the aesthetic of *Blade Runner*-era cyberpunk, *Carbongrad 1999* consists of clever variations on a single conceit: the seamless integration of Russian and Soviet everyday imagery into a gritty, urban high-tech landscape.

Visitors to Zubkov's VKontakte and Instagram accounts are treated to photorealistic images of an old Russian woman in customary drab garb (ill-fitting sweater, gray skirt, flower-patterned headscarf) feeding flying robot drones as if they were birds, a middle-aged man in knee-high rubber boots carrying rusty buckets of water in each of his arms (including the two robotic ones sprouting from his back), and an orange-jacketed worker using a hose from his clunky water truck to clean off the graffiti from a giant, hovering mechanical sphere that looks like a mini-Death Star. Perhaps the most iconic of all the *Carbongrad* images is a bald, track-suited cyborg carrying a baseball bat studded with bolts and decorated with two stickers, one a robotic version of the woman holding a finger to her lips from the famous World War II "Don't Blab!" poster, the other apparently the eponymous heroine of *The Girl from the Future*, both partially obscuring a warning familiar to anyone who has ever stood in front of a Russian subway door: "No Leaning!"

Zubkov's combination of the cybernetic and quotidian is not, in itself, new; the artist himself freely acknowledges his debt to Simon Stalenhag, the Swedish artist known for his haunting paintings of retrofuturist machines set against the bucolic backdrop of his native countryside.[14] Zubkov shares more than just Stalenhag's aesthetic; equally important is how they both downplay the strangeness of their subject matter. Each artist engages in what Olga Meerson has called "re-familiarization" or "non-estrangement" (*neostranenie*), the process of describing something new and odd as if we were expected already to know all about it.

Zubkov's art casually asserts an important point about Russia's future: namely, that Russia has one. True, Zubkov describes his imaginary world as an "alternate present," but what makes it alternate are the futuristic elements that share space with familiar Russian realia. This combination of Russia and (retro) futurism might well be understood by analogy to the largely anglophone movement known as Afrofuturism. At its most basic, Afrofuturism pushes against the overwhelming whiteness of most twentieth-century science fiction simply by

---

14. Stalenhag is probably best known for *Tales from the Loop*, a narrative art book that inspired a science fiction series on Amazon Prime in 2020.

depicting a future that, at a minimum, has Black people in it, and, more boldly, moves Blackness from the background to prominence.

It is this minimum that Zubkov achieves in *Carbongrad 1999*. Unlike the more militant SovPunk discussed below, Zubkov's deployment of Russian and Soviet signifiers is unaccompanied by patriotic bluster. He achieves this understated "Russofuturism" by avoiding the most obvious signs of Russian statehood and national pride, creating an imaginary geography that is maximally distant from the sites of empire. If we had to place *Carbongrad* somewhere on the maps of Russia, it would be deep in the North. Russia outside the capitals can be romanticized, and certainly has been by blood-and-soil traditionalists, but the conservatives' chosen setting is usually the countryside. Zubkov's world is both provincial and urban, located firmly within the modern world yet far from the traditional loci of *significance* in Russia.[15] Zubkov's imaginary Russia is a palimpsest in which the past, present, and future overlie each other. Unlike DSDS's "2045" video, it seems indifferent to questions of Russia's destiny and unwilling to police the boundaries of the Russian cultural imagination. His futuristic Russia comfortably fits within the current maps of the country. Far from being expansionist, it retreats to the Russian heartland. William Gibson, one of the fathers of cyberpunk, famously asserted that "the future is already here. It's just not very evenly distributed." *Carbongrad* is a gentle, optimistic rebuttal: the future will make it even to the Russian provinces.

Zubkov paints a set of worlds that can comfortably domesticate any external influence without making a fuss, even Western pop action heroes. In the *Northern Spider* series, Spider-Man is reimagined as a resident of an unnamed Russian provincial city. His costume retains the familiar red and black color scheme but appears to be made of more realistic components, cobbled together from clothing that might conceivably be available to an ordinary person. There is no need to give this version of Spider-Man any particularly Russian stylistic attributes (no two-headed eagles or Russian flags); he is Russified simply by his inclusion in an environment that is clearly far from Queens. In one picture he shoots webs at a monstrous mecha-truck as a babushka looks on, a grocery bag in each hand. Another shows what looks to be the Russian Peter Parker's bedroom, complete with a cobweb made out of his webbing, a turn-of-the-century computer displaying a newspaper story about his first appearance that shows the Northern spider in an homage to the iconic cover of the first Spider-Man story, and a newspaper clipping suggesting that the Northern Spider got his powers during a school trip to a nuclear power plant.

---

15. Here I am obviously influenced by Anne Lounsbery's brilliant *Life Is Elsewhere*.

Zubkov works the same sort of magic in his *Russian Turtles* picture, which announces itself (in English) as "An alternative universe in which 4 mutated turtles were born in Russia in the mad 90s." Leonardo now carries an AK-47, Donatello sports a Sputnik tattoo, Michelangelo is holding a shawarma in a pose suggesting either a weapon or his next meal, and all of them are wearing sneakers and ski masks. Instead of their customary sewer, the Turtles seem to have made their home base in a junk yard. Situating the Turtles in the Russian 1990s is a clever choice, and not just because most of the original cartoon aired in that decade. The original Turtles' scrappy, DIY aesthetic, along with their status as muscle-bound brawlers, makes it easy to imagine them in the messy world of Russian gangsters and general instability.

The artist's casual incorporation of future tech and Russian reality, not to mention foreign popular culture, is a relaxed, optimistic alternative to both alternate history and future history. For Russia to persist in the future, or for the future to make its way into present-day Russia, not a great deal has to change. "Russianness" (as depicted in everyday realia) is neither extolled nor condemned; the persistence of visibly Russian tropes in an imagined future could be seen as a gesture toward a cyclical, determinist model of the nation's history, suggesting that Russia will not and cannot ever change. But the lived-in feeling of Zubkov's work points in a different direction: Russia can make its way into the future while still remaining visibly Russian. There is nothing to fear from new technology, just as there is nothing to fear from the influx of Western animated turtles and web-slinging teens. Russia can absorb the new without losing itself.

Soviet Space: The Final Frontier

The most sustained effort at imagining a post-post-Soviet future for Russia is the *USSR-2061* project, which I have referred to a few times in previous sections. Started by two young men on LiveJournal who go by the handles Archy13 and Felix, the *USSR-2061* project was a reaction to the unrelenting pessimism its founders saw in then-contemporary science fiction; in one of their videos, they note that the year 2011, when they began the project, was dominated by zombies in film and video games, as well as talk about the Mayan calendar's alleged prediction that the world would end in 2012 (SSSR-2061, "Divannaia futurologiia"). As an inspiration for a more optimistic approach, they looked to the past: 2011 was the fiftieth anniversary of Yuri Gagarin's pioneering space flight. So they decided to fantasize about what life would be like on the hundredth anniversary, in a future where the Soviet Union had at some point been restored.

Thus began an annual tradition: the announcement of a contest for best contributions on a given theme in a given format. Most of the competitions, including the inaugural one, were for artwork. The theme was not just a Soviet future, or even a Soviet future in space, but artistic works that supported the project's tag line: "a future that you want to live to see" (*do kotorogo khochetsia dozhit'*). The first competition was devoted to the colonization of Mars, the second to the asteroid belt, followed by a contest to imagine the UAZ truck of the future, a competition commemorating the thirtieth anniversary of the hit science fiction film *The Girl from the Future*, and contests for designing Martian robots and imagining what vacations would be like in fifty years' time. They also conducted two short-story competitions, which garnered hundreds of entries. The second competition was paid for by a very successful crowd-funding campaign on Boomstarter, with the winning entries collected in a book published by EKSMO (one of the biggest Russian publishers). The rest of the stories are available online in eleven volumes of e-books.[16]

Archy13 and Felix found the art easier to judge, because it was less time-consuming than reading hundreds of stories. The results, however, are not particularly memorable. Ironically, a project whose founders have repeatedly insisted on their lack of interest in retrofuturism has yielded an astonishing amount of backward-looking art (particularly in comparison to *Carbongrad*). The general aesthetic is a combination of Soviet propaganda posters, American Golden Age science fiction cover art, video games, and anime. So we have square-jawed cosmonauts, spaceships with Soviet symbols, girls whose outfits somehow combine the Komsomol and Japanese schoolgirl garb, serious people looking up at the sky, and robots. Lots and lots of robots.

Indeed, despite the video game influence, the robots remind us that most of this art was made as if cyberpunk never happened. *USSR-2061* is analog through and through, even though it is all created on computers and shared over social media. Even in the fiction, most of the technology involves heavy machinery and space travel. Some of this is dictated by the contests' themes, but the consistency with which the virtual and digital are ignored is worth considering. While Archy13 and Felix are adamant that they are not interested in alternate history, and that therefore the Soviet Union has to have collapsed in 1991 as part of the fictional background, *USSR-2061* remains rooted in 1961: this is a future that is less the continuation of our world than the sequel to the golden age of the Soviet

---

16. None of these e-books have any publishing information included in their files, including editors or date of publication. They may have been produced by the competition's directors, or they may have been released by a third party.

space program. The result is a vision that could be more nostalgic only if it had Soviet music constantly playing in the background.

The stories and art of *USSR-2061* remind us of the huge symbolic significance held by the space program, to an extent that NASA never matched. The Soviets were the first in space, both with Sputnik in 1957 and Gagarin in 1961. As a response, John F. Kennedy famously committed the United States' resources to putting a man on the moon, an event that held the attention of the entire world. But soon NASA's launches lost their luster (tedium punctuated only by horrible tragedies, such as the 1986 space shuttle *Challenger* explosion). Going to the moon the first time was romantic; going for the third was routine. And eventually the pictures sent back from rockets and space shuttles paled in comparison to science fiction films, thanks to the huge strides made in special effects and computer graphics in the 1970s and 1980s. But NASA's declining prestige was also the result of choices made by the government, choices that involved not just finances but public relations.

After the 1960s, the US government made little effort to excite its citizens about the space program, while the Soviet Union never stopped using Gagarin as a point of pride. The Soviet space program was the logical evolution of the USSR's decades-long romance with science and flight. Under Stalin, aviators were national heroes; the pilots who seemed to defy the laws of gravity exemplified the Soviet progressive ethos. With the space program, the Soviet Union could lay claim not just to scientific progress but to the broader universe and, by extension, the future. If, as the Stalin-era song puts it, Soviet citizens were born to "turn fairy tales into real life," then the space program would do the same for science fiction.

Gagarin remained a national hero long after his flight into space. Even in the last Soviet years, his image was on posters and postage stamps, and people still told jokes playing off the famous word he said before takeoff, *Poekhali* ("Let's go!" or "We're off!"). Though undoubtedly the product of numerous political decisions and motivated at least in part by a desire to show the rest of the world how powerful Soviet science was, the space program, along with the Soviet victory over the Nazis, was one of the few national accomplishments of which everyone was proud, regardless of political convictions. Cosmonauts were heroes, pure and simple.

After the Soviet collapse, the space program fell on hard times. Disconnected both from everyday reality and the priorities of the new Russian state, the Soviet cosmonauts were the leftovers of a vanished world. Veteran cosmonauts Sergei Krikalev and Alexander Volkov were on the Mir space station when the Soviet Union ceased to exist on December 26, 1991. Their return was postponed because the Baikonur landing area was located in the now independent country of Kazakhstan. This odd story earned Krikalev the sobriquet of the "Last Soviet

Citizen." Krikalev had already been on the station long before Volkov arrived; when they finally landed, Krikalev had spent twice as much time in space as originally planned, and time dilation meant that he was now .02 seconds younger than everyone who had been born on Earth at the same time as he was. Once a harbinger of the future, the cosmonaut had become a man who was literally from another country and another time.

It is fitting, then, that the imaginary relaunch of the Soviet Union be predicated on multiple rocket launches into space. The entries submitted to the contest varied in their prehistories of the new USSR, and even in their geography. Sometimes the USSR was reborn within its old borders, sometimes on a smaller scale, and sometimes as a global empire. But these geographies turn out to matter far less than the infinite scale afforded by space. As one entry to the competition puts it, "The history of the space fleet is inextricably linked to the history of the USSR" (Prudnikov). It's not simply a matter of colonization, though that definitely plays a role (and since the time of Alexander Bogdanov's 1908 novel *Red Star*, who can resist the chance to turn Mars communist?).[17] The symbolic geography of the Soviet Union always had a strong vertical component, from the aforementioned aviators to the cosmonauts. The contest's conditions reversed the temporality of Soviet history (or at least the history of the *original* Soviet Union). Now, the Soviet Union 2.0 arises on Earth as a function of the demand to describe Soviet outer space. The Soviet Union was always as much an idea as a place, and now, in its resurrection, the idea (and the ideal) comes first. Nostalgia for the USSR tends to involve a desire for a return to "greatness"; *USSR-2061* starts with greatness and builds from there. By choosing the space program as a point of departure, *USSR-2061* develops a model of revanchist greatness that is considerably less hysterical than the much more prominent alternative: the countless stories returning to or reenacting World War II discussed in previous chapters.

Space Begins at Home

By making space exploration the theme of the first competition and following it up with a mix of technological topics (the asteroid belt, cars) and more general ones (vacation in the future), Archy13 and Felix implicitly encouraged a dual approach to science fiction. The trappings of hard science fiction were meant to be combined with what the organizers call "social science fiction" (*sotsial'naia*

---

17. From Timur Suvorkin's "Pioneer Means First": "When America was the first on the moon, that hurt. But that defeat meant one thing: challenge accepted. Mars would have to become Soviet."

fantastika). The result was often two competing info dumps in a single story: one about technological advances; the other providing sociohistorical background, usually with a distinct ideological tinge.

While Archy13 and Felix's project is obviously based on disenchantment with the current order, their own statements are never particularly strident. Even their guidelines for imagining a future USSR are rather moderate, both sociologically and technologically. There will be no faster-than-light travel, no aliens, no singularity but also no collapse of the United States or global conquest by the new USSR. Nonetheless, many of the contestants looked at the competition as an argument to elaborate their thoughts on geopolitics and ideology. It is no surprise that the winning stories were published in a volume that would become part of EKSMO's series of "patriotic" science fiction, much of which was produced by writers associated with the liberpunk movement (see my *Plots against Russia* 169–77). Liberpunk is a Russian science fiction subgenre whose prime subject matter is liberalism as a dystopia. USSR-2016 is not a liberpunk project, but it functions as a kinder, gentler fellow traveler.

Thus in Olga Bondareva's USSR-2061 story, "The Glass Dream," we learn that "the black population in the USA" continues to protest, even after the passage of the 2038 Political Correctness Law, which affirms the concepts of "Afro-American," "Euro-American," and "Asian American." America is even worse in Yuri Khabibulin's entry, "Mother's Day." Since 2025, the United States has been the last country in the world to be ruled by "secret state feminism." At an international women's conference, the US representative bursts with pride at her country's rising abortion rates, the laws restricting the rights of "aggressive and stupid" men, and the successful propaganda in favor of lesbianism, whose goal is to reduce men to "slaves and subhumans."

In his *USSR-2061* story, "Red Means Blood," Pyotr Nazinov's protagonist laments the plight of capitalists in the West, who are "surrounded by cruelty, perversions, and pettiness." The West, he explains, "hates us, because they are afraid. We hate them because they hate us. They've always hated us. Always, throughout history they've exploited and deceived us." The West's treachery is a recurrent theme. In Miloslav Kniazev's "Fifth Medal," we learn that Russia, Belarus, Ukraine, and Kazakhstan passed national referenda to restore the USSR, after which they were immediately attacked by "the fascist countries of NATO." It is not enough that the USSR be ideal; the West has to be on the decline. As Yana Talyaka writes in "Not a Word of Lies": "Now the Soviet does not look abroad to the promised land; it is the foreigner who looks to the USSR." In another story, Sergei Tolstoi's "The New Person," the USSR's growth rate is so high that the decision to reform the USSR in 2022 was undeniably correct: "The only way the Western world could stop the USSR and keep its hegemony was through war."

What else could be expected from the United States and its allies? As volume 9 of the series, "The Little Earth" by Aleksei Savvin, puts it, "The USA is run not by its government, but by secret financial clans, and they hold hostage not just the Americans, but the entire world."

Still, the expansion into outer space does allow some of the writers to think more expansively about how a future USSR might create a radiant future that manages not to be totalitarian. Most of the wars that the various future Soviet Unions wage are wars of defense, rather than choice; the USSR tends to win over hearts and minds through soft power and an appealing example. In Andrei Khval'skii's "Summer Internship," which is a futuristic pastiche of a familiar revolutionary story, Commander Chapaev tells the faithful Petka that the USSR is not for everyone: "our scientists think that there are so-called 'genetic liberals' for whom what we would consider an unacceptable environment is natural to them, like the swamp to a swamp creature." The new USSR takes these poor, benighted souls into account ("We're not fascists, Petka!"). It signed the "Oslo Accord on the Rights of Psychos and Their Individual Psychic Climates" and has pledged to take care of these liberals while making sure they don't start an "epidemic of mental illness."

Talyaka's "Not a Word of Lies" also emphasizes the USSR's voluntary character: "We don't keep anyone if they don't like it. Compensate the state for your education, medical care, and everything else it's spent on you, and you're off. Try your luck. What's important is that the Soviet Union has not made foreign countries into forbidden fruit." Tolstoi's "New Person" uses virtually the same language: "the Soviet person may freely choose to live in communism, socialism, or try his luck in a market environment."

Sim Socialism

The element of choice is important when we remember that these stories are not merely descriptive of an imaginary future; they are describing "the future you want to live to see." Like the twenty-first-century Soviet citizens, readers, too, are implicitly choosing their own path. It just so happens that the Soviet path is always the better one. More often than not, the new Soviet Union arises from the will of the people or from international agreements among former Soviet republics. The contributors to *USSR-2061* apparently share the widespread Russian antipathy to revolution.

Taken together, the stories offer a significant revision of Marxist theory in sci-fi form. Instead of the workers coming to consciousness and starting a revolution, the inhabitants of Russia in the future, as well as readers today, come to consciousness in order *not* to start a revolution but to build communism through consensus.

An early contribution by Villy9, called "The Decision," brings this point home through a plotline that starts as clever metafiction but ends with all the subtlety of a bulldozer. The year is, of course, 2061, and an expert on our time (the second decade of the twenty-first century) is called into an experimental physics lab for his advice. Soviet scientists have opened a portal to another dimension, where it is 2010 and the Soviet Union has collapsed: "The problem is that on their Earth only one path for development remains: capitalism." This other world is so hopeless that it "has no future." Even the residents' imagination is stunted: "A large part of their creative output is probably devoted to the coming apocalypse." Yes, reader, this is our world.

Fortunately, the scientists and the historian realize that all they need to do is somehow communicate to their counterparts (that is, to us), that change is possible, and it is up to them: "We'll give them the idea for a small literary competition. Or an art competition. We'll call it . . . how about, USSR-2112." The rest, as they say, is (alternate) history.

It's a clumsy story, and the point it is making is rather obvious. But if we stretch its metafictional parameters a bit further than was their likely intent, "The Decision" reveals something important about the competition's ideology and genre. These stories are meant to have the effect that all good utopian fiction strives for: to convert the reader to the cause. What emerges is the inverse of Marxism. Marx's "scientific" conceit was to put utopia at the end of a set of predictable, understandable historical processes, while pre- and non-Marxist utopian thought tended to presume that a perfect world could be built anywhere, as long as its founders and residents tried hard enough. The Soviet Union always had a strong voluntarist strain, especially under Stalin: industrial output was supposed to increase as a matter of will. But there remained at least the fig leaf of a historical theory and systematic thought. *USSR-2061* conjures a communist future by returning to the utopian roots that Marx so despised. There is no need for a revolution, nor is there really much point to figuring out how a better future is to be realized. It will be built repeatedly, and almost effortlessly, on the Internet, in a kind of graphomaniacal slacktivism.

Examining all these post-Soviet futures, from the post-apocalyptic wastelands to the empires to the revived USSR, yields a result that would probably surprise Westerners more than Russians. Compared to all the other scenarios, the future USSR is about the triumph of optimism. Let the imperial and postnuclear futures dabble in Stalinism and state violence; the Soviet future is about Soviet-style contentment. That is to say, for many readers and netizens, the imaginary Soviet Union is their happy place.

And because it exists solely in the realm of the imagination, this USSR is collectivist in form but individual in content. Each post-Soviet dreamer is free to keep what they like and ignore the USSR's more problematic features (indeed, even to deny these features' very reality). *USSR-2061*'s anthology format is the perfect embodiment of this dynamic: it consists of several collections of independently conceived Soviet futures that cannot be consistent with each other in the details while still manifesting a shared desire for something that is different in all the authors' minds while sharing the same name and premise.

All of this begs the question: how do we look at SovPunk now that the Russian Federation has been committing war crimes in Ukraine? Is it yet another in a long list of examples of Russian cultural figures' willful ignorance of both Soviet and Russian imperialism? Or worse, another weapon in the Russian imperialist arsenal, part of the assumptions of cultural "greatness" used to justify Russian hegemony? In the spirit of academic wishy-washiness, my answer is: yes and no. The case of the *USSR-2061* project is rather clear. Everything about the contests and their results is based on unexamined nostalgic assumptions about a Soviet Union that was multinational rather than imperial. *USSR-2061* exports Soviet and Russian notions of greatness to outer space, thanks to the importance that the space program played in the Soviet national consciousness. While it is meant to be a futurist projection of 1961, it also inadvertently recapitulates 1921, when Yevgeny Zamyatin finished his dystopian novel, *We*. The narrator of *We* writes his journal in response to the state's call for widespread cultural production to be included in the rocket that is about to be sent into outer space; somehow, these works spread the state's ideology to the stars. The flaws in this mission reflect the flaws of the state, particularly its inability to effectively conceive of difference and individuality (how, after all, are these aliens supposed to read texts in a language for which they have no frame of reference)? The *USSR-2061* project exemplifies the totalizing narcissism that Zamyatin so effectively critiques.

I want to hold out a little hope for the less threatening varieties of SovPunk, such as *Carbongrad 1999*. *Carbongrad* is unaggressive and humorous, and it does not have to be deployed in the service of an imperial idea. But I have my doubts on such imagery's resistance to appropriation by more belligerent forces. I have yet to see images of Russian soldiers in Ukraine with tattoos of Zubkov's baseball-wielding cyborg. But I would not be surprised if I found one.

Conclusion
TRADING RUSSIAN FUTURES

There's a saying Russians like to use when talking about the past: "History does not tolerate the subjunctive mood."[1] Like so many phrases rendered in translation, it sounds better in the original, not to mention more comprehensible. Even English speakers who are familiar with the term "subjunctive" might scratch their heads over this one.

In Russian, the "subjunctive" does cover the territory familiar to speakers of Romance languages (verbs following clauses that express wishing, suggesting, demanding), but it is fighting a losing battle for survival in English ("it is imperative that the subjunctive remain in use"). But the subjunctive does double duty in Russian, including the counterfactual conditional ("If you had done what I told you, you wouldn't be in this mess today"). The counterfactual is the true subject of the Russian phrase, as is clear in the German quotation by the historian Karl Hampe that apparently inspired it: "Die Geschichte kennt kein Wenn" (History knows no "if").

How fitting, then, that Russians often attribute the phrase to Joseph Stalin, a man who, whatever one's opinions of him might be, played a role in history that was undoubtedly decisive and whose methods were unconditional. Stalin is an ironic source if we read the phrase against the grain and insist on the other, more familiar meaning of "subjunctive": an action in a dependent clause that only occurs by will of the subject of the main clause. What better

---

1. There is also the variation "History knows no subjunctive mood."

characterizes Stalinist voluntarism than the subjunctive? To borrow a phrase more closely associated with Stalin's wartime enemies, the subjunctive is the triumph of the will.

Or perhaps, in the twenty-first century, the triumph of the willful, thanks to the insistence that the consensual understanding of reality can be manipulated and manufactured. *Unstuck in Time* has devoted so much attention to science fiction and fantasy because these are the genres that reveal the deep structure of the post-Soviet Russian discourse of time, history, and geopolitics. History is always present, as well as subject to change when political exigencies demand, and the struggles the country faces (economic, political, and geopolitical) are always about more than they seem. Since Putin's return to the presidency in 2012, the Russian media narrative has been increasingly dominated by a framework that might best be called the *conspiratorial fantastic*: behind every opponent is a much more sinister enemy, rendering every conflict the superficial manifestation of a Manichean battle with a supreme evil. From globalists to sinister liberals to the US State Department, the Russian state, along with huge swaths of the culture industry, loves to uncover hidden enemies. In the run-up to the second invasion of Ukraine, they have found the perfect incarnation of evil: all Russia's enemies are Nazis.

Many (Greenfield; Skorkin; Young) have noted that the war(s) in Ukraine were prefigured by nearly unreadable military science fiction novels about Russia's Western neighbor serving as the battleground for World War III. To my mind, these novels are valuable not as predictions (again, looking to science fiction to predict the future is a gross misunderstanding of how the genre works) but as reminders of the increasingly fantastic/science fictional character of contemporary Russian discourse. Alternate history (including the Time Crashers subgenre) is not just a popular form of entertainment. It is the dominant mode of political thought, providing the logic and falsified content of increasingly propaganda-driven media. Russia is living in the subjunctive mode, in the sense of both the counterfactual conditional and the subordination to the speaker's will. As this book has demonstrated, this habit of substituting a fantastic, conditional-subjunctive Russia for empirical reality has been primarily in the service of reactionary goals, but there is nothing inherent in the structure that prevents creating an alternate Russia for oppositional or subversive purposes. To close out the book, I want to look at two examples, one embodying the goals of Putinist revanchism on the eve of the first invasion of Ukraine, and the other a set of satirical responses to the second, full-scale invasion that borrow from the conditional/subjunctive Russian playbook in order to evoke empathy, shame, and outrage rather than imperial grandeur and postimperial grievance.

The Aleph of Sochi

The first example is from the Olympic Games hosted by Russia in 2014. This was meant to be an important year for the Russian Federation. It definitely was, but not in the way that the leadership had clearly hoped. Russia's military incursion into Crimea on February 27, 2014, immediately eclipsed everything that had happened in the first seven weeks of the year, including the Winter Olympics in Sochi. This was supposed to be a moment of triumph for Russia on the world stage, one that could have withstood all the bad public relations that preceded it (the stories of corruption and wasteful spending, the Internet memes of the bizarre toilets found throughout the newly built complexes).[2] The opening ceremonies on February 4 were a meticulously choreographed celebration of Russia, its history, and its culture, a condensation of Putin-era ideology and a perfect example of history being treated as an ideological playground.

Denigrating the opening ceremonies as nationalistic kitsch is as unfair as complaining that the Eurovision contest trades in national stereotypes packaged with all the aesthetic restraint of an eight-year-old experimenting with makeup. These things must be understood according to their own generic conventions. It is the job of a host country's opening ceremony to turn its culture into kitsch while providing a stunning spectacle. In this regard, the Sochi Olympics worked like a charm.

Besides the usual speeches and processions of athletes, the opening ceremonies consisted of two staged components that bracketed most of the event, one arranged according to the sequence of the Russian alphabet, the other a dazzlingly quick march through most of Russian history. In other words, the first part was synchronic, the second diachronic (that is, moving through time). Thanks to this division into two parts, as well as the obvious symbolism in each, it is as though the entire event were designed for semiotic analysis at some strange intersection of Tartu and Vegas, where Siegfried, Roy, and Yuri Lotman shared a residency. Since the show was masterminded by Konstantin Ernst, the chief executive officer of Channel One, whose brilliance as an impresario is matched by his facility for propaganda, this comparison is not so far from reality: Ernst is Putin's most sophisticated supporter in the Russian media world (Yaffa 25–76). He is also a past master of the historical subjunctive, as producer of *Old Songs about the Main Thing*, a series of nostalgic New Year's specials (1995–2001) that featured songs from the middle-aged viewers' Soviet youth, with plots and settings that evoked a bygone Soviet era somehow untroubled by the crimes of the regime.

---

2. As Kobierecki writes, "Putin's aim in organizing the Olympics was not only to show Russia strong, but also civilized" (173).

Each half of the Olympics show exemplifies the willfulness and syncretism that underlies so many of the phenomena discussed throughout the present book. Though obviously designed for the live and television audiences, the show is based on the conceit that everything unfolds from the perspective of a little girl named Lyuba (she recites the names in the first half and watches the parade of history in the second). Lyuba's role as mediator helps soften the imperial bombast of the show (even her name means love), but a less receptive audience could easily see the presence of eleven-year-old Liza Temnikova in this role as unsettling or even uncanny; the seemingly innocent little girl is such a common horror trope that an earnest version can be difficult to accept. Her proximity to grand historical events and cultural accomplishments can be a reminder that the country's patrimony is the inheritance of the next generations, but it is also nakedly manipulative. Watching Lyuba in the Sochi opening ceremonies is particularly disturbing in 2022, when images of happy, innocent, blond girls and their mothers have been plastered all over Russian-occupied towns in Ukraine as a symbol of the invaders' beneficence, accompanied by the slogan "Russia is here forever!" ("They Don't Belong Here"). Childlike, innocent, apolitical, and passive, Lyuba occupies the same subject position as the ideal Russian television viewer: what happens is for her edification and approbation but is not a matter of her own responsibility.

In the second half of the show, all (or almost all) of Russian history unfolds before her eyes, a series of uninterrupted triumphs preceded by a light-bedecked troika pulling the sun behind it. The dancers construct St. Basil's Cathedral (a monument built to commemorate Russia's military conquest of Kazan), then Peter the Great raises an army. The show dwells on the army longer than one might expect from a peaceful historical highlights reel, morphing from its seventeenth-century origins all the way to the Soviet era.[3] The soldiers are followed by an imperial ball, which makes way for the Russian Revolution, Stalinist industrialization, the Worker and the Peasant Woman statue, and Gagarin and the Soviet space program. Apparently, the army itself is as much of an achievement as the country's national monuments and scientific innovations.

In fact, Russia's military was supposed to have an even greater role in this part of the ceremony, but the International Olympic Committee insisted that the

---

3. On the role of the military in the Sochi show, Jonathan Grix and Nina Kramereva note: "The use of military vocabulary in the context of the Olympics demonstrates an interesting paradox. Outwardly, that is to the Western onlooker, Russia wants to appear a benign and responsible, though strong and ambitious, agent in international relations, committed to soft power ideals. Inwardly, that is, to the domestic audience, Russia sends a message which is meant to ignite a certain hostility against an outside world and to juxtapose 'us against them' and thus to use the West as a dissociative group in this identity building enterprise" (470).

organizers remove the segment dedicated to the Soviet victory in World War II. It is a glaring absence, not only because it would have made the early emphasis on the army more legible, but because of the Great Patriotic War's centrality to Russian historical myth. The lack of World War II is also the opening ceremonies' most significant deviation from the literal and metaphorical time travel that has been the subject of *Unstuck in Time*. Otherwise, the ceremonies offer the viewers a brief taste of historical reenactment, a glimpse of the Soviet Union in 2012, and imperial and Soviet nostalgia from the viewpoint of someone too young to have a direct connection with any of the touchstones of Soviet history. Also typical is the show's utter lack of a vision of the future, in keeping with Putinism's insistent recycling of useful elements of the past. Once again, Rabfak called it, just two years before the Olympic Games: "Why is today yesterday and not tomorrow?"

Lyuba's first vision, which opens the show, is not weighed down by the march of history, since its structure is alphabetical. This makes the sequence confusing for Western audiences, since Lyuba's list goes according to the order of the Cyrillic alphabet.[4] But this is as it should be: Russia is the host country, after all, and in any case, the sequence would never work perfectly because of translation issues. *Hedgehog in the Fog*, for example, was never going to appear between "G" and "I," since the Russian title starts with the Cyrillic letter ё. Even if it did, however, there is also the question of cultural translation. The title refers to Yuri Norstein's beloved 1975 cartoon; outside of the former Warsaw Pact, the only people likely to know this brilliant short film are area specialists and animation buffs. Equally obscure were the references to the architect Alexey Shchusev, the poet Vasily Zhukovsky, and the parachute (Gleb Kotelnikov invented the knapsack parachute in 1911, a fact I must admit I learned from Wikipedia). But the audience for the show was domestic as well as international; nearly everything about this particular alphabet would have been legible to an educated Russian speaker.

Or perhaps "legible" is not an apt metaphor here; the show is based on the building blocks of literacy, but the alphabetical order means that the letters form neither words nor sentences. The letter sequence is introduced by a scene of Lyuba holding a *bukvar'*, an alphabet book for children. Such books use examples of familiar items ("A is for Apple") to teach what might not yet be a familiar letter. For the literate Russian audience, the letters are a given; it is the examples that must be learned or reinforced. The alphabet sequence presents the building

---

4. The words associated with the alphabet in Lyuba's vision are: Alphabet, Baikal, Sikorsky's Helicopters, Gagarin and Gzhel', Dostoyevsky, Catherine the Great, Hedgehog in the Fog, Zhukhovsky, Grain Sorting Machine, Empire, Tchaikovsky, Kandinsky, Moon Rover, Malevich, Nabokov, Space Station, Periodical Table, Ballets Russes, Sputnik, Tolstoy and Television, Ushanka, Fisht, Khokhloma, Tsiolkovsky, Chekhov, Chagall, Shchusev, Pushkin, We, Love, Eisenstein, Parachute, Russia.

blocks of Russian culture and civilization, which can subsequently be used to create more meaning. If the juxtapositions are odd, well, that is just how the alphabet works.

Except when it is not. Russia is the last word on the list because it ends with the last letter of the alphabet (*ia*); Tchaikovsky is drafted to represent the *i kratkoe*, the last letter in his name in Russian and a letter that can never appear at the beginning of a word. Most of the letters are paired with a single example, but *T* and *G* each have two: Tolstoy and Television, and Gagarin and Gzhel'. In the case of *G*, one can imagine an argument among the event's planners, "Yes, we have to have Gagarin, of course, but what about *gzhel*'? Everybody loves *gzhel*'." The juxtaposition of Leo Tolstoy and Television is even stranger. There would seem to be nothing intrinsically Russian about television, except that Russians use the Russian-American inventor Vladimir Zworykin's invention of the cathode-ray tube to call him the father of television. The invocation of Tolstoy and television together, then, suggests that Russia's cultural triumph is one of both form and content: Tolstoy wrote some of the world's greatest novels, while television became the planet's dominant medium in the second half of the twentieth century.

The Tolstoy/Television dyad is just the clearest example of the definition of Russia that is at work. In this timeless, context-free collection of Russian-related signifiers, everything is equally related (or unrelated). There is no room for judgment, whether aesthetic or moral. Like the Periodic Table (seventeenth in Sochi's alphabetic list of accomplishments, or eighteenth if we account for the doubled examples for *G*), it is a system unto itself: on the Periodic Table, it is not bismuth's fault that it is next to the poisonous polonium. Yet there is one crucial difference: if we recognize the atomic number as the crucial distinction among the elements, the order of the Periodic Table is a foregone conclusion. But the organizers of the opening ceremonies had a broad spectrum of options for most letters. Surely "Russia' was more obvious for "R" than "Ballets Russes," but they played fast and loose by using the last letter of the name to match it up with the last letter of the alphabet. In fact, the organizing principle of the Sochi alphabet is indifference rather than difference: émigrés such as Vladimir Nabokov and Marc Chagall are welcomed into the fold as if their exile never happened. Sergei Eisenstein and Pyotr Tchaikovsky's inclusion is predicated on the implicit denial of their (forbidden) homosexuality, at a time when the Russian Federation was enduring harsh criticism for adopting the "gay propaganda" law the year before. And the tenth letter—empire—embraces Russia's past as a conquering and occupying power while sending an ominous (and, ultimately, correct) signal about the country's attitude toward its neighbors. An empire incorporates a wide variety of difference (ethnicity, language, faith, history) while subjugating these variations to the transcendent signifier of empire itself. Empire delineates the boundaries of acceptable difference in the name of a grand sameness.

The ahistorical grab bag of Russia's achievements that constitutes the Sochi alphabet turns time into space: all the important elements of the country's history are laid out on a set of virtual pages. In 1945, Jorge Luis Borges published a story called "The Aleph," which posited a singular point in space (the Aleph) that somehow incorporates all other points. All time and space are visible to one who gazes upon the Aleph. Borges's Aleph is personal (in that it is understood in relation to the story's characters and the mundane plot in which they are embroiled) and metaphysical (questioning our very understanding of the universe). The Sochi opening ceremonies are another kind of Aleph; since the subject is Russia, the scale is smaller, but as a vehicle of empire, the Sochi Aleph, as seen by Lyuba, models the peculiar balance of pride and indifference that characterizes the post-Soviet subject position in twenty-first-century Russia. The Aleph of Sochi embodies the polemical syncretism that animates the alternate USSRs and quirky time travel that form the subject of this book.

The End of the Fucking World

The post-Soviet era's obsession with revisiting or reconstructing the Soviet past is a trap that writers, filmmakers, and readers have willingly set for themselves, encouraged by a state media and government that want to keep the people looking backward. History has become a nightmare from which there is little public desire to awake. One might expect a boom in stories involving time loops, but despite both the occasional time loop in Soviet film and fiction (such as the 1987 movie *A Mirror for the Hero* (Zerkalo dlia geroia) and the popularity of the American hit film *Groundhog Day*, time loops only make an occasional appearance in post-Soviet entertainment. There is Vladimir Pokrovskii's 2004 story "Groundhog's Day, or Greetings from the Man with Horns," about a man who repeatedly relives his own murder, and Aleksei Slapovskii's 2013 novel *Back* (Vspiat'), in which time starts to flow in reverse on a daily basis (if today is December 12, then tomorrow we will all relive December 11). And, of course, we have already seen the attempt to stop the forward flow of time in *The Man Who Could Not Die*.

I would like to close this book with one of the few works of popular entertainment that has appropriated the tools of regressive, backward-looking storytelling not just for resistance but also to offer glimmers of hope within despair: Oleg Kuvaev's long-running series of short cartoons about a young woman named Masyanya. Begun as a quick-and-dirty online Flash animation project in 2001, over the next two decades it morphed into a pop cultural phenomenon and was even, for a brief period, broadcast on Russian television before returning to its Internet roots. *Masyanya* (as the series is called) was an unlikely vehicle for such a serious purpose: the show is an irreverent, deliberately vulgar set of stories about the title character, her (eventual) husband Hryundel (from the word for "grunting"), their children, and their best friend, Lokhmaty (Shaggy). A typical episode lasts for just a few minutes, detailing the absurd misadventures of its heroes and satirizing life in contemporary Russia. That satire was not particularly political at first, in keeping with the tenor of the early 2000s. After a series of conflicts about the ownership of *Masyanya* and the site that hosted it (mult.ru), Kuvaev left Russia in 2006 and moved to Israel, where he resides to this day. *Masyanya* continued to take place primarily in Kuvaev's hometown of St. Petersburg, but the fact that he no longer lives in Russia has made possible the much more trenchant political commentary that he began to produce in Putin's fourth term.

Like many liberal-leaning artists and intellectuals, Kuvaev was astonished and horrified by Russia's 2022 invasion of Ukraine, sharing the uneasy mix of helplessness and shame experienced by so many of his compatriots in the Russian Federation and abroad (Gavrilova). Not addressing the war was impossible, and, in any case, his cartoons had become increasingly political since the outbreak of the COVID-19 epidemic. In his March 13, 2021, episode "Doppelganger," every Russian citizen is assigned an armed soldier who constantly points a gun at them to make sure they do not say or post anything disloyal. As of August 2022, when this conclusion was written, Kuvaev had posted three videos devoted to Russia's war in Ukraine, and each one is a variation on the conditional subjunctive, a pocket Russian universe that obliges viewers to challenge their understanding of the war through a kind of thought experiment.

The first, "Wakizashi" (March 22, 2022), centers around Masyanya's and Hryundel's attempt to shield Lokhmaty from the horrible truth of the Ukrainian invasion. Just as they survived the pandemic through isolating themselves in their apartment ("Self-Isolation," April 1, 2020), now they contrive to keep Lokhmaty confined to their home and cut off from all sources of information (Lokhmaty's nickname comes from his Ukrainian last name, Lokhmatenko). Like so many Time Crasher stories, and like Russian propaganda about Ukrainian "Nazis," this episode works through its multiple appeals to the experience of World War II. The basic premise is a burlesque on Robert Benigni's 1997 film *Life Is Beautiful*, about parents who convince their young son that their confinement in a concentration camp is just a game, and after Hryundel is forced to reveal the truth to Lokhmaty, he reassures his friend that they can convert an overhead closet shelf into a hiding place, so he can survive "like Anne Frank."

All of their attempts to live in their own bubble and ignore the outside world fail. Lokhmaty finds out the truth after days of frustration at his friends' flimsy excuses for the lack of Wi-Fi, television, or any source of news. Hryundel cannot keep Lokhmaty safe, because the police break in to arrest them both, despite Hryundel's pathetic attempt to demonstrate loyalty to the regime ("We're all for nuclear war! Death to everyone! Death to everyone!"). But the real problem is not their recent attempts to live in their own private worlds. As Hryundel tells Masyanya, "You always said, 'No politics, please! No politics!' So this is what you get." It is a reproach to Masyanya, to Kuvaev himself for avoiding politics for so long, and to the generation of Russians who spent years repeating that same tired phrase and tacitly exempted themselves of any responsibility for their government's actions. They have been living in their own conditional-subjunctive bubble for decades.

Now it turns out that Masyanya's approach to life has been a kind of cynical optimism. "Wakizashi" contains a telling callback to an earlier episode, "The Mirror," from October 10, 2018. This was Kuvaev's first cartoon since the Ministry of Justice expanded its definition of "extremism" and added nearly five thousand books, websites, and other media to its list of banned materials. The episode proper is a hilarious juxtaposition of Masyanya's readings from *The True Mirror of Youth* (Iunosti chestnoe zertsalo), a 1717 guide to manners and family life, and the uncouth antics of her children and husband in twenty-first-century St. Petersburg. The episode concludes with a brief, seemingly unrelated clip of Masyanya and Hryundel dressed in tuxes, performing on a stage (Masyanya is on vocals, while Hryundel is at the piano). She sings a song that has become almost as famous as her many catchphrases over the previous eighteen years. The refrain is "Eto ne pipets," which uses a euphemism for the obscene word *pizdets*; *pizdets*, from the Russian word for "cunt," in this context means something absolutely horrible, including possibly the end of everything. My translation (below) is not literal and does not rhyme, but is meant to convey the overall sense:

> We're not totally fucked [*eto ne pipets*]
> We're not totally fucked
> Things just really suck, but we're not totally fucked
> We're definitely not totally fucked.
> We'll live a bit longer
> We're not totally fucked
> We're not totally fucked
> Don't exaggerate, or I'll fuck you up
> Let's relax and hang
> And take the cucumber out of our ass
> Don't shout about every little thing

(Don't shout about every little thing)
Don't fill my brain with nonsense
We're not totally fucked
We're not totally fucked
Whatever they say on the Net, we're not totally fucked
It's all happened a million times before
It all sucks, but we're not totally fucked.

Her song took on a second life during the COVID-19 pandemic, since this was just the message many people wanted (and needed) to hear. But now, in "Wakizashi," Hryundel tells Masyanya that thousands have died in Ukraine, cities have been destroyed, the whole world is against Russia, and the state is imprisoning people over the slightest expression of dissent, and concludes: "This time we really are totally fucked" (*Na etot raz deistvitel'no pipets*). In response, Masyanya sings:

Now we're totally fucked
Now we're totally fucked
Now, at last, we're totally fucked.

Two years after encouraging her audience with the thought that things could always be worse, Masyanya has no more illusions about the direction of her country. Her words, and her demeanor as she sings them, could easily be interpreted as despair, but they actually are a turning point from critique to action. Her husband's words have sunk in, and not only those describing the slaughter in Ukraine; she has also taken to heart his earlier reproach about her desire to keep her distance from politics. Now Masyanya, who for two decades had been a symbol of Putin-era absurdism and directionless irony, has understood that her life "without politics" was a carefully curated illusion that is no longer tenable. In the best Russian moralistic tradition, she, like the eighteenth-century social critic Alexander Radishchev, embarks on a journey from St. Petersburg to Moscow. Physically, her trip is far less arduous than that of her predecessor; it's the twenty-first century, and she takes a high-speed train. But Kuvaev replaces her actual trip with a symbolic montage that completely disrupts the serialized world of *Masyanya*. Animation is replaced by a series of actual photos of the devastation in Ukraine: bombed-out buildings, desperate refugees, and an aid worker comforting a survivor. In the corner of each still is Masyanya's face, drawn in black-and-white, her mouth agape in horror and her eyes bulging out of her forehead. It is both the Masyanya we have come to know over the past twenty years and someone new. The scene lasts only thirty seconds, though it seems to go on much longer. The temporary shift in medium from animation to still photography has done its job: Masyanya's absurd little micro-world has burst like the bubble it has always been.

Now Masyanya walks along the streets of Moscow, a scene that is animated in black and white (only Masyanya is rendered in her usual color scheme). Like her train trip, this walk is more thematic than realistic. Everywhere she goes, Masyanya passes signs with pro-war slogans: "The final solution of the Ukrainian problem"; "Yes to war!"; "Bombs and rockets for Ukrainian children"; "The people are with the Führer" (the word "with" in Russian, usually a Cyrillic *s*, has been replaced with the Latin Z, a symbol of support for the war effort); "The whole world is Nazis! Except us!"; "Z. Catch the national traitors!"; and "Z. Stalin is a hunk!" (the "Zs" in the last two slogans are made to look like swastikas). Though the slogans steal the show, Masyanya's own role here is noteworthy: every time a slogan comes her way, her eyes turn to stare at it. She has finally stopped looking away.

Masyanya's newfound activism does not negate the value of twenty years of cartoons; to the contrary, her reputation for insouciance helps her achieve her goal. When she is confronted by two armed guards at the gates of the Kremlin, there is no realistic way for her to gain entry. Instead, Kuvaev breaks the cartoon's long-standing fictional frame: the guards are *Masyanya* fans. They laugh, in imitation of her well-known *Beavis and Butthead*-style chuckle, and immediately quote two of her most famous catch phrases: "Go fuck yourself, director!" and "Let's go have a smoke!" They let her in ("since you're Masyanya!"), chuckling and repeating the same catch phrases.

When Masyana makes her way into Putin's bunker, the Russian president, unlike his guards, has no idea who she is. Instead of using her apparently famous name, Masyanya describes herself with words that could belong to millions of women in the Russian Federation: "I'm the wife of my husband and the mother of my children." She tells Putin he is a war criminal who has dragged two countries into hell out of vanity and an inferiority complex but offers him a gift: a Japanese short sword (the *wakizashi* of the episode's title), which is "convenient for, you know . . ." When she gets back home, Hryundel whispers the news to her; the audience can't hear, but we know what he is saying: Putin has killed himself. ("Well, I was, I was very persuasive!")

"Wakizashi" is a powerful and shocking revenge fantasy, the sort of cartoon that could never have appeared on the Internet had Kuvaev remained in Russia. It is a persuasive work of political art, but even as it strives to show the complicity of ordinary Russians who have turned a blind eye to their government's actions for years, it still replicates the structure of the conditional-subjunctive fantasy world: this episode takes place in an alternative present in which Russians can breathe a sigh of relief. The tyrant is dead.

In the next episode ("How to Explain to Your Kids," May 12, 2022), Masyanya, Hryundel, and Lokhmaty stage a six-minute theatrical review of Russian and Soviet history in order to help their children understand what is happening in Ukraine. It's a sharp and uncompromising view of the rise of Putin and his territorial ambitions, yet still somehow lighthearted and funny thanks to Masyanya's vulgar, sarcastic narration and the men's over-the-top performances. The choice of home theater as an educational vehicle makes sense because it treats their apartment once again as an isolated pocket of humanism in contrast to a cruel and dangerous external world. Throughout the performance, and especially afterward, Masyanya is at great pains to make the children understand that they cannot talk about what they have seen at school. When the kids are about to leave for the day, she explains that, in her time, her parents also told her to keep her mouth shut about certain issues when she was not home, and now her own children will have to do the same. In fighting against state propaganda within the confines of her apartment and telling her children that what they hear at school is lies, she is teaching her son and daughter how to operate in two opposing worlds of meaning, each with its own sense of politics and history. The children are not time travelers per se, but they may as well be; they are learning to navigate multiple realities over the course of a single day.

In the last of the war-themed episodes to date ("Sankt-Mariuburg," July 11, 2022), Kuvaev creates yet another conditional-subjunctive world in an attempt to do for his viewers on YouTube what Masyana does for her children: use art to make them understand Russia's crimes in Ukraine. By the end of the episode, the viewers also learn how its story came to be, both diegetically (it's all a nightmare Masyana is having) and nondiegetically (St. Petersburg and Mariupol are sister cities, a fact Kuvaev exploits by having the atrocities of Mariupol occur in his native city and using a portmanteau of both cities' names to give the episode its title).

None of this is explained at the beginning, however; instead, viewers are suddenly thrown into a world of unrelenting horror along with Masyanya herself, whom Hryundel awakens early in the morning with the news that Russian cities are being bombed by China. Step by step, the family's sense of safety is whittled away: they can't escape by car because the roads are blocked; their building is destroyed by a bomb; Hryundel is killed by another bomb while his family waits for him in a shelter; Masyana dies after yet another explosion. Soon only Badya, her son, is left to detail his experiences in his diary as he hides alone, underground. Two Chinese soldiers throw a grenade into the cellar, and Badya dies as well. Throughout the episode, Masyana and Hryundel cannot help but be continually appalled that this is now their reality: "How can this be happening in the twenty-first century?" St. Petersburg's most famous monuments are ravaged by shelling, and in one of the most painfully ironic moments in the entire episode, Hryundel hears about people who have found safety in the Ukrainian city of Bucha (the site of mass slaughter by Russian troops in our world). On television, the president of China (speaking Russian in an unfortunately racist caricature), declares that there is no such thing as Russia, that Russians are really just Ukrainians who stole all their land from China.

When Masyanya awakens from her nightmare, she muses aloud about the importance of empathy, driving home a message that one hopes is already obvious. Just imagine the terrible things committed by your country were happening to you: how would you feel? In the panoply of alternate Russias, in which the fate of the nation depends on the intervention of ordinary "heroes" righting historical wrongs, Kuvaev's *Masyanya* stands out as a rare call to conscience and responsibility rather than nursing post-imperial grievances. If I were a Time Crasher who could intervene in the course of post-Soviet Russian literature and entertainment, I would find a way to make fewer triumphant war stories and more *Masyanyas*.

Works Cited

Entries for films and television series are at the end of the works cited.

"About DAU." https://www.dau.com/en/about-us.
Agamben, Giorgio. *Homo Sacer: Sovereign Power and Bare Life*, translated by Daniel Heller-Roazen. Stanford, CA: Stanford University Press, 1998.
Akopov, Eduard, Aleksei Kozuliaev, and Iulii Guzman. *Park sovetskogo perioda*. Moscow: Geleos, 2007.
Akunin, Boris. *Komediia. Tragediia*. Moscow: Zakharov, 2015.
Aptekman, Marina. "Forward to the Past, or Two Radical Views on the Russian Nationalist Future: Pyotr Krasnov's *Behind the Thistle* and Vladimir Sorokin's *Days of an Oprichnik*." *Slavic and East European Journal* 53, no. 2 (2009): 241–60.
Aptekman, Marina. "The Old New Russian: The Dual Nature of Style and Language in *Day of the Oprichnik* and *Sugar Kremlin*." In *Vladimir Sorokin's Languages*, edited by Tina Roesen et al. Bergen: Slavica Bergensia, 2016. https://boap.uib.no/books/sb/catalog/view/9/8/174-1.
Arsen'ev, Sergei. "Sergei Arsen'ev o svoem tvorchestve." December 20, 2011. http://samlib.ru/a/arsenxew_s_w/about.shtml.
Arsen'ev, Sergei. *Studentka, komsomolka, sportsmenka*. Moscow: EKSMO, 2012.
Bacon-Smith, Camille. "Training New Members." *The Fan Fiction Studies Reader*, edited by Karen Hellekson and Kristina Busse, 138–58. Iowa City: University of Iowa Press, 2014.
Ball, Tom. "Third Empire: Fantasy Novel Predicted Russian Invasion." *The Times*. March 28, 2022. https://www.thetimes.co.uk/article/ukraine-russia-war-third-empire-fantasy-novel-predicted-russian-invasion-0zmgv5fz8.
Baran, Emily B. "Contested Victims: Jehovah's Witnesses and the Russian Orthodox Church, 1990 to 2004." *Religion, State and Society* 35, no. 3 (2007): 261–78.
Baran, Emily B. *Dissent on the Margins: How Soviet Jehovah's Witnesses Defied Communism and Lived to Preach about It*. Oxford: Oxford University Press, 2014.
Baran, Emily B. "From Sectarians to Extremists: The Language of Marginalization in Soviet and Post-Soviet Society." *Soviet and Post-Soviet Review* 46, no. 2 (2019): 105–27.
Bauman, Zygmunt. "Times of Interregnum." *Ethics and Global Practice* 5, no. 1 (2012): 49–56.
Bellamy, Edward. *Looking Backward*. Mineola, NY: Dover Publications, 1996.
Bershidsky, Leonid. "Putin Does Live in Another Reality." March 3, 2014. https://www.recordnet.com/story/opinion/columns/2014/03/03/putin-does-live-in-another/38581942007/.
Beumers, Birgit. *Nikita Mikhalkov: Between Nostalgia and Nationalism*. London: I. B. Tauris, 2004.
Beumers, Birgit. "Nostalgic Journeys in Post-Soviet Cinema: Towards a Lost Home?" In *European Cinema in Motion: Migrant and Diaspora Film in Contemporary*

Europe, edited by Daniela Berghahn and Claudia Sternberg, 96–113. New York: Palgrave, 2010.

Bird, Robert. "Ilya Khrzhanovsky's 'DAU.'" January 24, 2017–February 17, 2019. Centre Pompidou, Paris, Théâtre du Châtelet, Paris, Théâtre de la Ville, Paris." *Art/Agenda*, March 12, 2019. https://www.art-agenda.com/criticism/256823/ilya-khrzhanovsky-s-dau.

Black, Holly, and Justine Larbaleister, eds. *Zombies vs. Unicorns*. New York: Margaret K. McElderry Books, 2010.

Boele, Otto, Boris Noordenbos, and Ksenia Robbe. "'Perestroika and the 1990s—Those Were the Best Years of My Life!' Nostalgia for the Post-Soviet Limbo." In *Post-Soviet Nostalgia: Confronting the Empire's Legacies*, edited by Otto Boele, Boris Noordenbos, and Ksenia Robbe, 203–23. New York: Routledge, 2020.

Boele, Otto, Boris Noordenbos, and Ksenia Robbe, eds. *Post-Soviet Nostalgia: Confronting the Empire's Legacies*. New York: Routledge, 2020.

Bogdanov, Alexander. *Red Star: The First Bolshevik Utopia*, translated by Charles Rougle. Bloomington: Indiana University Press, 1984.

Bonaut, Joseba, and Teresa Ojer. "Locating Generational and Cultural Clashes in the Transfer of Successful Formats between the United Kingdom, Spain and the United States: The Case of Life on Mars." In *Life on Mars: From Manchester to New York*, edited by Stephen Lacey and Ruth McElroy, 153–67. Cardiff: University of Wales Press, 2012.

Bondareva, Olga. "The Glass Dream." *SSSR-2061*, volume 2. E-book.

Bordoni, Carlo. *Interregnum: Beyond Liquid Modernity*. New York: Transcript, 2016.

Borenstein, Eliot. *Meanwhile, in Russia . . . : Russian Internet Memes and Viral Video*. New York: Bloomsbury, 2022.

Borenstein, Eliot. *Overkill: Sex and Violence in Russian Popular Culture*. Ithaca, NY: Cornell University Press, 2008.

Borenstein, Eliot. *Plots against Russia: Conspiracy and Fantasy after Socialism*. Ithaca, NY: Cornell University Press, 2019.

Borenstein, Eliot. *Soviet Self-Hatred: The Secret Identities of Postsocialism*. Ithaca, NY: Cornell University Press, 2023.

Borenstein, Eliot. "Suspending Disbelief: Cults and Postmodernism in Contemporary Russia." In *Consuming Russia: Popular Culture, Sex, and Society since Gorbachev*, edited by Adele Marie Barker, 437–62. Durham, NC: Duke University Press, 1999.

Borges, Jorge Luis. "The Aleph." *The Aleph and Other Stories*, translated by Andrew Hurley, 118–33. New York: Penguin, 2004.

Bormatova, Ekaterina. "'Ia ustal, ia ukhozhu': 20 let fraze, kotoruiu El'tsin nikogda ne govoril." *Ekaterinburg Onlain*. December 21, 2019. https://www.e1.ru/text/politics/2019/12/31/66418294/.

Boym, Svetlana. *The Future of Nostalgia*. New York: Basic Books, 2001.

Bradbury, Ray. *Fahrenheit 451*. New York: Simon and Schuster, 2011.

Bradbury, Ray. *The Stories of Ray Bradbury*. New York: HarperCollins, 1983.

Buckley, William F. "Our Mission Statement." *National Review*. November 19, 1955. https://www.nationalreview.com/1955/11/our-mission-statement-william-f-buckley-jr/.

Bulgakov, Mikhail. *Flight*, translated by Howard Colyer. Lulu.com. 2012.

Bulgakov, Mikhail. "Ivan Vasilievich." In *Russian Satiric Comedy: Six Plays*, edited and translated by Laurence Selnick, 157–98. New York: Performing Arts Journal Publications, 1983.

Burnosov, Iurii. "Moskva 22." *Besposhchadnaia tolerantnost'*, edited by S. V. Chekmaev, 241–60. Moscow: EKSMO, 2012.
Butler, Octavia E. *Kindred*. New York: Beacon, 2003.
Buttonwood. "Britain: Back to Being the Sick Man of Europe? Constructing a Scenario of British Decline Is All Too Easy." *The Economist*. July 19, 2017. https://www.economist.com/buttonwoods-notebook/2017/07/19/britain-back-to-being-the-sick-man-of-europe.
Carassava, Anthee. "Euro Crisis: Why Greece Is the Sick Man of Europe." *BBC News*. December 20, 2011. https://www.bbc.com/news/world-europe-16256235.
Card, Orson Scott. *Ender's Game*. New York: Tor, 2021.
Cavendish, Philip. "DAU: Outside and Beyond History." In "Soviet Playtime: Architectures of Power and Profligacy in DAU," edited by Philip Cavendish, Natascha Drubek, and Irina Schulzki. Special issue of *Apparatus: Film, Media and Digital Cultures in Central and Eastern Europe* 14 (2022). https://www.apparatusjournal.net/index.php/apparatus/article/view/304/588.
Charodeyy. "Kak menia prinimali v sektu 'svidetelei SSSR.'" February 15, 2020. https://charodeyy.livejournal.com/99377.html.
Chekmaev, Oleg, ed. *Modnoverie: Ot strashnogo do smeshnogo*. Moscow: Snezhnyi kom, 2017.
Chesnakov, Edvard, and Oleg Kashin. "Oleg Kashin: Est' svidetel'stva, chto Gorbachev dralsia do poslednego za sokhranenie Sovetskogo Soiuza." *Radio Komsomol'skaia Pravda*. December 8, 2020. https://radiokp.ru/podcast/otdelnaya-tema-s-olegom-kashinym/178065.
Chizhova, Elena. *Kitaist*. Moscow: AST, 2017.
Clowes, Edith. *Russia on the Edge: Imagined Geographies and Post-Soviet Identities*. Ithaca, NY: Cornell University Press, 2011.
Diachenko, Marina, and Sergei Diachenko. *Armaged-Dom*. Moscow: OLMA-Press, 2000.
Dick, Philip K. *The Exegesis of Philip K. Dick*, edited by Pamela Jackson and Jonathan Lethem. London: Gollancz, 2012.
Dick, Philip K. *The Man in the High Castle*. New York: Harper Voyager, 2012.
Dick, Philip K. *Martian Time-Slip*. New York: Harper Voyager, 2012.
Dick, Philip K. *Radio Free Albemuth*. New York: Harper Voyager, 2020.
Dick, Philip K. *Valis*. Boston: Mariner Books, 2011.
Drubek, Natascha, John Leman Riley, and Irina Schulzki, eds. "*DAU*: Sometimes This Space Can Hurt You." *Apparatus: Film, Media and Digital Cultures in Central and Eastern Europe* 10 (2020). https://www.apparatusjournal.net/index.php/apparatus/article/view/230.
Dumai sam, dumai seichas. "2045-i. Epizod 1: Otkrovenniia byvshego millionera." May 1, 2021. https://www.youtube.com/watch?v=OM1DQaKIVrA.
Dumai sam, dumai seichas. "Bound to Wake Up: Class Dream of Humanity." September 26, 2019. https://www.youtube.com/watch?v=w3NtIiBjPsE.
Dumai sam, dumai seichas. "The Real Stalin." February 20, 2020. https://www.youtube.com/watch?v=7GZBYgMlPcI.
Dumancic, Marko. *Men out of Focus: The Soviet Masculinity Crisis in the Long Sixties*. Toronto: University of Toronto Press, 2021.
Dustman, Christian, et al. "From Sick Man of Europe to Economic Superstar: Germany's Resurgent Economy." *Journal of Economic Perspectives* 28, no. 1 (2014): 167–88.
Dvorkin, A. L. *Sektovedenie: Totalitarnye sekty. Opyt sistematicheskogo issledovaniia*. Moscow: Khristianskaia biblioteka, 2000.

Eberstadt, Nicholas. "Russia the Sick Man of Europe." *National Affairs* (Winter 2005): 1–20.
Efremova, Tatiana. "Beyond Nostalgia: Remediating the Soviet Body in Russian Culture under Putin." PhD diss. New York University, 2022.
Elin, Alexander. "Nash durdom (golosuet za Putina)." Performed by Rabfak. https://www.youtube.com/watch?v=CgotKEcLjgg.
Elizarov, Mikhail, *The Librarian*, translated by Andrew Bromfield. London: Pushkin Press, 2015.
Englund, Will, and Kathy Lally. "In Russia, Volunteers Step Up." *The Washington Post*, February 2, 2013.
Epstein, Mikhail N. *After the Future: The Paradoxes of Postmodernism and Contemporary Russian Culture*, translated by Anesa Miller-Pogacar. Amherst, MA: Amherst College Press, 1995.
Fedorova, Lioudmila. "The Russia They Have Lost: The Russian Gangster as Nostalgic Hero." In *A Companion to the Gangster Film*, edited by George S. Larke-Walsh, 302–18. New York: Wiley-Blackwell, 2018.
Fedotov, Nikita. "Dvoinoi obman: Retsenzii na serial 'Nazad v SSSR.'" October 3, 2011. https://eot.su/smi/art-kritika/retsenziya-na-serial-nazad-v-sssr.
Filippov, David. "Yekaterinburg, the Russian City That Says: 'Don't Call Us Siberia.'" *The Independent*. January 7, 2017. https://www.independent.co.uk/news/world/europe/siberia-russia-city-yekaterinburg-urals-europe-asia-a7513506.html.
Fishman, Leonid. "My popali." *Drushba narodov*, no. 4 (2010). https://magazines.gorky.media/druzhba/2010/4/my-popali.html.
Frei, Max. *The Stranger*, translated by Polly Gannon. *Labyrinths of Echo*, volume 1. New York: Overlook Press, 2011.
Freud, Sigmund. "The Uncanny." *The Standard Edition of the Complete Psychological Works of Sigmund Freud*, volume 27: *(1917–1919): An Infantile Neurosis and Other Works*, 217–56. London: Vintage, 1999.
Fukuyama, Francis. *The End of History and the Last Man*. New York: Free Press, 1992.
Gabaldon, Diana. *Outlander*. New York: Dell, 1992.
Gabowitsch, Mischa. *Protest in Putin's Russia*. Malden, MA: Polity, 2017.
Gaiman, Neil, Kelley Jones, et al. *The Sandman*, volume 2: *Dream Country*. New York: Vertigo, 2011.
Garner, Ian. "From Stalingrad to the Stars: Science Fiction and Memory in Putin's Russia." April 15, 2020. https://www.igarner.net/articles/scifi-stalingrad.
Gavrilova, Alla. "Nastalo vremia, kogda molchat' nel'zia. Interv'iu s Olegom Kuvaevym o poslednem episode 'Masiani.'" July 12, 2022. https://www.newsru.co.il/israel/12jul2022/kuvaev_501.html?fbclid=IwAR2Rn-kxmSdHw3nRufe6uPLCHHp5q_bRWanygmin1-_YfYJjBdsQqB67VQQ.
Gibson, William. "The Future Is Already Here—It's Just Not Evenly Distributed." *The Economist*. December 4, 2003.
Gilman, Charlotte Perkins. *Herland: A Lost Feminist Utopian Novel*. New York: Pantheon, 1979.
Gleick, James. *Time Travel: A History*. New York: Vintage, 2017.
Glukhovsky, Dmitry. *Metro 2033*, translated by Natasha Randall. London: Gollancz, 2011.
Gramsci, Antonio. *Selections from the Prison Notebooks of Antonio Gramsci*, edited and translated by Quintin Hoare and Geoffrey Nowell-Smith. London: Lawrence and Wishart, 1971.
"Grazhdane SSSR arestovany v Krasnodare za prigotovlenie k ubiistvu ravvina." *Kommersant*. September 23, 2020. https://www.kommersant.ru/doc/4502519.

Greenfield, Nathan W. "Post-Soviet Pulp Fiction: Presages of the War in Ukraine." *University World News*. April 16, 2022. https://www.universityworldnews.com/post.php?story=20220415151814289.

Griffiths, Mark. "Moscow after the Apocalypse." *Slavic Review* 72, no. 3 (2013): 481–504.

Grix, Jonathan, and Nina Kramereva. "The Sochi Winter Olympics and Russia's Unique Soft Power Strategy." *Sport in Society* 20, no. 4 (2017): 461–75.

Hanson, Stephen. *Time and Revolution: Marxism and the Design of Soviet Institutions*. Chapel Hill: University of North Carolina Press, 1997.

Hayden, Lisa. "The Big Wheel Effect: Salnikov's Chilling *Department*." *Lizok's Bookshelf*. May 12, 2019. http://lizoksbooks.blogspot.com/2019/05/the-big-wheel-effect-salnikovs-chilling.html.

Hanukai, Maxim. "Resurrection by Surrogation: Spectral Performance in Putin's Russia." *Slavic Review* 79, no. 4 (2020): 800–824.

Heinlein, Robert A. "All You Zombies." In *The Fantasies of Robert A. Heinlein*. New York: Tor, 1999.

Henkin, David M. *The Week: A History of the Unnatural Rhythms That Made Us Who We Are*. New Haven, Yale University Press, 2021.

Herbert, Frank. *Dune*. London: Penguin, 2005.

Hoban, Russell. *Ridley Walker: The Expanded Edition*. Bloomington: Indiana University Press, 1998.

Hoet, Madelon. "The City and the Underground in *Metro 2033* and *Metro: Last Light*." In *The New Urban Gothic: Global Gothic in the Age of the Anthropocene*, edited by Holly-Gale Millette and Ruth Heholt, 113–30. New York: Palgrave, 2020.

Howanitz, Gernot. "Metro 2033—More than a Cinegame?" *Digital Icons* 8 (2012): 97–116.

Huntington, Samuel P. *The Clash of Civilizations and the Remaking of the World Order*. New York: Simon and Schuster, 2011.

Huxley, Aldous. *Brave New World*. New York: Vintage Classics, 2020.

Iampol'skii, Mikhail. "DAU: Ekstsess, isteriia, razrushenie." *Seans*. January 23, 2019. https://seance.ru/articles/dau-yampolski-fragmentum/.

"Iunost' Ostankinskoi bashni: Park sovetskogo perioda." July 13, 2019. https://vk.com/video-25424708_456239088.

Iur'ev, Mikhail. *Tret'ia imperiia: Rossia, kotoraia dolzhna byt'*. St. Petersburg: Limbus, 2019.

Ivanova, Natal'ia. "I ptitsu paulin izrubit' na kaklety." *Znamia*, no. 3 (2001). http://magazines.russ.ru/znamia/2001/3/rec_tolst.html.

Jameson, Frederic. *Archaeologies of the Future: The Desire Called Utopia and Other Science Fictions*. New York: Verso, 2005.

Jamison, Anne. *Fic: Why Fanfiction Is Taking Over the World*. New York: SmartPop, 2013.

Jones, Sharon L. "Ladies against Women Ladylike in Name Only." Associated Press. August 5, 1985. https://apnews.com/article/6fb53b18e341cd0a66f185f51203f02b.

Jowitt, Ken. *New World Disorder: The Leninist Extinction*. Berkeley: University of California Press, 1992.

Kalinin, Ilya. "Future-in-the-past/Past-in-the-future: Sovetskoe budushchee postsovetskogo proshlogo." *Seans*. May 14, 2013. https://seance.ru/articles/future_in_the_past/.

Kalinin, Ilya. "Nostalgic Modernization: The Soviet Past as 'Historical Horizon.'" *Slavonica* 17, no. 2 (2011): 156–66.

Kalinin, Ilya. "Soviet Atlantis: A Melancholy Fantasy of the Post-Soviet Subject." *Eurozine*, November 22, 2019. https://www.eurozine.com/soviet-atlantis/.

Kataev, Valentin. *Time, Forward!*, translated by Charles Malamuth. Evanston, IL: Northwestern University Press, 1995.

Keyes, Daniel. *Flowers for Algernon*. Boston: Mariner, 2005.

Khabibulin, Yuri. "Mother's Day." *SSSR-2061*, volume 4. E-book.

Khapaeva, Dina. "Putin Is Just Following the Manual: A Utopian Russian Novel Predicted Putin's War Plan." *The Atlantic*. March 26, 2022. https://www.theatlantic.com/ideas/archive/2022/03/putin-kremlin-foreign-policy-strategy/629388/.

Khval'skii, Andrei. "Summer Internship." *SSSR-2061*, volume 5. E-book.

Klimova, Mariia. "Ausdaidery: Kak dentist Sergei Taraskin vozglavil SSSR, RSFSR i Rossiiskuiu imperiiu." *Mediazona*. August 21, 2017. https://zona.media/article/2017/08/21/outsiders-1-president.

Kniazev, Miloslav. "Fifth Medal." *SSSR-2061*, volume 9. E-book.

Kobierecki, Michał. "Russia and Its International Image: From Sochi Olympic Games to Annexing Crimea." *International Studies* 18, no. 2 (2016): 165–86.

Kobrin, Kirill. "The Eternally Wonderful Present, or Russia's Need for a New Culture." *Open Democracy*. November 18, 2016. https://www.opendemocracy.net/en/odr/eternally-wonderful-present-or-russia-s-need-for-new-culture/.

Kobrin, Kirill. *Postsovetskii mavzolei proshlogo: Istoriia vremen Putina*. Moscow: Novoe russkoe obozrenie, 2017.

Kobrin, Kirill, and Mark Lipovetskii. "Strakh nastoiashchego: Russkaiia literatura segodnia." *Colta.ru*. June 12, 2017. https://www.colta.ru/articles/literature/15386-strah-nastoyaschego-russkaya-literatura-segodnya.

Kornbluth, Cyril M. *The Best of Cyril M. Kornbluth*. New York: Ballantine, 1977.

Koroliuk, Mikhail Aleksandrovich. *Spasti SSSR! Infiltratsiia*. Moscow: Alfa-Kniga. E-book.

Kozlenko, Ivan. "The Anatomy of Totalitarian Violence: From DAU to Babyn Yar." In "Soviet Playtime: Architectures of Power and Profligacy in DAU," ed. Philip Cavendish, Natascha Drubek, and Irina Schulzki. Special issue of *Apparatus: Film, Media and Digital Cultures in Central and Eastern Europe* 14 (2022). https://www.apparatusjournal.net/index.php/apparatus/article/view/312/590.

Kozlov, Ivan. "Soiuz nerushimyi." *Takie dela*. March 17, 2021. https://takiedela.ru/2021/03/soyuz-nerushimyy/.

kpt_flint. "Obraz budushchego ne nuzhen?" July 12, 2021. https://ru-2061.livejournal.com/147917.html.

Krasnov, P. N. *Za chertopokhom* (*Beyond the Thistle*). Berlin: Ol'ga D'iakov, 1922.

Krusanov, Pavel. *Ukus angela*. Moscow: Amfora, 2000.

Kukui, Il'ia. "Moia lichnaia granitsa s Institutom." *Apparatus: Film, Media and Digital Cultures in Central and Eastern Europe* 10 (2020). https://www.apparatusjournal.net/index.php/apparatus/article/view/230.

Kukulin, Ilya. "Longing for Fear and Darkness: 'Oppositional Grassroots Stalinism' in the 1970s–1980s and Its Influence on Legitimizing Political Elites in Today's Russia." In *Post-Soviet Nostalgia: Confronting the Empire's Legacies*, edited by Otto Boele, Boris Noordenbos, and Ksenia Robbe, 89–115. New York: Routledge, 2020.

Lavery, David. "The Emigration of Life on Mars: Sam and Gene Do America." In *Life on Mars: From Manchester to New York*, edited by Stephen Lacey and Ruth McElroy, 145–52. Cardiff: University of Wales Press, 2012.

Lavrov, Sergei. "70 samykh proval'nykh rossiiskikh fil'mov." April 7, 2014. https://filmz.ru/pub/72/28527_1.htm.
Le Guin, Ursula K. "Ursula K. Le Guin's Speech at National Book Awards: 'Books Aren't Just Commodities.'" *The Guardian*, November 20, 2014. https://www.theguardian.com/books/2014/nov/20/ursula-k-le-guin-national-book-awards-speech.
Lerner, Amanda. "Remembering the Future: Time Travel Narratives in Soviet and Post-Soviet Russia." PhD diss., Yale University. 2018.
Lévi-Strauss, Claude. "The Structural Study of Myth." *Journal of American Folklore* 68 (270) (October–December 1955): 428–44.
Limonov, Eduard. *SSSR—nash drevnii Rim*. Moscow: Ad Marginem, 2014.
Lipovetsky, Mark. "DAU. Dir. Ilya Khrzhanovsky. Paris: Phenomenon Films, 2019. 330 minutes. Color." *Slavic Review* 80, no. 2 (2021): 390–91.
Lipovetsky, Mark. "Introduction: *Ressentiment* Monsters." In *The Man Who Couldn't Die: The Tale of an Authentic Human Being* by Olga Slavnikova, translated by Marian Schwartz, vii–xix. New York: Columbia University Press, 2019.
Lipovetsky, Mark. *Postmodern Crises: From Lolita to Pussy Riot*. New York, Academic Studies Press, 2017.
Lipovetsky, Mark. "Sled Kysi." *Iskusstvo kino*, no. 2 (2001). http://kinoart.ru/archive/2001/02/n2-article21.
Lipovetsky, Mark, and Aleksandr Etkind. "Vozvrashchenie Tritona: Sovetskaia katastrofa i postsovetskii roman." *Novoe literaturnoe obozrenie*, no. 94 (2008): 174–206.
Livianos, Dmitris. "The 'Sick Man' Paradox: History, Rhetoric and the 'European Character' of Turkey." *Journal of Southern Europe and the Balkans* 8, no. 3 (2006): 299–311.
lomasm. "Da na kher Ona mne sdalas'." December 30, 2015. https://wfi.lomasm.ru/.
lomasm. "Krasnyi zavet. I tot, u kogo net protivogaza." December 30, 2015. https://wfi.lomasm.ru/.
lomasm. "S novym godom, liubimyi krasnyi plashch." December 30, 2015. https://wfi.lomasm.ru/.
lomasm. "Sleduia zavetam Il'icha." September 7, 2015. https://wfi.lomasm.ru/.
lomasm. "Vse radostnee zhit'." September 7, 2015. https://wfi.lomasm.ru/.
Lounsbery, Anne. *Life Is Elsewhere: Symbolic Geography in the Russian Provinces, 1800–1917*. DeKalb: Northern Illinois University Press, 2019.
Lukianenko, Sergei. *Chistovik*. Moscow: AST, 2016.
Lukianenko, Sergei. "Popadantsy k Stalinu." *Izvestiia*. May 25, 2010. http://izvestia.ru/news/362106.
Lukianenko, Sergei. "Vitia Solnyshkin i Iosif Stalin." *Zateriannyi dozor: Luchshaia fantastika 2017*, edited by Aleksei Sinitsyn, 389–98. Moscow: AST, 2016.
Maiakovskii, Vladimir. *Sochineniia v dvukh tomakh*. Moscow: Pravda, 1988.
Makanin, Vladimir. *Escape Hatch and The Long Road Ahead: Two Novellas*, translated by Mary Ann Szporluk. Ann Arbor, MI: Ardis, 1997.
Mammone, Andrea, and Guiseppi A. Vetri. *Italy Today: The Sick Man of Europe*. New York: Routledge, 2010.
Marin, Louis. "Disneyland: A Degenerate Utopia." *Glyph*, no. 1 (1977): 50–66.
Marinina, Aleksandra. *Gor'kii kvest*. 3 vols. Moscow: Eksmo, 2018.
McCartney, Gerry, et al. "Has Scotland Always Been the 'Sick Man' of Europe? An Observational Study from 1855 to 2006." *European Journal of Public Health* 22, no. 6 (2012): 756–60.

Medvedev, Sergei. *The Return of the Russian Leviathan*, translated by Stephen Dalziel. New York: Polity, 2019.

Meerson, Ol'ga. *Nesvobodnaia veshch': Poetika neostraneniia v tvorchestve Platonova*. Oakland, CA: Berkeley Slavic Specialties, 1997.

Melikhov, Grigorii. "V Orenburge osuzhdeny grazhdane SSSR." June 7, 2022. https://bloknot-rostov.ru/news/v-rostovskoy-oblasti-zaderzhali-uchastnikov-organi-1512713.

Mel'nikov, Viktor. "Dvizhenie 'zhivykh liudei-suverenov.'" *Iriney.ru*. March 11, 2019. https://iriney.ru/okkultnyie/dvizhenie-suverenov-zhivyix-lyudej/novosti-o-dvizhenii-zhivyix-lyudej-suverenov/dvizhenie-zhivyix-lyudej-suverenov.html.

Mendlesohn, Farah. *Rhetorics of Fantasy*. Middletown, CT: Wesleyan University Press, 2008.

Merzlikin, Pavel. "Pravitel'stvo v izgnanii: Kak moskovskii dantist vozrozhdaet SSSR." March 29, 2016. http://www.furfur.me/furfur/changes/changes/217141-back-in-ussr. Archived at https://web.archive.org/web/20200215003857/http://www.furfur.me/furfur/changes/changes/217141-back-in-ussr.

Miéville, China. *The City and the City*. New York: Del Rey, 2010.

Miller, Walter M., Jr. *A Canticle for Leibowitz*. New York: HarperCollins, 2006.

Mills, Brett. "American Remake—Shudder: Online Debates about Life on Mars and 'British-ness.'" In *Life on Mars: From Manchester to New York*, edited by Stephen Lacey and Ruth McElroy, 133–44. Cardiff: University of Wales Press, 2012.

"Miniust vnes 'Grazhdan SSSR' v spisok ekstremistov: Chto eto za organizatsiia?" *BBC News*. August 24, 2022. https://www.bbc.com/russian/news-62661646.

Moore, Alan, and Dave Gibbons. *Watchmen*. New York: DC Comics, 1987.

More, Thomas. *Utopia*, edited by George M. Logan. Cambridge: Cambridge University Press, 2016.

Morson, Gary Saul. *The Boundaries of Genre: Dostoyevsky's Diary of a Writer and the Traditions of Literary Utopia*. Evanston, IL: Northwestern University Press, 1988.

Nadkarni, Maya, and Olga Shevchenko. "The Politics of Nostalgia: The Case for Comparative Analysis of Post-Soviet Practices." *Ab Imperio*, no. 2 (2004): 487–519.

Nazinov, Pyotr. "Red Means Blood." *SSSR-2061*, volume 1. E-book.

"Neoizychestvo ne ravno 'nekrokommunizm.'" November 12, 2020. https://tradition.foundation/112020/kl_necrocommunism/.

"A New Sick Man of Europe." *The Economist*. April 12, 2007. https://www.economist.com/europe/2007/04/12/a-new-sick-man-of-europe.

Noordenbos, Boris. "To Be Continued: Post-Soviet Nostalgia in Sergei Miroshinechko's Time-Lapse Documentary Series *Born in the USSR*." In *Post-Soviet Nostalgia: Confronting the Empire's Legacies*, edited by Otto Boele, Boris Noordenbos, and Ksenia Robbe, 133–52. New York: Routledge, 2020.

O'Rourke, Breffni. "Western Press Review: Milosevic and the New 'Sick Man of Europe.'" *RFE/RL*. January 9, 1997. https://www.rferl.org/a/1083031.html.

obsession_inc. "Affirmational Fandom vs. Transformational Fandom." June 1, 2009. https://obsession-inc.dreamwidth.org/82589.html.

Ogle, Vanessa. *The Global Transformation of Time: 1870–1950*. Cambridge, MA: Harvard University Press, 2015.

Olesha, Yuri. *The Complete Plays*, edited and translated by Michael Green and Jerome Katsell. Ann Arbor, MI: Ardis, 1983.

Olesha, Yuri. *The Complete Short Stories and Three Fat Men*, translated by Aimee Fisher. Ann Arbor, MI: Ardis, 1979.

Olesha, Yuri. *Envy*, translated by Marian Schwartz. New York: New York Review of Books, 2004.
Olevskii, Timur, and Renat Davletgil'deev. "Kak ustroeny 'Otriady Putina': Rasskazyvaet rukovoditel' 'beshenykh babok,' napavshikh na shtab Naval'nogo v Krasnodare." *Nastoiashchee vremia*. June 5, 2017. https://www.currenttime.tv/a/28598148.html.
Orsi, David, ed. *The Clash of Civilizations 25 Years On: A Multidisciplinary Approach*. E-International Relations, 2018.
Orwell, George. *1984*. New York: Signet, 1961.
Oushakine, Sergeui Alex. "New Lives of Old Forms: On Returns and Repetitions in Russia." *Genre* 43 (Fall/Winter 2010): 409–57.
Oushakine, Sergeui Alex. "Remembering in Public: On the Affective Management of History." *Ab Imperio*, no. 1 (2013): 269–302.
Oushakine, Sergeui Alex. "Second-Hand Nostalgia: On Charms and Spells of the Soviet *Trukhliashechka*." In *Post-Soviet Nostalgia: Confronting the Empire's Legacies*, edited by Otto Boele, Boris Noordenbos, and Ksenia Robbe, 38–69. New York: Routledge, 2020.
Oushakine, Sergeui Alex. "'We're Nostalgic but We're Not Crazy': Retrofitting the Past in Russia." *Russian Review* 66, no. 3 (2007): 451–82.
Palaniuk, Chuck. *Fight Club*. New York: W. W. Norton, 2018.
Parfitt, Tom. "Document Proclaiming the Death of the Soviet Union Is Missing." *The Daily Telegraph*. February 7, 2013. https://www.telegraph.co.uk/news/worldnews/europe/russia/9854619/Document-proclaiming-death-of-Soviet-Union-missing.html.
"Park sovetskogo perioda." *Po Rossii na avto*. August 24, 2011. https://autotravel.ru/otklik.php/7943.
"'Park sovetskogo perioda' poiavitsiia u podnozhiia Ostankinskoi telebashni v Moskve." TASS. July 9, 2019. https://tass.ru/moskva/6646462.
"Piat' storonnikov 'Soiuza slavianskikh sil Rusi' zaderzhali v Rostovskoi oblasti." *Kavkazskii uzel*. Augsut 23, 2022. https://www.kavkaz-uzel.eu/articles/380390/.
Platonov, Andrei. *The Foundation Pit*, translated by Robert Chandler and Geoffrey Smith. New York: HarperCollins, 1996.
Pokrovskii, Vladimir. "Groundhog's Day, or Greetings from the Man with Horns." *Esli* 10 (2004): 49–76.
Polovinko, Viacheslav. "Den' Sovka." *Novaia gazeta*. March 20, 2019. https://novayagazeta.ru/articles/2019/03/20/79945-shinel-dzerzhinskogo-usy-stalina-i-brovi-brezhneva.
Postanovlenie Pravitel'stva RF ot 08.01.1992 N 23. "O poriadke ischisleniia vremeni na territorii Rossiiskoi Federatsii" (vmeste s "Pravilami opredeleniia granits chasovykh poiasov na territorii Rossiiskoi Federatsii"). January 8, 1992. https://archive.ph/20120708185031/http://gov.consultant.ru/doc.asp#selection-21.0-21.207.
Postanovlenie Soveta Respubliki VS RSFSR ot 23.10.91 N 1790–1 "Ob uporiadochenii ischisleniia vremeni na territorii RSFSR." October 23, 1991. https://web.archive.org/web/20110716070235/http://infopravo.by.ru/fed1991/ch01/akt10797.shtm.
Postanovlenie Sovmina SSSR ot 24.10 1980. N 925 (red. ot 13.09.1984). "O poriadke ischislenii vremeni na territorii SSSR." October 24, 1980. https://www.consultant.ru/cons/cgi/online.cgi?req=doc&base=ESU&n=932#2FsdgETeQrplJimL.
Propp, Vladimir. *Morphology of the Folk Tale*, edited by Louis A. Wagner, translated by Laurence Scott. 2nd ed. Austin: University of Texas Press, 2010.

Prudnikov, Vadim. "The Last Dawn." *SSSR-2061*, volume 9. E-book.
Putin, Vladimir. "Address by the President of the Russian Federation." February 22, 2024. http://en.kremlin.ru/events/president/news/67843.
"Putin Sets Off Meme Storm by Comparing Medieval Invaders to Coronavirus Quarantine." *The Moscow Times*. April 9, 2020. https://www.themoscowtimes.com/2020/04/09/putin-sets-off-meme-storm-by-comparing-medieval-invaders-to-coronavirus-quarantine-a69931.
Radishchev, Alexander. *Journey from St. Petersburg to Moscow*, translated by Andrew Kahn and Irina Reyfman. New York: Columbia University Press, 2020.
Ragozina, Sof'ia. "Zaishchishchaia 'traditsionnyi' islam ot 'radikal'nogo': Diskurs islamofobia v rossiiskikh SMI." *Gosudarstvo, religiia, tserkov' v Rossii i za rubezhom* 36, no. 2 (2018): 272–99.
Rand, Ayn. *Anthem*. Mineola, NY: Dover Thrift Editions, 2020.
"Retsenzii: Park Sovetskogo perioda." *Kinopoisk.ru*. 2006. https://www.kinopoisk.ru/film/271515/reviews/.
Robinson, Kim Stanley. *Red Mars*. New York: Bantam, 1993.
Rodionova, Roksana. "Zhivorozhdennye v SSSR." *Moskovskii komsomolets*. December 14, 2018. https://ulan.mk.ru/social/2018/12/12/v-buryatii-rasprostranyaetsya-dvizhenie-zhivykh-kotoroe-paralizuet-rabotu-gosorganov.html.
"'Rossiiskaia Federatsiia—eto okkupant.' Prezident SSSR zhiv i gotovitsia vernut' sebe vlast'. No eto ne Gorbachev." *Lenta.ru*. February 8, 2018. https://lenta.ru/articles/2018/02/08/psycho_war/.
Rudenko, Iuliia. "Oleg Ulanov: 'Moi knigi vne politiki!'" *Prosto liubit' zhizn'*. June 4, 2011. http://prostolubit.ru/2011/06/oleg-ulanov-moi-knigi-vne-politiki/.
"Russian Clocks Go Back for Last Time." *BBC News*. October 25, 2014. https://www.bbc.com/news/world-europe-29773559.
S.T.A.L.K.E.R.: Teni Chernobylia. Sbornik rasskazov. [No editor]. Moscow: Eksmo, 2007.
Sal'nikov, Aleksei. *Oposredovanno*. Moscow: Redaktsiia Eleny Shubiny, 2010.
Sal'nikov, Aleksei. *Petrovy v grippei vokrug ego*. Moscow: Redaktsiia Eleny Shubiny, 2017.
"Samoprovozglashennogo 'prezidenta SSSR' posadili v Moskve na vosem' let." *BBC News*. May 4, 2022. https://www.bbc.com/russian/news-61309542.
"Samoprovozglashennogo 'prezidenta SSSR' Sergeia Taraskina prichislili k ektremistam, ne dozhidaias' suda." *Open Media*. November 3, 2021. https://openmedia.io/news/n3/samoprovozglashennogo-prezidenta-sssr-sergeya-taraskina-prichislili-k-ekstremistam-ne-dozhidayas-suda/.
Savvin, Aleksei. "The Little Earth." *SSSR-2061*, volume 9. E-book.
Selin, Adrian. "Uroki smutnogo vremeni." November 1, 2013. https://spb.hse.ru/news/99591641.html.
Semin, Konstantin. "Pochemu obraz prekrasnogo budushchego bespolezen dlia agitpropa?" July 9, 2021. https://www.youtube.com/watch?v=dBdHAQ2DegM.
Semukhina, Olga. "From Militia to Police: The Path of Russian Law Enforcement Reforms." *Russian Analytical Digest* 151 (June 30, 2014): 1–5.
Shadrina, Tat'iana. "Pribytie i otpravlenie poezdov nachnut ob"iavliat' po mestnomy vremeni." July 31, 2018. https://rg.ru/2018/07/31/pribytie-i-otpravlenie-poezdov-nachnut-obiavliat-po-mestnomu-vremeni.html.
Sharafutdinova, Gulnaz. *The Red Mirror: Putin's Leadership and Russia's Insecure Identity*. Oxford: Oxford University Press, 2020.
Sheiko, Konstantin, and Stephen Brown. *History as Therapy: Alternative History and Nationalist Imaginings in Russia*. Stuttgart: ibidem, 2014.

Shiliaeva, Anna. "V Rostovskoi oblast piat' ekstremistov, otritsavshikh sushchestvovanie Rossiiskoi organizatsii." *Komsomol'skaia pravda—Rostov.* August 22, 2022. https://www.rostov.kp.ru/daily/27434/4636126/.
Shterin, Marat. "New Religious Movements in Changing Russia." In *The Cambridge Companion to New Religious Movements,* edited by Olav Hammer and Mikael Rothstein, 286–302. Cambridge: Cambridge University Press, 2012.
siesit siesit. "Chet priunyl . . ." *LiveJournal.* January 20, 2016. https://siesit.livejournal.com/55956.html.
siesit siesit. "Chto takoe Sovetpank (Soiuz man'iak)." *LiveJournal.* October 20, 2015. https://siesit.livejournal.com/53758.html.
siesit siesit. "Gde zhe ty, tovarishch Kurchatov?" *LiveJournal.* January 14, 2016. https://siesit.livejournal.com/55798.html.
siesit siesit. "I tebia, tovarishch Lenin, Vechno pomnit' budut." *LiveJournal.* January 28, 2016. https://siesit.livejournal.com/56120.html.
Silant'ev, Roman, and Sergei Chekmaev. *Destruktologiia: Kak bystro i nadezhno lishit'sia deneg i zdorov'ia. 10 shagov k uspekhu.* Moscow: Piatyi Rim, 2020.
Silant'ev, Roman, and Ol'ga Strelakova. *Nekromanty nashikh dnei ili obzor uslug po ozhivleniiu liudei, organizatsii, gosudarstv.* Moscow: Snezhnyi kom, 2020.
Sinitsyn, Andrei, ed. *Zateriannyi dozor: Luchshaia fantastika 2017.* Moscow: AST, 2017.
Skepsis. Comment 245. March 5, 2021. http://samlib.ru/comment/a/arsenxew_s_w/about.
Skorkin, Konstantin. "Post-Soviet Science Fiction and the War in Ukraine," translated by Julia Sherwood. *Eurozine.* February 22, 2016. https://www.eurozine.com/post-soviet-science-fiction-and-the-war-in-ukraine/.
Slapovskii, Aleksei. *Vspiat'.* Moscow: AST, 2013.
Slavnikova, Olga. *The Man Who Couldn't Die: The Tale of an Authentic Human Being,* translated by Marian Schwartz. New York: Columbia University Press, 2019.
"Slavnikova v Chekhovke: Pisatel'nitsu obokrali?" *NG Ex Libris.* December 2, 2004. https://web.archive.org/web/20160308005249/http://www.ng.ru/fakty/2004-02-12/2_slavnikova.html.
Smith, Paula. "A Trekkie's Tale." Originally published in 1974. https://web.archive.org/web/20050208104838/www.fortunecity.com/rivendell/dark/1000/marysue.htm.
Snegovaia, Mariia. "Ukrainskie sobytiia davno opisany v liubimoi knige Kremlia." *Vedomosti.* February 3, 2014. https://www.vedomosti.ru/opinion/articles/2014/03/02/stroiteli-tretej-imperii.
Snyder, Timothy. *The Road to Unfreedom: Russia, Europe, America.* New York: Crown Books, 2019.
Sokolov, Boris. "Staraia novaia Rus'." *Agentstvo politicheskikh novostei.* November 1, 2006. http://www.apn.ru/publications/article10805.htm.
Sokolova, Natalia. "Co-opting Transmedia Consumers: User Content as Entertainment or 'Free Labour'? The Cases of *S.T.A.L.K.E.R.* and *Metro 2033.*" *Europe-Asia Studies* 64 (2012): 1565–83.
Sorokin, Vladimir. *Day of the Oprichnik,* translated by Jamey Gambrell. New York: Farrar, Straus, and Giroux, 2011.
Sorokin, Vladimir. *Sakharnyi Kreml'.* Moscow: AST, 2008.
Sorokin, Vladimir. *Telluria,* translated by Max Lawton. New York: New York Review of Books, 2022.
"Sovetpank kak forma samovyrazheniia." eparhia.ru. February 16, 2016. https://eparhia.ru/useful/?id=150452.
SSSR-2061. "Divannaia futurologiia #1: Nachalo." May 4, 2021. https://www.youtube.com/watch?v=nYzGzo-YtVI.

Stalenhag, Simon. *Tales from the Loop*. Los Angeles: Design Studio Press, 2015.
Stat'ia No. 362. Postanovlenie Soveta narodnykh komissarov. "O perevode chasovoi strelki vpered na odin chas." June 16, 1930. https://istmat.org/node/49861.
Stillbro. "Istoriia vizual'nykh novel v Rossii: Do 'Beskonechnogo leta.'" June 30, 2019. https://stopgame.ru/blogs/topic/97227/istoriya_vizualnyh_novell_v_rossii_do_beskonechnogo_leta.
Stroop, Chrissy. "Is Being Trans a Religion? Why the Christian Right Wants You to Think So." *Religion Dispatches*. August 6, 2021. https://religiondispatches.org/is-being-trans-a-religion-why-the-christian-right-wants-you-to-think-so/.
Strugatsky, Arkady, and Boris Strugatsky. *Hard to Be a God*, translated by Olena Bormashenko. Chicago: Chicago Review Press, 2014.
Strugatsky, Arkady, and Boris Strugatsky. *Roadside Picnic*, translated by Olena Bormashenko. Chicago: Chicago Review Press, 2012.
Suslov, Mikhail. "Of Planets and Trenches: Imperial Science Fiction in Contemporary Russia." *Russian Review* 75 (October 2016): 562–78.
Suvorkin, Timur. "Pioneer Means First." *SSSR-2061*, volume 4. E-book.
Talyaka, Yana. "Not a Word of Lies. Gulag. Doom." *SSSR-2061*, volume 9. E-book.
Tarugin, Oleg, and Aleksei Ivakin. *The Shtrafbat's Constellation: From Stalingrad to Alpha Centauri*. Moscow: EKSMO, 2000.
"'They Don't Belong Here': Even after Five Months of Russian Occupation, Kherson Residents Haven't Lost Faith in the Ukrainian Army." *Meduza*. August 1, 2022. https://meduza.io/en/feature/2022/08/01/they-don-t-belong-here.
Tiapukhin, S. V. "Grafik raboty 'sutki cherez troe.'" May 22, 2020. https://www.audit-it.ru/articles/personnel/a110/1012994.html.
Tolstaya, Tatyana. *The Slynx*, translated by Jamey Gambrell. New York: New York Review of Books, 2016.
Tolstoi, Sergei. "The New Person." *SSSR-2061*, volume 5. E-book.
Twain, Mark. *A Connecticut Yankee in King Arthur's Court*. New York: W. W. Norton, 2018.
Ulitskaya. Ludmila. *The Funeral Party*, translated by Arch Tait. New York: Shocken, 2002.
Van Zaichik, Khol'm. *Delo zhadnogo povara*. Moscow: Azbuka, 2000.
Varlamov, Il'ia. "'Grazhdane SSSR' ostalis' bez prezidenta i bez strany." November 27, 2020. https://varlamov.ru/4106655.html.
Varlamov, Il'ia. "'Grazhdane SSSR' protiv Rossii, evreev i Mirovogo pravitel'stva." September 2, 2019. https://varlamov.ru/3578963.html.
Viazovskii, Aleksei, and Garik Viazovskii. *Polnaia entsiklopediia popadantsev v proshloe*. 23rd ed. Posted on June 12, 2020. http://samlib.ru/i/isaew_a_w/popadanec23.shtml.
Viazovskii, Aleksei, and Garik Viazovskii. *Polnaia entsiklopedia popadantsev v proshloe*. 24th ed. Posted on November 16, 2020. http://samlib.ru/i/isaew_a_w/popadanec24.shtml.
Villy9. "The Decision." *SSSR-2061*, volume 2. E-book.
Vodolazkin, Eugene. *The Aviator*, translated by Lisa C. Hayden. London: Oneworld Publications, 2019.
Voinovich, Vladimir. *Moscow 2042*, translated by Richard Lourie. New York: HarperVia, 1990.
Vonnegut, Kurt, Jr. *Slaughterhouse-Five*. New York: Dial, 2009.
Wells, H. G. *The Time Machine*. New York: W. W. Norton, 2008.
Wijermars, Mariëlle. *Memory Politics in Contemporary Russia Television, Cinema, and the State*. New York: Routledge, 2019.

Willis, Andy. "Memory Banks Failing! Life on Mars and the Politics of Re-imagining the Police and the Seventies." In *Life on Mars: From Manchester to New York*, edited by Stephen Lacey and Ruth McElroy, 57–68. Cardiff: University of Wales Press, 2012.

Winslow, Barbara. "How Ladies against Women Flummoxed Phillis Schlafly." *Meeting Ground On-Line*. July 12, 2014. http://meetinggroundonline.org/how-ladies-against-women-flummoxed-phyllis-schlafly.

Yaffa, Joshua. *Between Two Fires: Truth, Ambition, and Compromise in Putin's Russia*. New York: Tim Duggan Books, 2020.

Yakhina, Guzel. *Zuleikha*, translated by Lisa C. Hayden. London: Oneworld Publications, 2019.

Young, Cathy. "The Sci-Fi Writers' War: They Predicted and Possibly Inspired the Conflict in the Ukraine, and Now They're Fighting It." *Slate*. July 11, 2014. https://slate.com/news-and-politics/2014/07/science-fiction-writers-predicted-ukraine-conflict-now-theyre-fighting-it.html.

Yurchak, Alexei. *Everything Was Forever until It Was No More: The Last Soviet Generation*. Princeton, NJ: Princeton University Press, 2006.

Zabirko, Oleksandr. "The Magic Spell of Revanchism: Geopolitical Visions in Post-Soviet Speculative Fiction." In *Ideology after Union: Political Doctrines, Discourses, and Debates in Post-Soviet Societies*, edited by Aleksandr Etkind and Mikhail Minakov, 251–305. New York: ibidem, 2020.

Zamyatin, Yevgeny. *We*, translated by Clarence Brown. New York: Penguin, 1993.

Zhegulev, Il'ia. "Tysiachi liudei vstupili v profsoiuz 'Soiuz SSR': Oni schitaiut sebia grazhdanami Sovetskogo Soiuza i otkazyvaiutsia platit' za usluti ZhKKh." *Meduza*. December 27, 2018. https://meduza.io/feature/2018/12/27/tysyachi-lyudey-vstupili-v-profsoyuz-soyuz-ssr-oni-schitayut-sebya-grazhdanami-sovetskogo-soyuza-i-otkazyvayutsya-platit-za-uslugi-zhkh.

Zhilova, Anna. "'Muzh sestry s"el svoi passport RF!': Chitateli E1.RU—o sekte 'grazhdan SSSR.'" *Ekaterinburg onlain*. January 14, 2020. https://www.e1.ru/text/gorod/2020/01/14/66442459/.

Zhilova, Anna. "Sekta 'grazhdan SSSR'—zastriavshie v proshlom ili obyknovennye moshenniki?" *Ekaterinburg onlain*. January 24, 2020. https://www.e1.ru/text/gorod/2020/01/24/66456643/.

Films and Television

Back to the Future. Robert Zemeckis, director. Amblin Entertainment, 1985.

Back to the USSR (Nazad v SSSR). Valerii Rozhnov, creator. Magnum Productions, 2010.

Chernobyl: Exclusion Zone (Chernobyl': Zona otchuzhdeniia). Pavel Danilov, Vasilii Kutsenko, Vitalii Shliappo, Igor Tudiasev, Dmitrii Yan, directors. TNT and TV3, 2014–2017; feature film, 2019.

Citizen Nobody (Grazhdanin Nikto). Vladimir Yankovsky, director. UPS Ukrainian Production Studio, 2016.

The Dark Side of the Moon (Obratnaia storona luny). Aleksandr Kott, creator. Kinoslovo and Sreda, 2012–2018.

DAU: Degeneration. Ilya Khrzhanovsky, director. Phenomen Berlin Filmproduktions, Phenomen Ukraine, Phenomen, 2020.

DAU: Nora. Son. Ilya Khrzhanovsky and Jekaterina Oertel, directors. Phenomen Berlin Filmproduktions, Phenomen Ukraine, Phenomen, 2020.
Day Watch (Dnevnoi dozor). Timur Bekmambetov, director. Bezelevs Productions, Pervyi Kanal, and TABBAK, 2006.
Fight Club. David Fischer, director. Fox 2000 Pictuers, Regency Enterprises, and Linson Films, 1999.
The Fog (Tuman). Artem Aksenenko and Ivan Shurkhovetskii, directors. VVP Alians and STS Media, 2010.
The Fog 2 (Tuman 2). Ivan Shurkhovetskii, creator. VVP Al'ians, 2012.
The Game. David Fincher, director. Propaganda Films, 1997.
Goodbye, Lenin! Wolfgang Becker, director. X-Filme Creative Pool, 2003.
Groundhog Day. Harold Ramis, director. Columbia Pictures, 1993.
Hedgehog in the Fog (Ezhik v tumane). Yuri Norstein, director. Soyuzmultfilm, 1975.
Idiocracy. Mike Judge, director. Twentieth Century Fox, Ternion Pictures, and Major Studios Partners, 2006.
Ivan Vasilievich Changes His Profession (Ivan Vaslievich meniaet professiiu). Leonid Gaidai, director. Released in English as *Ivan Vasilievich: Back to the Future.* Mosfil'm, 1973.
Jurassic Park. Steven Spielberg, director. Universal Studios and Amblin Entertainment, 1993.
Kidnapping, Caucasian Style (Kavkazskaia plennitsa). Leonid Gaidai, director, Mosfil'm, 1967.
Life Is Beautiful (La vita e bella). Roberto Benigni, director. Melampo, Cinematografica, Cecchi Gori Group, and Miramax Films, 1994.
Life on Mars. Matthew Graham, Tony Jordan and Ashley Pharoah, creators. BBC One and BBC Four, 2006–2007.
The Manchurian Candidate. John Frankenheimer, director. M. C. Productions, 1962.
Masiania, written and directed by Oleg Kuvaev.
"Doppelganger." Episode 142, March 12, 2021. https://www.youtube.com/watch?v=qVkQif8opaA.
"How to Explain to Your Kids" (Kak ob"iasnit' detiam). Episode 161, May 12, 2022. https://www.youtube.com/watch?v=gqAlCAAFokA&t=479s.
"The Mirror" (Zertsalo). Episode 130, October 10, 2018. https://www.youtube.com/watch?v=r9loc1UQ9ZI.
"Sankt-Mariuburg." Episode 162, July 11, 2002. https://www.youtube.com/watch?v=s-GLAIY4DXA.
"Self-Isolation" (Samoizoliatsiia). Episode 143, April 1, 2020. https://www.youtube.com/watch?v=ZWzVBUlCxow.
"Wakizashi" (Vakizashi). Episode 160, March 22, 2022. https://www.youtube.com/watch?v=kzx_N8AjiKw.
Mirror for a Hero (Zerkalo dlia geroia). Vladimir Khotinenko, director. Sverdlovskaia kinostudiia, 1987.
Mister Nobody (Gospodin Nikto). Vladimir Iankovskii, director. UPS Ukrainian Production Studio, 2016.
Night Watch (Nochnoi dozor). Timur Bekmambetov, director. Bezelevs Productions, Pervyi Kanal, and TABBAK, 2004
Park of the Soviet Period (Park sovetskogo perioda). Iulii Guzman, director. Iug TV, Slovo, and A. G. Pictures, 2006.
The Promised Heavens (Nebesa obetovannye). El'dar Riazanov, director. Mosfil'm, Slovo, Cinebridge, 1991.
Psycho. Alfred Hitchcock, director. Shamley Productions, 1960.

"The Russians Are Here." *Frontline*, Season 1, Episode 20. Ofra Bikel, director. June 13, 1983.
Sleeper. Woody Allen, director. United Artists, 1973.
Stalker. Andrei Tarkovsky, director. Mosfil'm, 1979.
The Truman Show. Peter Weir, director. Paramount Pictures, Scott Rudin Productions, 1998.
We Are from the Future (My iz budushchego). Andrei Maliukov, director. A-1 Kino Video, 2008.
We Are from the Future 2 (My iz budushchego 2). Andres Puustusmaa, director. A-1 Kino Video, 2010.

Index

Abramovic, Marina, 118
Adonyev, Sergei, 117
affective attachment to state, 19, 64–65, 74–76, 98, 114
Afghanistan, 45
Afrofuturism, 156–57
Agamben, Giorgio, 66
AgitProp (YouTube channel), 142–43
Akopov, Eduard, 110
Akunin, Boris, *The Mirror of St. Germain*, 52
"The Aleph," 172
alienation, 13, 45, 51
Allen, Woody, 53
"All You Zombies," 27
alternate history, 10–12, 59, 82, 99–100, 167; time travel and, 11. *See also* present-day alternative USSR
Anderson, Benedict, 63
Andrei Kapitan (username), 145
Angel's Kiss, 133
Anna Karenina, 146
anticommunism, 87. *See also* Cold War; East/West conflict
anti-entropy, 39, 92–93, 153
antisemitism, 75, 80
anti-utopia, 127, 142
apocalypse. *See* post-apocalyptic futures
Aptekman, Marina, 139n4
Archy13 (username), 158–59, 161–62
Armaged-dom, 125
Arsenyev, Sergei Vladimirovich, 38, 48; "Sergei Arsenyev on His Work," 23; *Student, Komsomol Girl, Athlete*, 22–29, 35–36, 99
atheism, 81
Atomic Heart, 155
Aum Shinrikyo, 78
Aviator, 55–58

Back, 172
Back to the Future, 19, 21
Back to the USSR, 50–52
Banderites, 7
Bauman, Zygmunt, 4
Becker, Wolfgang, *Goodbye, Lenin!*, 90–95, 98, 121

Bekmambetov, Timur, 17
Belarus, 105, 122
Bellamy, Edward, *Looking Backward*, 53–55, 76, 134
Benigni, Robert, 173
Berlin Wall, 87, 91–93
Beumers, Birgit, 7
Beyond the Thistle, 139
Bird, Robert, 120n19
Black, Holly, 143
Boele, Otto, 7
Bogdanov, Alexander, *Red Star*, 161
Bolsheviks, 64
Bondareva, Olga, "The Glass Dream," 162
books, in post-apocalyptic fiction, 128–31
Bordoni, Carlo, 4
Borges, Jorge Luis, "The Aleph," 172
Boris Godunov, 4
Boym, Svetlana, 7, 21, 61
Bradbury, Ray: *Fahrenheit 451*, 128; "A Sound of Thunder," 100
Branch Davidians, 78
Brezhnev, Leonid Ilich, 57, 63, 87, 95–97, 101, 109, 149
Buckley, William F., Jr., 87
Bulgakov, Anton, 68–69
Bulgakov, Mikhail: *Flight*, 89; *Ivan Vasilievich*, 55
Burnosov, Yuri, "Moscow 22," 53–54
Butler, Octavia E., 10
Butterfly Effect, 10, 27, 33n9, 49, 100

calendar, 2–3
A Canticle for Leibowitz, 13–14, 127–28
capitalism: critiques of, 12, 23, 49–50, 52, 91–93, 102, 105–6, 144, 154, 162, 164; dominance of, 124, 146–47; Soviet reconstructions and, 108, 110. *See also* liberal democratic paradigm
Carbongrad 1999 (*Russia 2077*), 156–58, 165
Card, Orson Scott, *Ender's Game*, 130
Cavendish, Philip, 121
Center for Combating Extremism (Center E), 77–79
Chagall, Marc, 171

INDEX

Chapaev, Vasily Ivanovich, 112
Chekmaev, Sergei, 80
Chernenko, Konstantin, 88
Chernobyl disaster, 100–102, 125, 127, 132
Chernobyl: Exclusion Zone, 13, 99–102, 121, 150
China, 102, 133, 138, 177–78
Chizhova, Elena, *The China Expert*, 12
Christofascist Posse Comitatus movement, 71
Citizen Nobody, 103n9
citizenship, 65, 68, 70–71, 73, 163
Citizens of the USSR, 65–85, 86n2, 150; ideology and conspiracy theories, 74–76; nostalgia and, 65–67; passports and, 69–74; as secular extremists and a cult, 76–80; shrinking of public sphere and, 80–82; *styob* (ironic overidentification), 82–85
The Clash of Civilizations, 133–34, 138
Colbert, Stephen, 83
The Colbert Report, 83
Cold War, 78, 91, 101, 127; end of, 87–88, 123–24, 133, 146. *See also* East/West conflict
colonialism, 121–22. *See also* imperialism
Command & Conquer franchise, 153
Complete Encyclopedia of Popadantsy to the Past, 18
conditional subjunctive, 13, 15, 105, 173–74, 176–77; counterfactual, 166–67
A Connecticut Yankee in King Arthur's Court, 10, 20, 53
conspiracy theories, 74–76, 101, 105
corruption, 27, 45, 94, 103n9, 107, 137–39, 154, 168
cosmonauts, 28, 93, 160–61. *See also* space program, Soviet
cosmos, 35, 49–50, 52
COVID-19 (coronavirus) pandemic, 7, 75n5, 173, 175
Crimea, 87, 168
cults. *See* new religious movements
curatorial fandom, 61
Curry, Tim, 153
cyberpunk, 12, 149, 156, 157, 159
cynicism, 32–35, 103n9, 112, 174
Czechoslovakia, 123

The Daily Show, 83
The Dark Side of the Moon, 13, 24, 39–49, 99–108, 121–22
DAU, 13, 108, 117–22

Day of the Oprichnik, 9, 14, 124, 133, 134, 139–42
Day Watch, 17
"The Decision," 164
decree time, 1–2
degeneration, 23, 126, 129–32
Degeneration, 118–19
degradation, 26, 104, 126, 139
Demkin, Sergei, 68–69
democracy. *See* liberal democratic paradigm
Destructology, 80
determinism, 19, 57, 158
Dick, Philip K., 3n2, 59–60, 67, 122; *Exegesis*, 59; *The Man in the High Castle*, 11, 59; *Radio Free Albemuth*, 59; *Valis*, 59
dictatorship, 5, 18, 100
difference, 138, 165, 171–72. *See also* pluralism
Doctor Who, 10
A Dream of a Thousand Cats, 63–65
Drugaia Rossiia coalition, 60
Dumai sam, dumai seichas (DSDS), "2045," 143–45, 157
Dumancic, Mark, 29
Dune, 14
Dvorkin, Alexander, 78–79
Dyachenko, Marina and Sergei, *Armaged-dom*, 125
dystopias: fantasy and, 147–48; liberalism as, 26, 162; medieval, 14, 133–34, 138–42; politics and, 146; post-apocalyptic, 125–32, 143; Soviet reconstructions, 112; Time Crasher stories, 26–28, 53–58, 104. *See also* anti-utopia

Eastern European countries, 123
East Germany, 91–93, 95, 98, 123
East/West conflict, 133–37, 146, 162–63
economic conditions, 4, 64, 69, 76, 123–24, 167; prosperity, 31, 63, 101–2, 143
Efremova, Tatiana, 7, 118n14
Eisenstein, Sergei, 171
EKSMO, 162
Elin, Alexander, 8. *See also* "Our Nuthouse Is Voting for Putin"
Elizarov, Mikhail, *The Librarian*, 84
emigration, 68, 88–90, 115, 171
empathy, 31, 167, 178
empire, 132–34, 137, 171–72. *See also* imperialism
Ender's Game, 130
Endless Summer, 154–55
The End of History and the Last Man, 123–24
Enlightenment, 137

INDEX

Eno, Brian, 118
entropy, 39, 92–93, 153
Envy, 88
Epstein, Mikhail, 109
Ernst, Konstantin, 168
escapism, 21, 62
ethics, 38, 44, 92, 118–21
ethnogenesis, 63
Etkind, Alexander, 8
Etush, Vladimir, 111
Eurasianism, 133, 134n3, 140–41, 144
Eurasian Symphony, 133
Everything Was Forever until It Was No More, styob, 82
extremism, 77–82, 119n17, 174

fairy tales, 12, 27, 48, 51–52, 93, 160
fandom and fan fiction: curatorial vs. transformative, 61; Mary Sue figure, 48; politicized, 134; Time Crashers and, 18, 20–21, 23, 25, 48, 52, 56, 61–62; *USSR-2061* and, 145
fantasy: genre, 13, 20, 42, 134–35, 167; immersive, 60; *nauchnaia fantastika* (scientific fantasy), 20; regressive, 39–44; utopias and dystopias as, 147–48; wish-fulfillment fantasies, 13, 25, 41, 47, 52, 56, 135–36, 150
Fedorova, Lioudmila, 7
Felix (username), 158–59, 161–62
"Fifth Medal," 162
Fight Club, 50
Fishman, Leonid, "My popali," 26n4
Flight, 89
Flowers for Algernon, 55
The Fog and *The Fog 2*, 30–32
folkloric tropes, 51–52
Fomenko, Anatoly, 62
Foundation for Traditional Religions, 80
Foundation Pit, 120
Frei, Max, *Labryinths of Echo*, 62
Freud, Sigmund, 24, 25, 42, 129, 147; on the uncanny, 14–15, 27
Frolova, Lidia, 73
Fukuyama, Francis, 123–24
Funeral Party, 88–90, 94, 98
future, 123–65; future shock, 87; imperialism and, 132–42; past and, 8–14, 56–58; as progress, 132; radiant, 4, 99, 145–47, 155, 163; retrofuturism, 124, 144, 156, 159; Russofuturism, 157; SovPunk visions of, 12, 124, 133, 148–65; Time Crasher stories in, 53–58; Western framing of, 123–24, 146. *See also* dystopias; medieval futurism; optimism; pessimism; post-apocalyptic futures; utopias

Gagarin, Yuri, 28, 106, 158, 160, 169, 171
Gaidai, Leonid: *Ivan Vasilievich Changes His Profession*, 55; *Kidnapping, Caucasian Style*, 22n2, 111
Gaiman, Neil, *Sandman*, 63
The Game, 50
Garner, Ian, 10n9, 54n13
gender dysphoria, 22–28
geopolitics, 66, 105, 107, 134, 162, 167
Germany, 87; Reichsbürger (Reich Citizens), 70–72, 74. *See also* East Germany
Gibbon, Dave, 6
Gibson, William, 157
gigantism, 136, 138
The Girl from the Future, 156, 159
glasnost, 96
"The Glass Dream," 162
Gleick, James, 19
Glukhovsky, Dmitry, *Metro 2033*, 9, 126, 129–32
GM Reds, 155
Goodbye, Lenin!, 90–95, 98, 121
Gorbachev, Mikhail, 16, 22, 64, 67, 96–97, 101
Gorky Park, 13
Gorky Quest, 115–18, 120–21
Gramsci, Antonio, 3–4
grandfather paradox, 10, 18–19, 49
Great Patriotic War. *See* World War II
Great White Brotherhood, 78
Greenfield, Nathan W., 167
grief, 98, 155
Grix, Jonathan, 169n3
Groundhog Day, 154, 172
"Groundhog's Day, or Greetings from the Man with Horns," 172
Gulag, 55–56, 111, 139, 149
Gumilev, Lev, 14, 63
Guzman, Yuli, 110

Hampe, Karl, 166
Hanson, Stephen, 2n1
Hanukai, Maxim, 7n4
Hard to Be a God, 14
haunted houses, 120
Hayden, Lisa, 148n8
Heaven's Gate, 78
Hedgehog in the Fog, 170
Heinlein, Robert, "All You Zombies," 27
Herbert, Frank, *Dune*, 14

Herland, 134
heroes, agency of, 18–19, 25, 37–39, 47–52, 57
historical fiction, 11, 53. *See also* Time Crasher stories
history. *See* past; Soviet nostalgia; World War II
Hitler, Adolf, 16, 23, 28; "Hitler wins" stories, 10, 11, 12, 59, 99
Hoban, Russell, *Ridley Walker*, 127
holidays, 2–3
homoeroticism, 141–42
homophobia, 23–24, 53–54, 162, 171
horror genre, 120
Huntington, Samuel, 133–34, 138
Huxley, Aldous, *Brave New World*, 55, 128, 146

Iampol'skii, Mikhail, 118n15
ideology, 4, 108, 109, 112, 121; Citizens of the USSR and, 74–76; Putinist, 167–72; in utopian fiction, 9, 12, 76, 146–47, 162–64
Idiocracy, 53
Immortal Regiment, 7, 31
imperialism, 19, 121–22, 132–42, 165, 168, 177. *See also* territorial expansion; Ukraine, Russian invasion of
incest, 19, 21, 39, 47
Indirectly, 148–50
individualism, 39, 51, 112, 138, 165
interregnum, 3–5
irony, 151–52, 175. See also *styob*
Ivakin, Aleksei, 54n13
Ivanova, Natalia, 127
Ivan The Terrible, 16, 55; oprichnina, 14, 126, 137
Ivan Vasilievich (play), 55
Ivan Vasilievich Changes His Profession (film), 55

Jahn, Sigmund, 93
Jameson, Frederic, 9, 146–47
Japan, 78
Jehovah's Witnesses, 78, 79
Jones, Kelley, 63
Jowitt, Ken, 98
Judge, Mike, 53
Jurassic Park, 61, 110
justice, 45, 76, 137–40
Juvenal, 137

Kalinin, Ilya, 7, 32n7, 61n1
Karlson on the Roof, 43
Kasparov, Garry, 60
Kataev, Valentin, *Time, Forward!*, 1
Kennedy, John F., 160

Keyes, Daniel, *Flowers for Algernon*, 55
Khabibulin, Yuri, "Mother's Day," 162
Khanga, Elena, 111
Khodorkovsky, Mikhail, 43–44, 49
Khristos, Maria Devi, 78
Khruschchev, Nikita, 97, 109
Khrzhanovsky, Ilya, *DAU*, 13, 108, 117–22
Khval'skii, Andrei, "Summer Internship," 163
Kidnapping, Caucasian Style, 22n2, 111
Kirkorov, Filipp, 43–44
Kniazev, Miloslav, "Fifth Medal," 162
Kobierecki, Michał, 168n2
Kobrin, Kirill, 8, 52, 123n1
Kobzon, Iosif, 111
Kornbluth, Cyril M., "The Marching Morons," 53
Koroliuk, Mikhail, *Save the USSR!*, 20, 39, 48, 52
Kotelnikov, Gleb, 170
Kozlenko, Ivan, 121
Kozuliaev, Aleksei, 110
kpt_flint (username), 145–46
Kramereva, Nina, 169n3
Krasnov, Pyotr, *Beyond the Thistle*, 139
Krikalev, Sergei, 160–61
Krusanov, Pavel, *The Angel's Kiss*, 133
Kukui, Il'ia, 118n14
Kukulin, Ilya, 7
Kuvaev, Oleg, 172–78

Labryinths of Echo, 62
Ladies Against Women, 83
Landau, Lev, 117
Larbaleister, Justine, 143
law enforcement, 44–45, 107; extralegal (*see* oprichnina). *See also* police procedurals
Left/Right conflict, 143, 146
Le Guin, Ursula, 147
Lenin, Vladimir, 64, 69, 76, 91, 97; mausoleum, 114; Red Cape memes and, 152; statues of, 94, 112
Lerner, Amanda, 46n6, 47n7
Lévi-Strauss, Claude, 39–40
liberal democratic paradigm, 51, 124, 137–38; as dystopia, 26, 162. *See also* capitalism
liberpunk movement, 80n9, 162
The Librarian, 84
libraries, 130–31
life-cycle rituals, 30
Life is Beautiful, 173
Life on Mars, 13, 39–40, 42, 45n4, 46n6
Limonov, Eduard, 60; "The USSR Is Our Ancient Rome," 61–62

INDEX

Lindgren, Astrid, 43
linear time, 6
"Liompa," 88
Lipovetsky, Mark, 8, 52, 91, 110n13, 120n18, 127
A List of Blessings, 89
literacy, 128–29, 170
"The Little Earth," 163
Living People, 68, 75
Looking Backward, 53–55, 76, 134
Lounsbery, Anne, 157n15
Lukyanenko, Sergey: *Night Watch* series, 17; "Popadantsy," 18; *Rough Draft*, 62; "Vitya Solnyshkin and Joseph Stalin," 16–19, 29, 39

magical helper figure, 51–52
Makanin, Vladimir, *Escape Hatch*, 9
The Manchurian Candidate, 78
The Man Who Couldn't Die, 90–91, 94–98, 121, 172
"The Marching Morons," 53
Marin, Louis, 109
Marinina, Alexandra, 108; *Gorky Quest*, 115–18, 120–21
Mars, 3, 147, 161
Martian time slip, 3
Marxism, 76, 123–24, 142, 146, 163–64
Mary Sue figure, 48, 52, 57, 153
Masha and the Bear, 125, 150
Masyanya, 172–78
Mayakovsky, Vladimir, *Verses on My Soviet Passport*, 69–70, 72
medieval futurism, 13–14, 133, 136–41
Medvedev, Dmitry, 46, 49, 68, 77, 107
Medvedev, Sergei, *The Return of the Russian Leviathan*, 61
Meerson, Olga, 156
melancholia, 93, 98, 153, 155
Mendelsohn, Farah, 11
Metro 2033, 9, 126, 129–32, 153
Miéville, China, *The City and the City*, 60–61
militarization, 29. See also World War II
millenarianism, 66–67
Miller, Walter M., Jr., *A Canticle for Leibowitz*, 13–14, 127–28
A Mirror for the Hero, 172
The Mirror of St. Germain, 52
Mitki subculture, 152
Moore, Alan, 6, 137
morality, 29, 32–33, 35, 38, 51–54, 72, 77, 79, 101, 112, 119, 140, 171, 175
More, Thomas, *Utopia*, 54, 134

Morson, Gary Saul, 140, 146
"Moscow 22," 53–54
Moscow 2042, 53n10
Mother of God Center, 78
"Mother's Day," 162
mourning, 98, 155
Mundfish Studio, 155
Mussorgsky, Modest, 4
mutation, 126, 127, 130

Nabokov, Vladimir, 171
Nadkarni, Maya, 7
National Review, 87
nauchnaia fantastika (scientific fantasy), 20
Navalny, Alexei, 84–85, 143
Nazinov, Pyotr, "Red Means Blood," 162
Nazis: Russian collaboration with, 30; Ukrainian nationalism and, 7, 34, 167, 173, 176. See also Hitler, Adolf; World War II
Necromancers of Our Times, 79–80
neopaganism, 80
New Chronology, 62, 83
New Medievalism, 136–39
"The New Person," 162–63
new religious movements (NRMs), 78–80
Nicholas I, 87
Night Watch, 17
1984, 112, 127, 133, 146
Noordenbos, Boris, 7
Norenstein, Yuri, 170
Norka, Sergei, 5
Northern Spider, 157
nostalgia. See Soviet nostalgia
"Not a Word of Lies," 162–63
nuclear disasters, 99–102. See also Chernobyl disaster

October Revolution, 3, 21, 88
Odyssey, 42
Oedipus story, 39–43, 49
Ogle, Vanessa, 2n1
Olesha, Yuri: *Envy*, 88; "Liompa," 88; *A List of Blessings*, 89
oligarchs, 43–44
Olympic Games (Sochi 2014), 168–72
One Day in the Life of Ivan Denisovich, 139
online communities and projects, 23, 52, 84, 124, 130, 145–46; *Masyanya*, 172–78. See also SovPunk
oprichnina, 14, 126, 137–42
optimism, 26, 94, 124, 128, 143, 146, 157–58, 164–65, 174

INDEX

Orange Revolution, 34
O'Reilly, Bill, 83
Other Russias, 60–62
Ottoman Empire, 87
"Our Nuthouse Is Voting for Putin" (performed by Rabfak), 8, 83–84, 124, 170
Oushakine, Sergeui Alex, 7, 8n6
Outlander, 11
Oxxymiron, 143

paradoxes (in time travel), 10, 18–21, 27, 42, 49. *See also* Butterfly Effect
Park of the Soviet Period (film), 13, 108–15, 118
Park of the Soviet Period (tourist attraction), 108–10, 114, 121
parricide, 39, 71
past: historical reenactments, 35, 51, 112, 118, 170 (*see also* reconstruction projects); political uses of, 4–8, 35–39, 168–72. *See also* Soviet nostalgia; Time Crasher stories; time travel; World War II
patriotism, 30–31, 39, 45, 64, 107
Pelevin, Victor, 60
Pepe the Frog, 152
perestroika, 4, 30, 46, 62, 64, 95, 104, 114, 146
Periodic Table, 171
Perkins, Charlotte Gilman, *Herland*, 134
pessimism, 36, 126, 142–43, 146, 158
Peter the Great, 64, 169
The Petrovs in and around the Flu, 148
Pink Floyd, 45, 46
Platonov, Andrei, *The Foundation Pit*, 120
Plato's *Republic*, 119; Allegory of the Cave, 127, 140
pluralism, 81, 138. *See also* difference
Plutonium Players, 83n10
Pokrovskii, Vladimir, "Groundhog's Day, or Greetings from the Man with Horns," 172
police procedurals, 40, 42–45, 47, 107
political assassination, 25, 27, 38
politics: rejection of, 37–39, 49, 139. *See also* geopolitics
popadantsy, 9–10. *See also* Time Crasher stories
"Popadantsy," 18
portal quest historical fiction, 11. *See also* Time Crasher stories
post-apocalyptic futures, 9, 14, 124–32, 135, 142–43, 148, 164
postmodernism, 110n13, 119, 125
post-sots, 8, 110n13
power, 63, 66, 68, 71, 76–77, 84–86, 94, 101–2, 128, 134, 142, 147; soft power, 163, 169n3

present-day alternative USSR, 12–13; belief in continued existence of USSR, 59–60, 65–85; morbidity and mortality metaphors, 87–98; Other Russias, 60–62; reconstruction projects, 107–22; Soviet antiquity and, 61–63; territory and, 122; in Time Crasher stories, 99–107; voluntarist approach to, 62–65
presuppositionalism, 81
The Prisoner, 112
Prometheus, 127
The Promised Heavens, 84
Propp, Vladimir, 51
Psycho, 153
public sphere, 65, 80–82, 102
Pugacheva, Alla, 43–44
Puppets, 84
Pushkin, Alexander, 4
Putin, Vladimir: capitalism and, 110; centralized power, 5, 68, 135; Huntington and, 133–34; ideology, 167–72; opposition to, 84–85, 175–77; Orthodox Church and, 81; patriotism and, 107; retrohistorical orientation, 4–8, 60, 83–84, 111, 114; return to presidency, 46, 167; sovereignty and, 14, 64, 66, 77, 82, 132; suppression of civil society, 77, 81–82. *See also* Ukraine, Russian invasion of

QAnon, 74–75
Quantum Leap, 10

Rabfak, 8, 83–84, 124, 170
radiant future, 4, 99, 145–47, 155, 163
Radishchev, Alexander, 175
Rand, Ayn, *Anthem*, 128
Reagan, Ronald, 38
realism, 131. *See also* socialist realism
reconstruction projects (simulations of Soviet Union), 107–22
Red Cape memes, 151–52
Red Mars, 3, 147
"Red Means Blood," 162
Red Star, 161
Reichsbürger (Reich Citizens), 70–72, 74
religion, 77–81, 152
Repentance, 114
repressive forces, 30, 80–82, 92, 104, 137, 174–75
retrofuturism, 124, 144, 156, 159
Return of the Russian Leviathan, 61
Reunova, Valentina, 68
revanchism, 8, 68, 83, 122, 161, 167

revolution, 53, 64, 69, 143–45, 153, 163–64, 169. *See also* October Revolution
Riazanov, Eldar, 84
Rip van Winkle time travel trope, 53, 55, 86–87
Roadside Picnic, 132
Robinson, Kim Stanley, *Red Mars*, 3, 147
robots, 19, 132, 156, 159
Romanov, Mikhail, 4
Romanov dynasty, 137
Roosevelt, Franklin Delano, 16
Rough Draft, 62
Rozhnov, Valery, *Back to the USSR*, 50–52
rubles, 11, 24, 41, 69, 72, 117
Russian Federation: conditional-subjunctive, 13, 15, 105, 166–67, 173–78; disruption of time in, 1–14; documents, 71–73; establishment of, 64 (*see also* USSR, collapse of); territory of, 69, 75, 122, 123. *See also* Putin, Vladimir
Russian nationalism, 19; antisemitism and, 75, 80. *See also* affective attachment to state
Russian Orthodox Church, 78–79, 81, 152
Russian Revolution, 169
Russian Turtles, 158
Russofuturism, 157
Russophobia, 34

Salnikov, Aleksei: *Indirectly*, 148–50; *The Petrovs in and around the Flu*, 148
Sandman, 63
satire, 54, 127, 131, 140, 173
Save the USSR!, 20, 39, 48, 52
Savvin, Aleksei, "The Little Earth," 163
Schlafly, Phyllis, 83
Schmitt, Carl, 66
science fiction, 53, 99, 131; history and, 167; liberpunk, 80n9, 162; *popadantsy*, 9–10 (*see also* Time Crasher stories); social science fiction, 161–62; on space exploration, 160–65; time travel and, 19 (*see also* time travel); utopias in, 146–47
sectarianism, 80–82, 85
Selin, Adrian, 4n3
Sellars, Peter, 118
Serebrennikov, Kirill, 148
sexual transgressions, 39–43
sexual violence, 13, 118–19, 140–42
Shakespeare, William, 55, 128
Shaov, Timur, "Soviet Tango," 113
Sharafutdinova, Gulnaz, 4n3
Shchusev, Alexey, 170
Shevchenko, Olga, 7
Shevchuk, Yuri, 121

The Shtrafbat's Constellation, 54n13
Shushkevich, Stanislav, 86n2
"sick man of Europe," 87
siesit siesit (username), 150–53
Silantiev, Roman, 79–82
simulation, 97. *See also* reconstruction projects
Skepsis (username), 23–25
Skorkin, Konstantin, 167
Slapovskii, Aleksei, *Back*, 172
Slaughterhouse-Five, 5–6, 8
Slavnikova, Olga, *The Man Who Couldn't Die*, 90–91, 94–98, 121, 172
Sleeper, 53
The Slynx, 9, 126–30, 132
Smith, Paula, "A Trekkie's Tale," 48
Snegovaya, Maria, 133
Snyder, Timothy, 8
Sobyanin, Sergei, 104
socialist realism, 38–39, 57, 153
Society for Krishna Consciousness, 78
Sokolov, Boris, 139n4
Solovyov, Vladimir, 111
Solzhenitsyn, Alexander, 53n10; *One Day in the Life of Ivan Denisovich*, 139
Sorokin, Vladimir: *Day of the Oprichnik*, 9, 14, 124, 133, 134, 139–42; *Sugar Kremlin*, 14; *Telluria*, 14
Soros, George, 77
Sovereign Citizens, 70–72, 74, 75n6
sovereignty, 14, 64, 66, 70, 77, 82, 132
Soviet nostalgia, 7–8; conditional-subjunctive, 105; critiques of, 97; for "greatness," 66, 76, 101, 161, 165 (*see also* power); oprichnina and, 138–39; politics and, 119; reconstruction and reenactment projects, 108–17; restorationist groups and, 65–67 (*see also* Citizens of the USSR); restorative, 21, 61; in Sochi Olympics ceremony, 170; SovPunk and, 150–55, 160, 165; *styob* (ironic overidentification) and, 83–85; Time Crasher stories and, 18, 21, 39–47, 52–54, 57, 101
Soviet Park (public art project), 61
Sovietpunk. *See* SovPunk
SovietPunk: Nostalgia for the Present, 155
"Soviet Tango," 113
Soviet Union. *See* USSR
SovPunk, 12, 124, 133, 148–65
space program, Soviet, 28, 93, 106, 158–61, 165, 169
speculative fiction: post-Soviet Russian, 9–14. *See also* alternate history; fantasy; *popadantsy*; science fiction; Time Crasher stories

INDEX

Spider-Man, 157
Sputnik, 160
Stagnation (Brezhnev era), 46, 47, 57, 63, 96–97, 101
Stalenhag, Simon, 156
Stalin, Joseph: Citizens of the USSR and, 69, 74, 76; collective justice, 138; future orientation, 94, 109, 110, 124; industrialization, 169; repression and terror, 23, 31, 97, 101, 113–14, 120, 126; revolution from above, 64; subjunctive and, 166–67; Time Crasher stories about, 16–18, 27, 29, 31, 55, 101
Stalker, 132
S.T.A.L.K.E.R., 132, 150
Star Trek, 48, 153
state: affective attachment to, 19, 64–65, 74–76, 98, 114; as imagined community, 63; voluntarist approaches to Soviet statehood, 62–65
steampunk, 12, 149
Strelakova, Olga, 79–80
Stroop, Chrissy, 81
structuralism, 39, 51–52
Strugatsky brothers (Arkady and Boris), 26n4; *Hard to Be a God*, 14; *Roadside Picnic*, 132
Student, Komsomol Girl, Athlete, 22–29, 35–36, 99
styob (ironic overidentification), 82–85, 140
subjunctive: conditional, 13, 15, 105, 173–74, 176–77; counterfactual conditional, 166–67
Sugar Kremlin, 14
"Summer Internship," 163
Suvorkin, Timur, 161n17
sympathetic magic, 150
Syomin, Konstantin (Semin), 142–43, 145

Tales from the Loop, 156n14
Talyaka, Yana, "Not a Word of Lies," 162–63
Taraskin, Sergei, 67–69, 75–76, 82
Tarkovsky, Andrei, 132
Tarugin, Oleg, 54n13
Tchaikovsky, Pyotr, 171
teleology, 4–5, 57, 124
television, 171
Telluria, 14
Temnikova, Liza, 169
territorial expansion, 104, 121–22, 135–36, 177. *See also* imperialism; Ukraine, Russian invasion of
Tesak (Maxim Martinskevich), 119
The Third Empire, 9, 14, 124, 133–40, 142

time: linear, 6; post-Soviet discourse of, 1–14, 167; timelessness, 3, 5–6; voluntarist approaches to, 1–3, 62. *See also* future; past; present-day alternative USSR
Time, Forward!, 1
Time Crasher stories: authorial self-insertion, 20–21, 25, 48–49; defined, 10–11; as fan fiction, 18, 20–21, 23, 25, 48, 52, 61–62; hero's agency in, 18–19, 25, 37–39, 47–52, 57; historical consciousness in, 31–36; origins of genre, 19–21; persistent Soviet Union, 99–108; preventing collapse of Soviet Union, 12, 16–19, 24–28, 83, 99; rejection of politics, 37–39, 49; set in 1970s, 42–47; set in the future, 53–58; set in World War II, 19, 21, 23, 28–37, 46, 53, 57, 161, 167, 173; Soviet nostalgia in, 18, 21, 39–47, 52–54, 57, 101; uncanny, 21–28, 33, 41–42; video games and, 154–55; voluntarist approach to time, 62
time loops, 154–55, 172
The Time Machine, 11, 19–20
Time of Troubles, 4–6
time travel, 10–11; as disruptive, 56; free will and, 49; paradoxes, 10, 18–21, 27, 42, 49; Rip van Winkle trope, 53, 55, 86–87. *See also* Butterfly Effect; Time Crasher stories
Tolstaya, Tatyana, *The Slynx*, 9, 126–30, 132
Tolstoi, Sergei, "The New Person," 162–63
Tolstoy, Leo, 88, 146, 171
Torgunkov, Sergei, 68, 75
totalitarian sects, 78–80
transformative fandom, 61
transgender identity, 25, 27–28, 81
"A Trekkie's Tale," 48
The True Mirror of Youth, 174
The Truman Show, 50
Twain, Mark, *A Connecticut Yankee in King Arthur's Court*, 10, 20, 53

UFMS (Administration of the Federal Migration Service), 73
Ukraine, Russian invasion of: in 2014, 7, 133, 136; in 2022, 7, 60, 81–82, 109, 121–22, 133, 136, 155, 165, 167, 169, 173, 175–78; Ukrainian nationalism and "Nazis," 7, 34–35, 167, 173, 176
Ulanov, Oleg, *Unusual Travel Agent*, 50n8
Ulitskaya, Lyudmila, *The Funeral Party*, 88–90, 94, 98
uncanny: Freud on, 14–15, 27; post-Soviet, 21–28, 33, 41–42, 60–61, 97, 169
"Union Maniac" community, 150–52

Union of Slavic Forces of Rus, 67, 81–82
Union of the SSR Labor Union, 69
United Kingdom, 45n4
United States: Christian Right, 81; cults in, 78; Fourteenth Amendment, 71; imagined collapse of, 100–102, 105–6, 136; politics, 38; Russian émigrés in, 88–90; Sovereign Citizens groups, 70–72, 74, 75n6; SovPunk portrayals of, 162–63; space program, 160
The Universe of Metro 2033, 130
Unusual Travel Agent, 50n8
USSR: affective attachment to, 19, 64–65, 74–76, 98, 114 (*see also* Soviet nostalgia); central planning, 1, 97, 124; collapse of, 1, 5, 11–12, 16–19, 24–28, 64–66, 83, 86–98, 99, 101, 123–24, 135 (*see also* Russian Federation); ideology, 4; life cycle of, 21; material culture, 121; restorationists, 67 (*see also* Citizens of the USSR); Soviet antiquity, 61–63; Soviet subjectivity, 114–15; space program, 28, 93, 106, 158–61, 165, 169; voluntarist approach to time, 1–3, 62
USSR-2061, 124, 145–46, 158–65
"The USSR Is Our Ancient Rome," 61–62
utopias: aesthetics, 12; anthropology of, 37; ideology and, 9, 12, 76, 146–47, 162–64; More's *Utopia*, 54, 134; in nineteenth-century literature, 14, 53–55, 134–35; Other Russias, 60; satire and, 127; SovPunk, 148–65; Stalinist, 94; in Time Crasher stories, 26, 28, 50

Van Zaichik, Holm, *Eurasian Symphony*, 133
Varlamov, Ilya, 77
Verses on My Soviet Passport, 69–70, 72
Victory Day, 7, 30–31
video games, 14, 126, 129–32, 144, 150, 153–55, 158–59
Villy9, "The Decision," 164
violence, 13, 29, 82, 121, 140–42, 152, 164
Vissarion, 78
"Vitya Solnyshkin and Joseph Stalin," 16–19, 29, 39
VKontakte, 150, 156
Vladimirovich, Vladimir, 8
Vodolazkin, Eugene, *The Aviator*, 55–58

Voinovich, Vladimir, *Moscow 2042*, 53n10
Volkov, Alexander, 160–61
voluntarist approaches: to Soviet citizenship, 163; to Soviet statehood, 62–65; Stalinist, 164, 167; to time, 1–3, 62
Vonnegut, Kurt, *Slaughterhouse-Five*, 5–6, 8

The Walking Dead, 143
watchmen, 44, 137, 142
Watchmen (Moore and Gibbons), 6
We (Zamyatin), 127, 165
We Are from the Future, 30–33
We Are from the Future 2 (sequel), 30, 33–35
Wells, H. G., *The Time Machine*, 11, 19–20
Westworld (1973 film), 111
Wijermars, Marielle, 139
Willis, Andy, 45n4
wish-fulfillment fantasies, 13, 25, 41, 47, 52, 56, 135–36, 150
Witnesses of the USSR, 79
World War II: commemorations of Soviet victory in, 6–8, 30–32, 33n9, 170; as formative trauma, 125; Time Crasher stories about, 19, 21, 23, 28–37, 46, 53, 57, 161, 167, 173. *See also* Hitler, Adolf; Immortal Regiment; Nazis

Yakhina, Guzel, *Zuleikha*, 149
Yankovsky, Vladimir, 103n9
Yegorov, Mikhail, 33n9
Yeltsin, Boris, 5, 16, 22, 27, 66, 97, 127
Yorchak, Alexei, *Everything Was Forever until It Was No More*, styob, 82
Young, Cathy, 167
Yuriev, Mikhail, *The Third Empire*, 9, 14, 124, 133–40, 142

Zabirko, Oleksandr, 10n9, 34n10, 37n1
Zamyatin, Yevgeny, *We*, 127, 165
Zhukovsky, Vasily, 170
"Zombies vs. Unicorns," 143
Zubkov, Evgeny: *Carbongrad 1999* (*Russia 2077*), 156–58, 165; *Northern Spider*, 157; *Russian Turtles*, 158
Zuleikha, 149
Zworykin, Vladimir, 171